mother grains

RECIPES *for the* GRAIN REVOLUTION

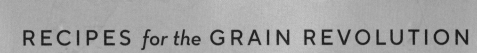

mother grains

ROXANA JULLAPAT

Photography by Kristin Teig

W. W. NORTON & COMPANY
Independent Publishers Since 1923

For information about permission to
reproduce selections from this book, write to
Permissions, W. W. Norton & Company, Inc.,
500 Fifth Avenue, New York, NY 10110

For information about special discounts for
bulk purchases, please contact W. W. Norton
Special Sales at specialsales@wwnorton.com
or 800-233-4830

Manufacturing by ToppanLeefung
Book design by Ashley Tucker
Production manager: Lauren Abbate

Library of Congress
Cataloging-in-Publication Data

Names: Jullapat, Roxana, author. |
    Teig, Kristin, photographer.
Title: Mother grains : recipes for
    the grain revolution / Roxana Jullapat ;
    photography by Kristin Teig.
Description: First edition. | New York :
    W. W. Norton & Company, Independent
    Publishers since 1923, 2021. | Includes index.
Identifiers: LCCN 2020035519 | ISBN
    9781324003564 | ISBN 9781324003571 (epub)
Subjects: LCSH: Cooking (Cereals) | Grain. |
    LCGFT: Cookbooks.
Classification: LCC TX808 .J85 2021 |
    DDC 641.3/31—dc23
LC record available at
    https://lccn.loc.gov/2020035519

W. W. Norton & Company, Inc.
500 Fifth Avenue, New York, N.Y. 10110
www.wwnorton.com

W. W. Norton & Company Ltd.
15 Carlisle Street, London W1D 3BS

1 2 3 4 5 6 7 8 9 0

To the women who raised me—
my grandmother Eugenie,
her sister Elena, and
my tías Vicky and Nela.
And above all, to my mother,
Rose Marie, for teaching me
table manners and battle cries
with equal intensity.

Contents

Introduction

It's 3:00 a.m. I walk into an empty bakery, turn on the lights, disable the alarm, start a pot of coffee, and fire up the ovens. From the walk-in refrigerator I pull rolling carts packed with unbaked Sonora wheat croissants and start brushing them with egg wash. The first shift of bakers arrives soon after and helps me finish egg-washing the croissants. Then they head to their assigned stations to tackle daily tasks—sprinkling sugar over blue cornmeal scones, portioning semolina loaf cakes, mixing spelt muffin batter, assembling brown rice coffeecakes, and traying rye chocolate chip cookies. The bakery is divided into two departments: bread and pastry. If I'm working in pastry, I'll take over the main oven—a rotating beast that can accommodate thirty large baking trays at once—and two smaller convection ovens, baking every single pastry in the oven that suits it best. If I'm working the bread station, I will refresh the starter, make the baguette dough, and bake in the deck oven the sourdough breads that were shaped the day before. Then I go through the motions of making rich doughs for rolls and focaccia, poaching and baking bagels, and I start packing bread and pastries for our wholesale accounts. Another bread baker comes in at 5:30 a.m. and shapes the baguettes and rolls that I started earlier. By the time the wholesale orders are out the door it is 6:30 a.m. I take a minute to regroup, get a second cup of coffee, and mix bread dough for the next day. The rest of the crew goes through its prep list and gets to work. One or two more bakers, whom we call the closers, join us later in the morning to take care of larger projects. By noon, the morning bakers have gone home. I will stay for a few more hours. I might pour myself a third cup of coffee and, on occasion, wonder, how did I get here?

I was born in Orange County, California, to immigrant parents who came to the United States in the late 1960s. My father, Carlos, left his native Costa Rica just before turning twenty, while my mother, Khaisri, left Thailand after graduating from nursing school. Their paths crossed years later while they were both living in Los Angeles, and they married shortly after. When I was just two years old, tragedy struck my family when my mother passed away, prompting my father to sell everything and move back to Costa Rica with my older brother and me. A few years later, my father married my stepmother, Rose Marie, a Costa Rican–born teacher of French and Spanish descent. My new family would shape my childhood in many colorful ways.

I grew up immersed in all things Costa Rican—language, culture, and, of course, food. Gallo pinto, tropical fruits, and dulce de leche were staples of my life, along with torta chilena, a homemade puff pastry that my step-grandmother prepared masterfully. From an early age, I was a voracious and curious eater and always felt at home in the kitchen. My European step-grandmother, Yenita, whose whole house smelled of melted butter, and her sister, Elena, instilled in me a sense that cooking was to be enjoyed and not an obligation. Throughout my youth I looked forward to making meals for my siblings and would eagerly participate in preparing the lavish feasts my family would serve when they entertained, which was frequently. Whether it was Rose Marie's sweet corn lasagna on Sundays, Tía Vicky's pata de cerdo (traditional uncured ham) every Christmas, or Tía Nela's queque seco (page 125), I wanted a part in all of it.

I graduated from college with a journalism degree and, feeling a bit burned out on academia and thinking about a break before grad school, I left Costa Rica and returned to L.A. for cooking school. Little did I know that restaurant work as a baker and pastry chef would become my bread and butter.

I met my husband, Daniel Mattern, at the Southern California School of Culinary Arts. Dan started working at L.A.'s celebrated restaurant Campanile in 1998 while still in school. I was hired a few months later. Under the tutelage of Nancy Silverton and Mark Peel, we were introduced to the importance of seasonality, the idea of selecting your ingredients based on what's available and in abundance—something we've continued championing throughout our careers. After less formative jobs, I landed the role of pastry chef for highly acclaimed L.A. restaurants

Lucques and A.O.C. and reconnected with Dan, who had been the chef de cuisine at A.O.C. for the past few years. We've been an item in and outside of the kitchen ever since.

Our cooking adventures eventually took us to Portland, Oregon, where we worked at Clarklewis, a rebellious restaurant embracing whole-animal butchery, foraging, and biodynamic agriculture, which were novel ideas at the time. Homesick for sunny California, we returned to L.A. and cooked at Ammo, a small restaurant known for its farm-to-table fare; then in 2011 we opened Cooks County, which we ran for four years in the Fairfax District. Cooks County gave us the opportunity to fully manifest the ideas that would come to make up our cooking philosophy—carefully sourcing our meats and fish, buying all of our produce at local farmers' markets, making our own preserves and condiments, and baking our own bread. As the restaurant became more popular, grain farmers and small mills would give us samples of their products to try. Nan Kohler, founder and miller of L.A.'s Grist & Toll, was one of the first to knock on my door. Had I known then how transformative her flours would become and how much impact she would have on my life both professionally and personally, I would have shown proportional enthusiasm. I began using whole grains in our breads and pastries and, for the first time, paid attention to how these new ingredients could transform the way I baked. My breads and desserts with these flours were received ardently by our customers, and this gave me a peek into a world of possibilities. In early 2015, Dan and I decided to step out of the kitchen for a bit to spend more time consulting, teaching, and, above all, cooking at home.

Without a demanding kitchen job for the first time in years and with a fair amount of free time on my hands, I traveled. For two years, I experimented with heirloom grains from suppliers all over the country and around the world. I went to Bhutan, where I tasted Himalayan crepes thin and thick and sampled earthy Bhutanese red rice. Then I headed to Turkey, where whole ancient wheat berries are common in savory dishes seasoned with sumac, aromatic olive oil, and copious lemon juice. Back in Costa Rica, I discovered heirloom blue corn grown organically in the northern region of Nicoya. Finally, over Christmas in London, I was delighted to discover small bakeries that gracefully displayed baked goods made with whole-grain rye, spelt, and einkorn. In between trips, I toured Southern California farms that were spearheading the local grain movement. I visited the University of Washington's Bread Lab—an ambitious project bringing together scientists, growers, and nationally recognized bakers—and I met a handful of academics making a difference in the world of grain.

I had never before considered grain a seasonal ingredient, even after working in some of California's most produce-driven kitchens. How can we make seasonal food if we don't know when and where our grains were planted, harvested, and milled into flour? I learned that local grains are significantly more nutritious and climate-friendly than conventionally grown wheat, and I became committed to convincing others to open their minds, hearts, and wallets to diversified grain consumption.

Inspired for the first time in years, and without a rigorous restaurant job to distract me, I could focus on how to incorporate more heirloom grains into my recipe repertoire. As luck would have it, our plan to open Friends & Family coincided with a successful harvest for the Southern California grain farmers. I wanted Friends & Family to reflect this grain revolution. My goal was to prepare traditional, time-honored baked goods while showcasing everything local growers and millers had to offer. Would it be okay not to offer a single loaf of white bread? Thankfully, our customers have demonstrated nothing but eagerness to try the unique flavor spectrum filling our pastry case, bread rack, and restaurant menu. Like us, they notice our grain-centric recipes are that much more interesting and taste that much better. Food made from these grains is not just good for the environment and the community; it's also damn tasty!

The reemergence of ancient grains, combined with consumer interest in alternatives to the mass-produced, nutrient-deficient foodstuffs of yesteryear, have shifted plenty of mind-sets. People are curious about grain varieties, how flour is milled, and how best to use it. This renaissance has allowed us to become a local grain mecca of sorts. Our newsletter, in-house discussions, and baking classes have further made our bakery a hub for the alternative food community, attracting producers and consumers alike.

The local grain movement didn't appear out of thin air; it was brewing in the fields of farmers growing grain to restore the soil as part of their sustainability practices, in the fermentation tanks of brewers nationwide, and on the benches of many a baker seeking better flour. But it took the trifecta of grower, miller, and consumer demand to provide the necessary resources for us to bake with local whole-grain flours every day. It truly required a network of friends and family to make Friends & Family the flourishing bakeshop that it is today.

...W 2/18

HW 2/18

TRI 2/15

SPELT 2/9

SUN 2/5

HW 2/18

Why Mother Grains?

The eight grains highlighted in this book are barley, buckwheat, corn, oats, rice, rye, sorghum, and wheat. I focus on this core group for the following reasons:

They can all be considered ancient grains. Advances in genetics have enabled us to trace the origins of ancient grains with precision. To know the extent of their journey through time and geography is to fully appreciate their role as economic and cultural catalysts, reinforcing our determination to preserve and protect their genetic richness.

All eight grains are grown domestically and are available nationwide. These ingredients are available in grocery stores, online shops, farmers' markets, and artisan mills across the country. Some may require more effort to track down, but in today's growing market, accessibility is only increasing. And when you *do* ask for these unique products, you only encourage suppliers to increase their output to meet the increasing demand.

American growers excel at these grains. The majority of farmers who grow these grains are doing an outstanding job of seed saving, land stewardship, and grain husbandry. By supporting these grains and the people who grow them, we validate their efforts to adapt varieties to local microclimates, bettering the species for future generations.

All eight grains can be grown adequately with a lesser eco footprint. Growing grains where they thrive naturally reduces the need to import foreign goods—a process that burns ample fossil fuels. If the grower is near a local mill and distributor, the impact is reduced even further. By supporting such production we vitalize the local grain industry, better allowing it to supply the immediate community. For an independent business owner like me, a local grain hub furthers my community's sustainability goals, even if the model may not be applicable at a macro level.

I am a grain advocate. While reflecting on my lifelong relationship with flour and baking, I was struck by the fact that our conventional, global flour supply reflects only a handful of wheat varieties. This is especially shocking considering the diversity of flavorful, nutritious grains found in nature. Industrialization drastically reduced grain diversity, followed by a post–WWII mentality prizing efficiency and convenience over flavor and nutrition. Think of the expression "the best thing since sliced bread." It suggests a general consensus that bread at its best is uniform, identical slices. Our ability to put bread on the table is a feat of human ingenuity, but along with that ingenuity we've lost something more than nutritional value. By discussing ancient grains (including more recent heirloom varieties), discovering delicious ways to prepare them, and mentoring a new school of bakers to appreciate their many virtues, we can promote diversity across the industry. As bakers, anytime we choose to buy flour made from ancient grains, minimally processed by an artisanal miller, we're making a conscious decision to preserve the seeds of our ancestors for future generations.

Know the Difference
Ancient, Heirloom, Artisan, Alternative, Whole, and Landrace

The terms *ancient*, *heirloom*, *artisan*, *alternative*, *whole*, and *landrace* are often used interchangeably, depending on the catchy marketing angle of the moment. However, it's important to understand what differentiates them.

Ancient grains are grains or pseudocereals unaltered by domestication. Ancient grains have maintained their original form for millennia, while other grains have been modified to create resistant, higher-yield varieties. Some people believe that ancient grains are a rare product, grown by indigenous people on faraway continents. This misconception excludes important American ancient grains, like corn, which is native to our continent, and sorghum, which has been grown in the American South for centuries.

Heirloom or heritage grains are species maintained by gardeners and farmers, particularly in specific regions or communities. These cultivars are often genetically different from their ancient ancestors, but altered by traditional breeding methods such as grafting. There's no official or legal requirement for classifying a plant as "heirloom," although it's generally understood that an heirloom variety is at least a hundred years old. Breeders also refer to heirloom grains developed in the last fifty years as "modern heirlooms." Over the last thirty years, heirloom grains have become increasingly popular in response to the rise of post–WWII monocultures. Manitoba, Red Fife, Turkey Red, Edison, Glenn, Star, and Sonora wheat are all examples of heirloom varieties widely used today. Many of the recipes in this book call for specific heirloom varieties worth pursuing, such as Öland wheat in the Cardamom Buns on page 300 or Bloody Butcher cornmeal in the Hatch Chile and Cotija Corn Bread on page 117. If rare or difficult to find, an apt substitution will be suggested.

Artisan grains refers to the cultivation, harvest, milling, and use of a grain variety. Artisan is a buzzword often applied to any non-mass-produced food. In this case, it refers to grains used to produce stone-ground flours, never refined to extract the bran or germ, thus ensuring a higher nutritional value. It's generally assumed that producers of artisan flour have an expansive understanding of the scientific and historical way these foods are made, often following time-honored methods passed down through generations.

Alternative grains is the most ambiguous term of all. It generally refers to grains aside from the mainstream cereals: wheat, corn, and rice. Grains like quinoa, millet, amaranth, and teff are often marketed as alternative grains.

Whole-grain products contain germ, endosperm, and bran, as opposed to refined flour, which has been stripped of germ and bran to extend their shelf life. According to the Whole Grains Council, a whole grain must contain bran, germ, and endosperm in the same proportion as when the grain was growing in the fields.

Landrace grains refers to crops improved by traditional agricultural methods. This long-term husbandry process is usually carried out by small farms. It typically involves retaining, replicating, and improving the quality and performance of a crop by allowing the species to adapt to specific places and environments over time.

Milling Your Own Flour

The increased availability of grain varieties at local mills, farmers' markets, and other specialty stores has led to a growing interest in home milling. Personally, I prefer purchasing flour milled by a trained professional over grinding my own flour. As someone who has spent twenty-plus years immersed in the craft of baking, I wholeheartedly identify with a miller's commitment to detail, technique, and nuance. Just like baking, milling is a complex process that requires experience, dedication, and skill to execute successfully. Therefore, I leave the milling to the milling experts.

That being said, milling your own flour at home is certainly a worthwhile pursuit. Witnessing the process firsthand will enrich your understanding of whole grains and baking with whole-grain flour. To mill your own grain you'll need—drumroll please—a mill! There are various types of mills, but a stone mill is the most reliable, durable, and user-friendly option. It's also the best option for the grain; unlike the large roller mills used to make commodity flour, this method preserves the nutrients in the grain. Stone milling works by crushing the grain between a stationary base, or bedstone, and a turning stone, or runner stone. Tabletop stone mills for home use range widely in size and price, starting at around $400. KoMo is a popular brand.

You can buy whole grains to mill at well-stocked grocery stores, artisan mills, and homesteader shops. The process is fairly simple. Just put the whole kernels in the hopper and see the flour come out through the spout. Depending on the mill you're working with, you can select the size of the grind. In the vast majority of cases, you want the finest particle possible, but as you grind more and more at home, you may come to realize that each individual variety of grain responds differently to the settings of the mill—spelt grinds easily, for example, while durum is more stubborn. You may also choose to sift the resulting flour to remove larger pieces of hull or bran that make it into the flour. As a rule of thumb, I sift only if I'm making pastries, quick breads, cakes, or muffins. When making bread, I don't sift at all.

It's highly recommended that you store whole grains in the freezer and then grind them from frozen. The friction in the mill will inevitably warm up the flour, and the lower temperature helps keep the grain cool as it grinds, reducing the chance of rancidity down the road. Keep in mind that because home-milled flours contain the entire grain, they'll be very thirsty, which means the amount of liquid in a recipe will probably have to increase. If you're a beginner, I recommend that you start with milling for your bread recipes. Because bread making generally calls for a high water content and plenty of time to allow the flour to hydrate, it tends to be more successful with home-milled flour than other baking projects.

Home-milled flour will keep for two weeks at room temperature or three months in the freezer or refrigerator. Always label the flour container with the variety used and the milling date .

Principles of Working with Mother Grains

When it comes to working with ancient grains, the following principles will guide you through purchasing and maximizing their use in your home kitchen.

Selection

Take a minute and ask yourself what you want this flour to do. Is your desired result strength rather than tenderness, or heartiness as opposed to lightness? Flour performance is tied closely to protein content. High-protein flours are ideal for bread, while soft or lower-protein flours are best for pastry. Some recipes, such as my Chocolate Chip Cookies (page 251), work well with a large range of flours, regardless of protein content.

Flavor should also play a significant role in your recipe selection. Think of grain the way you think of wine. You'll need to get acquainted with different varieties to be able to describe their flavor. When confronted with a new flour, grab a handful and take a good sniff or even taste the raw flour to analyze its flavor profile. Is it nutty or perfumed? Bitter or sweet? Sour or neutral? Some flours are so outright delicious you'll want to showcase them with little manipulation. If you're feeling unsure, ask your suppliers. They'll likely know the flour better than anyone and can select the ideal product for your desired outcome.

Read the Sourcing section of the book on page 336 before making any purchases. I've included vendors from all over the country, all at the forefront of the grain movement.

Provenance

Knowing where your grain and its resulting flour comes from is paramount for bakers dabbling in ancient grains. Whenever possible, favor flour grown in your region. In doing so, you'll choose the freshest grains, most recently harvested and milled. Plus, locally grown grain doesn't require long-distance

Opposite: (1) Rye Flakes, (2) Black Rice, (3) Rolled Oats, (4) Rye, (5) Sonora Wheat, (6) Popcorn, (7) Blue Cornmeal, (8) Barley, (9) Kamut, (10) Freekeh, (11) Red Rice, (12) Steel-Cut Oats

transportation, thus requiring less energy to produce. Proximity to the grain's source will also enable you to ask pertinent questions (Is the flour organic? When was the grain harvested? How was it stored?) of your supplier.

Freshness

It's hard to conceptualize flour as perishable after a lifetime of working with the white refined stuff found at the grocery store. Germ and bran, the main fat and fiber sources in the kernel, are sifted out in the refining process. Extracting these components, which have the potential to oxidize, greatly extends flour's shelf life. Whole-grain flours, on the other hand, have their germ and bran intact. This means they can turn rancid within a relatively short period of time.

After buying one too many bad bags, I've grown distrustful of supermarket flour. But over time I've learned to navigate the flour shelf with a bit more confidence. Judging by the sell-by date isn't enough. Shop at busy stores where product moves quickly. Open the bag as soon as you get home and take a good smell. You'll know right away if the flour is rancid. Rancid flour has a strong, off-putting smell, not unlike rancid oil. If you deem the flour stale, return it. You'll likely be reimbursed, and the store will know its flour has turned the corner and shouldn't be sold.

Purchasing flour from an artisan mill or local distributor is much less risky. Small-scale, detail-oriented operations maintain rapid movement of product, making it less likely that flour will go bad.

Storage

Now that you've taken the steps to procure good flour, let's make sure you store it properly. Refrigerating or freezing flour and whole kernels, anywhere from three to twelve months, will keep it from turning rancid. Due to space constraints, we don't refrigerate all our flour at the bakery. However, we go through it so quickly that it doesn't have a chance to spoil. At home I store my growing collection of grain and flour samples in a cool pantry. I try to use the flour within three months of purchase but don't always succeed. More than once I've been pleasantly surprised to pull a forgotten bag of year-old flour from my pantry and found it usable. But I've also been unlucky, making a batch of rancid cookies where the culprit was undoubtedly old flour. To keep track, I recommend labeling the bag with the date of purchase.

Good Judgment

When developing recipes for home bakers, we food industry folk often look to universal ingredients, ensuring that readers can obtain similar results regardless of location. But every crop, every single bag of ancient grain flour, is unique by nature. The recipes have been tested and retested with flours produced all over the country, but I invite you to view these recipes as guides, rather than strict formulas. Have confidence in the recipe, but feel free to exercise your own judgment.

How to Use This Book

I wrote this cookbook with everyone from professional baker to novice home cook in mind. *Mother Grains* is a guide to navigating the grain spectrum, a source of ideas for pairing flours with other ingredients in unique ways, and a reference for simple techniques that bring out the best in every ingredient you have.

Spending your whole paycheck at a fancy supermarket or buying expensive appliances is not a prerequisite for using this book. I've made it a point to find viable substitutions for each potentially elusive ingredient and provided suggestions for swapping ingredients in a way that doesn't sacrifice the flavor of the final product.

In addition to recipes, you'll find information on the history, cultural significance, and global relevance of each grain. I've provided prep pointers for many recipes, outlining which steps can be done in advance. It's important to take a minute and think about what you're creating prior to starting a project. Walk yourself mentally through the steps it takes to transform the raw materials into something delectable. In the professional kitchen, we call this "prep"—thinking ahead to break down the cooking process into small, manageable steps. It's what allows restaurants to serve brunch for three hundred on a Sunday morning or bake three hundred pies the day before Thanksgiving. Most of these recipes require little prep, and with a few ingredients on hand you'll be able to bake mouthwatering treats in under an hour. That being said, a few recipes do require time and planning ahead. Save these for a special occasion or a rainy weekend project.

So go ahead! Preheat that oven and bake away! If I entered your kitchen to find half-full bags of whole-grain flour in your pantry and a worn copy of this book, stained all over the pages, my mission would be accomplished.

My Baking Philosophy

1. Respect the vitality of the ingredients. Most of the flavor in anything you make will come from the ingredients themselves and less from what you do to them. Take every step necessary to make sure that the integrity of the ingredients doesn't suffer, whether it's sourcing seasonal fruits and vegetables from organic producers, cutting fruit right before turning it into a jam, using flour as freshly milled as possible, mixing batters just before baking, or favoring small batch sizes to ensure everything is as fresh and vibrant as possible.

2. Exercise restraint. It may be tempting to add a variety of flavors into a dish (spices for warmth, fat for richness, citrus for brightness), but to achieve a well-balanced concoction, you must make sure that every ingredient has a purpose and is added in the right proportion. A small amount can be effective in making an impact on flavor. You don't have to swing heavy one way; even an increase of ¼ teaspoon of salt or 1 teaspoon of acid can make something taste better.

3. Bake treats we all want to eat. Although the flavors and textures of some of the whole-grain flours I favor can be challenging to some, I always aim to create craveable recipes rooted in comfort and nostalgia, but incorporating a thoughtful twist or pertinent update (making chocolate chip cookies with rye flour, using brown rice flour in coffee cake to yield a pillowy crumb, pairing buckwheat and cardamom in a crispy waffle that is mild enough for kids but interesting enough for parents to be excited about).

4. Look to cultural, historical foodways for ideas. It's always a sure bet to put together things that come from the same geographic region or the same culinary tradition even if you've never been to those places (making babka with rye flour, sprinkling fennel pollen over semolina cookies, or adding sorghum syrup to pecan pie). It's an effective way to transport yourself to different countries or eras, turning food into a catalyst for thought and memory. I'm amazed at how the combination of hazelnuts and brown butter tastes French, or cumin and green chiles make you think of Mexico, and rice and beans take me back to my childhood in Costa Rica.

5. There is always room for whole-grain flour. To date, I haven't encountered a recipe that doesn't benefit from the addition of whole-grain flour. From pasta and bread, to pies and doughnuts, even a small amount can make a difference in flavor and texture. My experimentation process always starts the same way: deduct a percentage of refined flour and replace it with a whole-grain counterpart. Think about it this way: in every recipe you make, replace one-quarter of the flour with a new whole-grain flour. In time you will find yourself using a larger percentage of whole-grain flours across the grain spectrum.

6. Follow the recipe and scale with precision. More experienced bakers break this rule all the time. I do it myself. But if you want to obtain the results promised by the recipe author, you must follow it to the letter. In baking it's also imperative to stick to the amounts the recipe calls for, since commonly used ingredients have the ability to alter the end result significantly. Treat every ingredient as if it were salt. Even the tiniest amount in excess can have an undesired effect.

7. I prefer using coated, nonstick molds. Coated, nonstick bakeware costs more, but it's generally sturdier and longer-lasting. It does require more care; avoid using corrosive cleaning materials or scraping with sharp objects.

8. Parchment paper is your best ally. At home and at the bakery, I always have a stack of unbleached precut parchment paper sheets that are available in regular grocery stores. My favorite kind is the eco-friendly brand If You Care (see Sourcing on page 336). Even when I'm using nonstick bakeware, I line every sheet, pan, or mold with parchment paper for safe release and easy cleanup. Parchment paper also comes in handy when rolling certain doughs over the kitchen counter with a rolling pin. It's a cleaner way to roll and will spare you having to sprinkle extra flour on the work surface. It's also good for wrapping dough before storing it in the refrigerator. For lining baking sheets, nonstick silicone baking mats can be very useful. They are inexpensive, heat-resistant, durable, environmentally friendly, and easy to clean. They come in very handy when making poached breads, such as the Spretzels on page 295.

9. Preheat the oven. Always bake at the right temperature, positioning the oven rack in the required position. If you suspect your oven is off caliber, I recommend buying an oven thermometer to ensure accurate temperature. They're reasonably priced and easy to find at restaurant supply stores or online.

10. For evenly baked goods, rotate the pan. Many of my recipes will ask you to rotate the pan or mold halfway through the baking process to ensure even baking. When baking on two separate sheets at once, it's also advisable to switch their positions in the oven, moving the top sheet to the bottom rack and vice versa, so that you get an even color.

11. Yes, sifting is key. Sifting is a multipurpose step in many recipes, and you must never skip it. It helps break up lumps of dry ingredients as well as aerating them. My favorite tool for sifting is a fine-mesh sieve or tamis. When working with flours high in fiber, it's possible to end up with some of the bran in the sifter; just pour the captured bran back into the sifted ingredients.

12. Straining makes a difference. Just like sifting, straining may seem unnecessary, but it means the difference between eggy and silky-smooth lemon curd. Every liquid sauce, juice, curd, filling, or custard in this book will need to be strained through a fine-mesh sieve, sometimes twice.

13. Use butter at room temperature sometimes but not always. Use soft, room-temperature butter when the recipe requires you to cream it. This is the case for most cakes and cookie doughs. Always use cold butter, straight from the refrigerator, whenever the recipe asks you to cut the butter into cubes that will eventually be blended into the dry ingredients (e.g., biscuits, scones, pie dough). The best way to temper butter is to let it sit for one hour at room temperature before preparing a recipe. If for any reason the butter seems melty and oily, put it back in the refrigerator for ten minutes. In many cases you can use cold butter in recipes that call for softened butter, but you will have to increase the mixing time since it will take longer to cream.

14. No, I don't use eggs at room temperature. It's true that room-temperature eggs will whip quicker than cold ones. They are also easier to incorporate into creamed doughs and batters. However, to prevent the risk of foodborne illness, I've made it a habit to always work with refrigerated eggs. It's a required health code practice I must comply with at the bakery, and I've adopted it at home. You can choose to work with room-temperature eggs though, removing them from the refrigerator one hour before preparing a recipe.

15. Store nuts, seeds, and dried fruits in the refrigerator. To prevent nuts and seeds from drying out and turning rancid, store them in the refrigerator. Put a label on the bag or container with the date of purchase for future reference. They will keep for approximately six months under refrigeration.

16. Toast nuts and seeds to maximize their flavor. Many of the recipes in this book require you to toast nuts and seeds. Even when the nuts are on top of a cake that must be baked, they should be pretoasted.

17. You don't need expensive tools. In twenty years of experience I've come to learn that many times it is just better to use your hands. Stick to simple tools and traditional methods. It's possible to use the breadth of baking techniques to keep each recipe engaging and fun without spending a fortune on the latest kitchen gadget.

18. Watch the sweetness level. I've noticed a welcome departure from overly sweet goods across the industry, probably influenced by recent nutrition data. Even a sugar lover like me can get behind this trend. Sugar is important in recipes from a food science perspective, but we still have the ability to make decisions that affect the level of sweetness, from adding the right amount of dried fruits to exercising restraint when we frost a cake.

19. **For increased flavor, bake on the dark side.** This is perhaps the hardest lesson to teach novice bakers, and just when you think they know what you mean, they might start to burn things—also a valuable part of the learning experience. The process by which baked goods brown is known in food science as the *Maillard reaction*. It was identified by French chemist Louis Camille Maillard in 1912, and it's responsible for producing hundreds of flavor compounds. A properly baked bread or pastry will be moist in the middle with a fully caramelized exterior. Many breads and pastries will actually suffer from underbaking; they will lose volume as they cool, their centers will become doughy, and their crusts will be soggy and lackluster.

20. **Value whimsy and imperfection.** I celebrate that the world of baking has room for so many aesthetics and styles. I love looking at intricately decorated chocolates, glossy éclairs, and stenciled viennoiserie. However, the breads and pastries that I like to make are nothing like that. I believe in letting baked goods show their true nature. If a scone expands and cracks when it bakes, there's no reason to hide this intrinsic characteristic. Even when pastries are made the same way, time after time, they may vary slightly when you look at them all together. These pastries tell the story of a handcrafted product, made with artisan ingredients, in a small-scale operation. There's beauty in their imperfection.

About Weights and Measurements

The recipes in this book include volume measurements in cups and tablespoons and their weight equivalent in grams whenever the amount exceeds ¼ cup. You may use whichever you feel more comfortable with. Always use a reliable digital scale and a trusty set of measuring cups and spoons. Keep in mind that weight measurements are more accurate. I've chosen to use grams (metric system) instead of ounces (imperial system) to make these recipes more translatable and user-friendly. In an increasingly connected world, where we can share recipes with bakers around the globe, I've grown to value the more standardized metric system. Even among my colleagues, I've noticed an increased shift toward the metric system for its simpler, decimal-based structure. For ingredient equivalences in ounces, refer to the Equivalence Chart on page 338.

The Baker's Pantry

COCOA AND CHOCOLATE

Chocolate chips. Good chocolate is worth the splurge. Stick to bittersweet chocolate chips with 60 to 70 percent cacao solids. There are many reputable brands made in many different countries; among my favorites are Valrhona, TCHO, and Guittard. Unfortunately, many high-end brands don't make chips. If that is the case, you may choose to chop the chocolate in chunks with a chef's knife. The extra step will pay off.

Cocoa powder. The recipes in this book call for Dutch-processed cocoa powder. This type of cocoa has been neutralized and is usually a lot darker than natural cocoa powder. I prefer it because it's always unsweetened with an intense chocolaty flavor.

DAIRY AND EGGS

Butter. Always use unsalted butter for baking. You will be able to control how much salt the recipe should have. It was generally believed that unsalted butter was fresher since salt was added to the butter to extend its shelf life. But nowadays butter is made in such industrial amounts to meet public demand that both kinds are considered fresh.

Buttermilk. I prefer buttermilk to most forms of dairy when I'm baking. It reacts with the baking soda to produce desirable results and adds a pleasant tang. It's always low in fat because it's a by-product of butter making.

Cream. When shopping for cream, look for heavy cream or whipping cream. In the United States, they're virtually the same product by a different name with almost identical fat content.

Eggs. Choose large eggs, which weigh about 1.7 ounces or 50 grams, for making the recipes in this book. I prefer farm-raised, cage-free organic eggs.

Milk. For the purposes of this book, always use whole milk. Never use fat-free (skim) milk in its place. Whole-grain flours benefit from the fat in dairy.

Sour cream. Sour cream contributes to the flavor of many recipes while also adding richness. Choose full-fat sour cream, never reduced-fat. Crème fraîche can be used in its place.

DRIED FRUITS

Look for dried fruits that are still plump. Reject fruits that have a sugary exterior, which means they have been around too long and are starting to dry out. Keep dried fruits in a freezer bag or airtight container, write the date of purchase on it, and store in the refrigerator. Never swap dried fruits with freeze-dried fruits. Freeze drying aims at rapidly locking in the fresh flavor of the fruits, while dried fruits develop a flavor of their own over a long drying period.

FLAVOR ENHANCERS

Almond and vanilla extracts. Always buy real extract over artificial. Storing it in a dark and cool place will preserve its intensity for a long time. Extracts can be so pricey that it might be tempting to go for the cheaper version. Instead, sub in amaretto, dark rum, or bourbon to do the trick.

Almond paste or marzipan. This confection made out of almonds, sugar, and almond extract can be eaten on its own or used as an ingredient. Marzipan and almond paste are virtually the same, but the name *marzipan* often refers to European confectionary shaped and dyed into figures resembling small fruits or animals. When purchasing in the United States, you can buy either one. My preferred brand is Mandelin (see Sourcing on page 336), made here in California. It adds a profound almond intensity to many of my recipes.

Rose water and orange-flower water. These Middle Eastern staples are powerful flavor enhancers. They aren't as concentrated as an extract, so they can be added in larger quantities. Their unusual flavors can add a new and unexpected dimension to savory and sweet preparations. They're affordable and easy to find in Middle Eastern markets or well-stocked supermarkets. Popular brands are Cortas and Indo-European.

Spices. Always buy spices in the smallest amount possible so they won't sit on your spice rack for too long. Whole spices last a long time (up to two years), but ground spices should be used within a year. When in doubt, give the spice jar a good smell; if no longer heady and aromatic, it's time to throw it away.

Vanilla beans. These pricey and flavorful pods can transform a recipe from average to sublime. Unfortunately, the availability and price of vanilla beans fluctuates often in the world market, and it can be tricky and expensive to find high-quality beans. Always choose aromatic, plump, and moist beans. Purchase one or two beans at a time and store in the refrigerator. Most of my recipes call for just half of a vanilla bean; you can refrigerate the other half to use later.

LEAVENERS

Baking powder and baking soda. These artificial leaveners are irreplaceable in baking. They tend to lose their potency the longer they sit in your pantry. Date the container on the day that you open it and use it within nine months. Always add the amount the recipe calls for and never use one in lieu of the other.

Instant yeast. I prefer to use instant yeast over active dry yeast because it's made of finer granules and therefore dissolves more easily. In theory, instant yeast can be added directly into the dry ingredients, but I always recommend dissolving it in lukewarm water before combining with the rest of the ingredients. This step will promote the yeast to activate more efficiently.

NUTS AND SEEDS

Buy raw nuts and seeds whenever possible. You can toast them when you need them to maximize their flavor. Remember that nuts and seeds have a high fat content and can turn rancid. To extend their shelf life, store in the refrigerator in a freezer bag or airtight container labeled with the date of purchase.

OILS

Coconut oil. Solid at room temperature and liquid at higher temperatures, coconut oil is the ideal replacement for butter, solid or melted, in plant-based recipes. It's an increasingly popular and easy-to-find ingredient that can also be used in cooking because of its clean, mild flavor.

Nonstick spray. Nonstick pan spray made from olive, coconut, and other vegetable oils is widely available in the market. I use it habitually to ensure pans and molds are greased adequately.

Olive oil. I like using olive oil not only as a source of fat but also as a flavor component (see Olive Oil Polenta Cake, page 127). I recommend always using extra virgin olive oil. My favorite variety is Arbequina olive oil produced here in California.

Vegetable oil. Use a mild-flavored vegetable oil. Grapeseed oil is one of my favorites for its neutral taste, but canola or avocado oil will work just as well. I avoid using corn-based and cottonseed oils because they're considered less sustainable.

REFINED FLOURS

All-purpose flour. Always purchase the best refined flour you can. I make it a point to buy domestic organic unbleached all-purpose flour. At home I use Whole Foods 365 all-purpose flour, but I also recommend King Arthur, a brand popular among professional bakers. At Friends & Family, we purchase Central Milling refined flours, which are available online, and many of my colleagues recommend Camas Country Mill flours (see Sourcing on page 336).

Bread flour. Just like all-purpose flour, refined bread flour is useful when working with other grains. It will help compensate for the mechanical challenges that arise when using low-gluten flours. There are many brands of good bread flour to choose from. At home, I prefer using King Arthur's organic unbleached bread flour with a protein content of 12 to 14 percent.

SALTS

Fine sea salt. I use finely ground sea salt in bread making because it dissolves quickly and therefore can be easily incorporated into the dough. Avoid using coarse salt; its large granules can affect the crumb of the bread because they rip into the strands of gluten. Salt will inhibit rapid fermentation, helping the dough rise at a slower pace and thus producing a more flavorful bread. Always adhere to the amounts called for in the recipe. Besides retarding fermentation and adding flavor, salt will toughen the dough slightly, contributing to its texture. Without salt, bread dough would run amok, resulting in an overfermented, sour, and sloppy mess. In the absence of fine sea salt, you can use kosher salt, but the former is always preferable.

Kosher salt. With the exception of bread recipes and a few savory ones, all the recipes in this book call for kosher salt. I recommend choosing a brand free of additives. My go-to is Diamond Crystal.

White Flour: Friend or Foe?

Even in a cookbook about whole-grain flours, there's a place for refined flour. Used in combination with the many whole-grain flours in this book, all-purpose allows other grains to shine. Because it's neutral in flavor and higher in gluten, it can provide the perfect canvas for more flavor-forward flours to take center stage. These recipes were developed to use the minimum amount necessary of refined flour—just enough to get the job done without taking anything away from the more interesting whole-grain flour. Think of all-purpose flour as the building blocks of the house, while the accompanying whole-grain flour is the pretty yard and the paint on the walls.

Mechanically, refined flour's main job in whole-grain baking is to troubleshoot issues that whole grains might present (lack of gluten, gritty texture, starchy aftertaste, or bitter flavor, for example).

As a rule, every single bread, morning pastry, or cookie we bake at Friends & Family must contain whole-grain flour. Some baked goods have a higher percentage than others, but at least 20 percent of the flour content in any recipe must come from whole grains. The recipes in this book mirror this practice.

As I've become proficient at baking with whole-grain flours, I find myself increasing their percentage in my recipes more frequently. After using this book, you may start to feel the same way. Under the mentorship of Nan Kohler, miller and founder of Grist & Toll, I've learned to use 100 percent whole Sonora wheat flour as my all-purpose flour for pastry making and Glenn or Starr wheat as my predominant bread flour. You can try this too. I look forward to a day when baking entirely with whole-grain flour is the norm.

Artisan sea salt. I use artisan sea salts as a finishing touch to add crunch and salty minerality to sweet and savory dishes. Because sea salt is harvested close to the source, each one conveys a sense of terroir. My favorite coarse salts are Maldon from England, Jacobsen from the Pacific Northwest, Flor de Sal from Portugal, and Fleur de Sel de Guérande from France.

SUGAR

Granulated sugar. Use your preferred brand of organic or conventional granulated sugar in the amount the recipe calls for and never replace it with sugar alternatives such as Sucanat, monk fruit sweetener, or stevia. Besides adding sweetness, sugar is responsible for many reactions in the baking process, from aiding caramelization to softening batters. Cutting back or adding extra sugar can unleash a disastrous chain reaction.

Dark brown sugar. I favor the assertive and deep flavor of dark brown sugar. Avoid substituting light or golden brown sugar, which has a much milder flavor. Dark brown sugar contains a higher percentage of molasses. It adds caramel notes to baked goods and promotes soft and yielding textures.

Turbinado sugar. This sugarcane-based sugar is minimally processed to preserve its natural molasses. It's ideal for sprinkling over cookies, muffins, or scones. Because of its large crystal size it won't melt at moderate temperatures in the oven.

Baking Tools

BAKING DISHES

Baking dishes range in size, depth, and material. They're in every gift registry and can cost a fortune. I find the classic 13-by-9-inch rectangular baking dish a multipurpose size to have at home, as well as a 9-inch pie pan for anything from pies to cobblers and crumbles. Although fancier manufacturers like Emile Henry, Staub, and Le Creuset offer beautifully designed baking dishes in these sizes, affordable Pyrex glassware is still my go-to.

BAKING SHEETS

I prefer multipurpose baking sheets over cookie sheets that may not have a rim or edge. You don't need to have expensive coated nonstick baking sheets. Heavy-duty aluminum ones are affordable and easy to find. Just make sure to line with parchment paper whenever the recipe asks you to do so. Dimensions may vary, but rimmed 18-by-13-inch sheets are pretty common and fit in most ovens. I recommend having two of them on hand.

BANNETON

Used for proofing bread dough, bannetons are baskets made from different materials (from rattan and wicker to plastic) in a wide variety of shapes. I recommend a round banneton, 8 to 9 inches in diameter, that can fit loaves ranging from 1 to 2 pounds. With the exception of plastic bannetons, they cannot be washed and therefore must be cleaned with a dry brush. Keep in a dry area to prevent them from molding.

BENCH KNIFE

An important item in bread making, a bench knife is the best tool to cut and divide bread dough. You can also use it to scrape the dough stuck to the work table, making cleanup a lot easier.

BISCUIT OR COOKIE CUTTERS

To make biscuits, scones, cookies, doughnuts, and more, a set of multisized round cutters with plain or fluted edges is indispensable. I prefer metal cutters over plastic ones. They're durable and dishwasher safe.

CAKE PANS AND TART PANS

I prefer using coated nonstick pans across the board because they're durable and easy to clean. The majority of the cake recipes in this cookbook, call for a 9-inch springform pan because it doesn't require inverting the cake to release it, thus preserving the integrity of the top. For brownies, blondies, and other sturdy items, I recommend using 9-inch round or square cake pans. Most American Bundt pans range from 9 to 10 inches, and you can use either size. My preferred tart pan is 9 inches in diameter with a removable bottom to prevent breakage when removing from the mold.

COOLING RACK

Use a wire rack about the size of your baking sheet to cool hot pots and pans and protect your counter surfaces from heat damage. A wire rack is ideal for cooling bread and other baked goods fresh out of the oven because air can circulate underneath, preventing the bottom from getting steamy.

DIGITAL SCALE

I recommend a digital scale with weights in grams and ounces and a capacity of 5 to 10 pounds. I find it useful when the scale is large enough (approximately 6 square inches) to fit a medium-size bowl on top. Taylor makes durable, affordable, and easy-to-find scales with these characteristics.

DIGITAL THERMOMETER

Digital thermometers are important to ensure the oil for frying doughnuts is the correct temperature or to determine whether a loaf of bread is done by checking its internal temperature. They're affordable and easy to find. Just make sure yours reads temperatures from 75° to 400°F.

DUTCH OVEN

Dutch ovens have become the vessel of choice for baking bread at home. A lidded 4½- to 5½-quart cast-iron Dutch oven provides a perfect environment for breads to develop open crumbs and crusty exteriors. The lid traps the steam released by the loaf in the hot environment, keeping the exterior of the bread supple so it may expand and reach a desirable oven spring. Many manufacturers offer stylish and pricey Dutch ovens in round and oval shapes. If you don't already own one, I recommend starting with an affordable brand such as Lodge and upgrading to a higher-caliber pot in due time.

FOOD PROCESSOR

As a baker, I use my food processor frequently to make nutmeals and buttery crumbles or even to mix doughs. It's also useful for making purees, such as the pumpkin puree for the Barley Pumpkin Bread on page 43 and the date paste for the Power Oat Bars on page 145.

HEAT-RESISTANT RUBBER OR SILICONE SPATULA

My heat-resistant flexible spatula serves multiple purposes daily, from scraping a bowl clean of its contents to stirring hot caramel sauce on the stove. Because you need only one, I recommend you buy a high-quality one. My preferred brand is Le Creuset.

KNIVES

For baking purposes, it suffices to have a durable and sharp chef's knife, a smaller paring knife, and a high-quality serrated knife. Make sure your chef's and paring knives remain sharp with a honing steel or take them to your favorite kitchenware store regularly to have them sharpened professionally.

LAME

This slashing tool composed of a blade attached to a handle is used to score the tops of loaves of bread. A lame can be used to make decorative designs, but its main purpose is to create a vent on the surface for the bread to release pressure as it expands in the oven. Lames are cheap and easy to find, but in a pinch a sharp paring knife will do.

LOAF PANS

Loaf pans are the perfect vessel to bake anything from a buttery cake to a loaf of bread. I find the standard 8½-by-4½-by-2¾-inch loaf pan to be easy to find and ideal in size. I also like to bake in a mini loaf pan mold with eight cavities about 3¾ by 2½ inches in size. They make the best power bars and charming mini banana breads.

MEASURING CUPS, MEASURING SPOONS, AND LIQUID MEASURING CUP

When measuring dry ingredients by volume, use measuring cups and spoons. To be as precise as possible, fill the cup or spoon to the top and remove excess with the back of a knife. Use a liquid measuring cup or measuring spoons to measure liquids accurately, including melted butter and oil. For thicker liquid ingredients such as sour cream or applesauce, I like to use dry measuring cups because they make leveling a lot easier.

OFFSET SPATULA

An offset spatula will come in handy to spread batter evenly into a mold. It's also helpful to loosen cakes, tarts, and cookies from their pans, and it makes it easy to frost a cake. It can also be used to flip panfried items in a sauté pan.

PASTRY WHEEL CUTTER

Similar to a pizza cutter, a pastry wheel cutter will enable you to score and cut doughs cleanly. It's indispensable to cut croissants, crackers, or the dough strips to make the Cardamom Buns on page 300. I prefer the cutters that have a double head, one with a plain-edged wheel and another with a fluted-edged wheel.

PLASTIC DOUGH SCRAPER

Usually made of a flexible plastic that you can hold directly in your hand, a dough scraper works a lot like a rubber spatula. It helps scrape the bottom of the bowl clean or remove dough stuck on a work surface without damaging the surface.

STAND MIXER

This is one of the most valuable items a home baker can own. Stand mixers are not cheap, but they do tend to last for a lifetime. The first one I ever owned lasted twenty years. It's important to use the attachment (paddle, whisk, or dough hook) that the recipe calls for since each is designed to perform a specific task.

WHISK

A stainless-steel whisk can do most mixing jobs without the hassle of using your electric stand mixer.

WOODEN ROLLING PIN

Many bakers prefer a rolling pin with handles, but I prefer mine without. I have owned a long French wooden rolling pin since I went to cooking school. French rolling pins don't have handles. The ends can be tapered or perfectly cylindrical. Never wash your rolling pin under running water and it will outlive you. Instead wipe it clean with a wet kitchen towel.

WOODEN SPOONS

Wooden spoons can perform most tasks fancy tools were created for. They can beat, mix, and scrape. They're also inexpensive and made out of sustainable materials. I use my wooden spoons every day. My home collection is proof that there's a wooden spoon for every job. Whenever I travel, I always bring back a wooden spoon. Their use is so universal that you can find them almost anywhere in the world made from local wood. They're inexpensive, easy to find, and great for stirring and making jam. They can acquire the taste of garlic, onions, and other strong flavors, so I recommend keeping spoons used for savory cooking separately. Because their surface is porous, they can harbor bacteria. To sanitize them, wash your spoons by hand, scrubbing them vigorously with dish soap and hot water, and dry them immediately afterward.

Opposite: An offset spatula is ideal to spread fillings evenly.

barley

HORDEUM VULGARE L.

To live and thrive like a gladiator, eat more barley.

Barley devotees love to point out the eating habits of ancient Roman gladiators. Recent studies have found that gladiators—known in Latin as *hordearii*, or barley men—were fed well to meet the demands of their strenuous sport, despite being an enslaved class destined to die in combat. In 1993, a gladiator cemetery was discovered amid the ruins of Ephesus, an ancient Roman city located in present-day Turkey. Scientists at the University of Bern in Switzerland analyzed the remains of twenty-two believed gladiators. Their bones revealed that they consumed a diet heavy in beans and grains—barley and wheat, specifically—with minimal animal protein. This carb-heavy regime helped gladiators build subcutaneous fat, in turn providing protective padding during combat. Much like sumo wrestlers, larger gladiators were made more visible by their striking size. This proved an asset in the Coliseum, where they were loved and lauded by audiences until their untimely deaths. I like to think the term *barley men* references not only the gladiators' dietary staple, but also the ancient Romans' regard for barley's immense nutritional value.

Much like that of the hordearii, our modern diet incorporates barley in various ways, sometimes unbeknown to us. You may not frequently dine on classic American beef barley soup and yet regularly consume notable quantities of barley in the form of malt. This

Opposite: Malted Almond Bars (page 53)

is especially true if you are a beer drinker, but also accurate for those of us who consume common processed foods like breakfast cereals, nutrition bars, or malted milk almost every day. Barley currently ranks fourth as the world's most important grain, following wheat, rice, and corn. Its uses run the gamut from farm animal feed to fermented and distilled beverage production to food manufacturing. And barley's reputation as food fit for gladiators is not at all unfounded. Rich in antioxidants, vitamins, and minerals, it contains more protein than corn, rice, sorghum, or rye. Of all the whole grains, barley contains the highest amount of fiber, with up to 17 percent depending on the variety, compared to 12 percent in wheat, the second highest. Fiber is typically found only in the grain's exterior hull, but barley's anatomy is unique because fiber is woven through the entire barley kernel. This fiber reduces blood pressure, lowers LDL (bad) cholesterol, prevents diabetes, and, according to the FDA, reduces risk of coronary heart disease.

Barley has historically played an important role in the societies that grow and consume it. It became the base of the English measurement system in the early fourteenth century when Edward II determined an inch to be "three grains of barley, dry and round, placed end to end lengthwise." Christopher Columbus brought barley to the Americas in 1449, but it wasn't cultivated in North America until English and Scandinavian settlers grew it for beer making. The origins of Scots Bere, the first variety of barley grown in the United States, can be traced back to the Orkney Islands, in eighth-century Scotland. It's still in production there today. Scots Bere was first grown along the East Coast of the United States, and then a Canadian shipping firm, Hudson's Bay Company, took it to the Pacific Northwest. Later on, Jesuits took a relative of the same barley to California.

Barley is a highly adaptable crop, growing in disparate regions like the Arctic Circle, the Andes, and Ethiopia—where more varieties of barley are found than anywhere else. Its adaptability and short growing season facilitate cultivation across the United States. According to the National Barley Growers Association, American farmers plant 3.5 million acres of barley a year, yielding 200 million bushels. About 90 percent of this crop is grown in the Pacific Northwest and northern plains.

How to Purchase and Use

Berries

When buying whole berries, look for hulled barley—also known as *barley groats*—or hull-less barley, a variety with a loose outer layer that comes off easily during harvesting. Because less processing is required, it remains high in fiber. I avoid buying pearled barley, which has been polished with the purpose of removing as much of the outer fiber-rich layer as possible. But if hulled or hull-less barley proves hard to find in your area, pearled berries will do. While it can't be considered a whole grain, it still packs a respectable fiber punch at 5 grams per ounce. The cooked berries have a chewy, pasta-like texture and a wholesome, nutty flavor. They are great in grain salads, porridges, soups, and stews. Whole-grain barley berries can take 30 to 45 minutes to cook but can be prepared easily in a rice cooker. My preferred brand for hull-less barley is Bob's Red Mill. When hull-less barley isn't available, I opt for pearl barley. If your local miller or homebrew shop offers other hulled varieties, I strongly recommend giving them a try, always keeping in mind that cooking times may vary.

Flour

Barley flour isn't as popular as it deserves to be considering that it's very similar to wheat flour. With its creamy color, subtle sweetness, and mild, malty flavor, barley flour lends softness and moisture to a recipe. Autumn is my favorite time to bake with barley flour. It provides a complementary canvas for quintessential fall flavors and spices. As a flavor component, barley flour adds unexpected undertones of browned butter, vanilla bean, and butterscotch. It performs well in recipes that normally have a tighter crumb, such as quick breads, or in treats like brownies and blondies that have a naturally dense and chewy structure. Although it produces tighter and denser crumbs, the texture is always moist, silky, and soft. It's often used in combination with wheat flour (my preferred ratio is one part barley flour to one part all-purpose flour) to make up for the lack of strength in barley flour. Although barley contains gluten, this gluten is weaker than the kind in wheat and does not hold well in many recipes where gluten is crucial, such as bread. I do like adding a small percentage of barley flour to enriched breads such as the Potato Rolls on page 62. The addition of barley can push bread recipes a few notches into the sweet spectrum without robbing them of their savory qualities. King Arthur's barley flour is finely ground and performs really well in all the baking recipes in this chapter. It may not be readily available in every supermarket but can be ordered through the online store. King Arthur also offers barley flakes and diastatic malt powder, a common ingredient used by professional bakers to promote active fermentation, supple texture, and enhanced browning in breads and pastries. Independent millers around the country, such as Grist & Toll in California and Palouse Heritage in Washington, ship barley flour milled from heirloom varieties like Scots Bere and purple barley across the country. Availability of these heirloom flours can be seasonal and pretty limited, so I advise you to purchase them when you see them to avoid the heartbreak of coming back only to find out they've run out. Store flour in a cool pantry and try to use it within 3 months of purchase. To keep track, I recommend labeling the bag with the date of purchase.

Malt

Malting requires soaking grain in water to encourage germination and then hot drying it to halt the process. These steps enable the barley to develop enzymes that can convert grains' natural starch into sugar. It's estimated that three-quarters of the barley produced in the United States is destined for malting.

The term *malt* actually refers to a category of products—including malted grain, diastatic malt, and nondiastatic malt—made by the malting process, rather than one specific, tangible product. Malted grain is central to the production of beer, whiskey, and malt vinegar, while diastatic malt and nondiastatic malt are used widely in bread and pastry making. *Diastatic* refers to malts with a high level of enzymatic activity, which helps convert starch into sugar. Bakers use diastatic malt, usually in powder form, as an additive in doughs to encourage yeast performance, improving rise and caramelization. In nondiastatic malt the enzymes have been deactivated by heat. It's typically used by bakers to add color and viscosity. The most common form of nondiastatic malt is barley malt syrup, also known as *malt extract*, which you can find in health food stores. I like to use it as a sweetener or flavor enhancer in place of honey or molasses in many of my recipes. My go-to brand of barley syrup is Eden Foods from Michigan, which can be found in stores across the country. King Arthur's barley syrup is also excellent although not as widely distributed. Throughout this chapter you'll find different creative ways to incorporate barley malt syrup. Use it to varnish the top of an autumnal Barley Pumpkin Bread (page 43) or make an elegant glaze to coat decadent Malt-Glazed Brownies (page 51). Be adventurous and make the Malted Almond Bars (page 53) with their tacky caramel layer or the Persimmon Sticky Pudding (page 57) bathed in soul-warming malted butterscotch sauce.

Barley Pumpkin Bread

MAKES 1 LOAF, ABOUT 8 SLICES

Equipment: 8½-by-4½-inch loaf pan

1 cup (110 g) barley flour

¾ cup (105 g) all-purpose flour

¼ teaspoon baking powder

1 teaspoon baking soda

¼ teaspoon kosher salt

¼ teaspoon ground cloves

¼ teaspoon freshly grated nutmeg

½ teaspoon ground cinnamon

1⅓ cups (260 g) sugar

2 large eggs

¾ cup (180 ml) vegetable oil

1 cup (250 g) pumpkin puree, canned or homemade (see page 45)

1 teaspoon minced Candied Kumquats (see page 47) or finely grated zest of 1 orange (optional)

¼ cup (40 g) golden raisins

2 tablespoons barley malt syrup (optional)

Technically, this fall staple should be called kabocha squash bread, but that doesn't sound half as inviting (or comfortingly familiar) as good ol' pumpkin bread. I'm certainly not the first to encounter this dilemma, and like many other bakers, I use the generic "pumpkin" to describe anything made with the numerous winter squashes that lend themselves so beautifully to baking.

I often say barley is the ultimate fall flour—with its caramel undertones it sets the perfect stage for the spice-forward flavors of the season. For me, the magic of this pumpkin bread lies in complementing the warmth of winter squash with the malty notes of barley. In addition to using barley flour in the batter, I brush the baked loaf with molasses-like barley malt syrup as soon as it comes out of the oven, making this an incomparable, heart-warming sweet. Just as important is the adequate use of spices. Refrain from buying spice blends labeled "pumpkin pie spice" and instead opt for combining the right proportions of your favorite warm spices. And the old rule still stands: while whole spices keep for several years, ground spices should be used within a year. To test whether they've lost their essence, give them a good smell. If they're no longer heady and aromatic, it's time to throw them away. The Californian in me can't help including a bit of citrus zest, candied or fresh, but the purists among us can omit it in favor of the traditional pumpkin and spice.

1. Place an oven rack in the middle position and preheat the oven to 325°F.

RECIPE CONTINUES

2. Cut a 12-by-7-inch rectangle of parchment paper. Lightly coat the loaf pan with nonstick spray, line it with the parchment paper rectangle, and fold the excess paper outward to the sides. This paper sling will make the step of unmolding the pumpkin bread much easier.

3. Sift the flours, baking powder, baking soda, salt, and spices into a medium bowl and make a well in the center with your hands.

4. Whisk the sugar, eggs, vegetable oil, pumpkin puree, and minced kumquats (if using) together in a separate mixing bowl. Pour the pumpkin mixture into the well of the dry ingredients and whisk to combine. Stir in the raisins until well distributed throughout the batter.

5. Transfer the batter to the prepared loaf pan and smooth out the top with a spatula.

6. Bake for 30 minutes. Then rotate the pan and bake for another 15 minutes, until a toothpick inserted in the center comes out clean. Rotating the pan about halfway through the baking process will ensure that the loaf bakes evenly. As soon as the bread comes out of the oven, brush the top with the barley malt syrup (if using). Let cool in the pan for at least 1 hour.

7. Carefully run an offset spatula or paring knife along the sides of the pan and pull the sling of parchment paper from the pan to remove the pumpkin bread. Slice into 1-inch pieces with a serrated knife and enjoy with a cup of coffee or tea, for breakfast or as an afternoon snack. It will keep for 2 days at room temperature if stored in an airtight container. In fact, I recommend toasting a day-old slice, then smearing it with butter. It also makes a delicious dessert, worthy of a Thanksgiving table, if served warm with a dollop of whipped cream, lightly sweetened with brown sugar.

Making Your Own Pumpkin Puree

There's nothing wrong with canned pumpkin puree, but it will never compare to the homemade version. Choose homemade over canned in recipes where the texture and flavor of pumpkin are front and center, such as pumpkin bread or pumpkin pie.

Place an oven rack in the middle position and preheat the oven to 375°F. Cut a small kabocha or butternut squash in half with a large chef's knife and scrape out the seeds. Put the halves on a roasting pan cut side down, add ½ cup water to the bottom of the pan, and cover with aluminum foil. Bake for 50 to 60 minutes or until very tender. To check whether the squash is done, carefully invert one of the halves and press the flesh with the back of a fork—if it mashes easily, like a cooked potato, the squash is ready. Cool until safe to handle, but not completely—it's better to work with the squash while it's still a bit warm because it will be easier to puree (just like mashed potatoes). Scoop out the flesh with a spoon, put it in a food processor, and puree until smooth. Depending on the size of your squash, you may have to work in batches. Let the puree cool completely, and refrigerate until ready to use. The pumpkin puree will keep in the refrigerator for 1 week or in the freezer for up to 2 months. In the fall, when we're prone to baking pumpkin treats often, it's a good idea to pack 1-cup portions in separate freezer bags that you can thaw out and use as needed.

Candied Citrus Peel

Candying citrus peel is a simple technique that makes bitter, astringent peels soft and sweet, with a tart bite that makes them almost as addictive as candy. In fact, during the early days of the Grande Cuisine when Marie-Antoine Carême cooked for the French aristocracy, candied citrus basically *was* candy. Candied citrus has, however, been around since before the fourteenth century and is believed to have originated in Arabic culinary traditions.

Although you can add your own tweaks or spin (such as adding spices to the candying syrup or spiking it with liquors like limoncello), the basic process of candying citrus peel is simple: blanch or soak the peel to remove the bitterness, boil in a simple syrup of sugar and water, then toss in granulated sugar and let dry. You can also omit the sugar coating in favor of a glossy syrup sheen instead (this is particularly handy if you're using your citrus peel as garnish or decoration). The sugar prevents the growth of microorganisms that lead to spoilage; as a result, the candied peels can last for up to a year. With this technique you can candy just about any type of citrus, including lemon, lime, grapefruit, orange, and even yuzu. Italians, in particular, make ample use of candied citrus. The classic Christmas sweet bread panettone is studded with candied lemon and orange peels, while cannoli can more often than not be found with a garnish of orange peel. In France, orangettes are made by dipping candied orange peel in tempered bittersweet chocolate, yielding an iconic bite-size treat. The English are famous for packing their fruitcakes and figgy puddings with bits of candied zest. In Costa Rica where I grew up, the candying technique is central to making toronja rellena, an elaborate preparation in which an entire grapefruit is gutted, the shell candied and filled with a milk-based taffy called *cajeta*.

Candying is somewhat laborious but always a good investment of your time. You will find plenty of opportunities to use the candied peels, and you can store them in the freezer until ready to use. Fold chopped candied peel into batters and doughs for cakes, quick breads, muffins, and scones. Use it as a garnish for cakes or incorporate it into the filling sandwiched between layers. You can add candied citrus to ice creams, sorbets, and even cocktails. Always buy organic fruits without blemishes for candying. Never discard the candying syrup, which is as flavorful and aromatic as the candied fruit. Use it to glaze sweet breads, pound cakes, or fritters. Overall, it's a veritable "secret sauce" ingredient that adds an extra burst of flavor.

Candied Kumquats

Candied kumquats have been a staple in every pastry kitchen I've worked in. They're especially useful in holiday desserts, adding Californian brightness to a Christmas panettone or Easter hot cross buns. The candying method is very simple and can be used to candy any type of citrus zest. The trick is to blanch the citrus peels three times in a row, "washing away" a bit of their bitterness and softening them so they easily absorb the candying syrup. The candied fruit can enhance many goodies such as the Buckwheat Fruit-Nut Bread on page 99 and the Barley Pumpkin Bread here.

MAKES 1 QUART

2 pounds (910 g) kumquats, stems removed

3½ cups (700 g) sugar

½ vanilla bean

1. Fill a medium pot halfway with water and bring to a boil over high heat. Carefully drop the kumquats into the boiling water and blanch for 1 minute. Drain the kumquats in a colander and discard the blanching water. Repeat two more times with fresh boiling water. Set the blanched kumquats aside.

2. Put the sugar in a separate, clean pot and add 4 cups (about 1 liter) water. Split the vanilla bean lengthwise with a paring knife and scrape the pulp with the back of the knife. Put the pod and pulp in the pot. Bring this mixture up to a boil. Lower the heat, add the blanched kumquats, and bring the candying syrup to a simmer. Cut a parchment paper circle a bit larger than the circumference of the pot and place it over the kumquats, just touching the syrup to keep the kumquats submerged. Allow the kumquats to simmer in their syrup for 90 minutes or until the skin of the kumquats is translucent and can be pierced easily with your fingernail. Let cool completely.

3. Transfer the candied kumquats and their syrup to a glass container. Cover and let stand at room temperature overnight. The next day, place them in the refrigerator and keep indefinitely.

Macadamia Brown Butter Blondies

MAKES 12 BLONDIE WEDGES

Equipment: 9-inch cake pan

½ cup (65 g) whole macadamia nuts, raw or unsalted dry-roasted

1 cup plus 2 tablespoons (2¼ sticks/250 g) unsalted butter

½ vanilla bean

¾ cup (85 g) barley flour

¾ cup (105 g) all-purpose flour

1¾ teaspoons baking powder

1½ teaspoons kosher salt

1⅓ cups packed (285 g) dark brown sugar

2 large eggs

1 teaspoon vanilla extract

We've baked these brown butter blondies every day since opening Friends & Family in 2017. To make them stand out in a case full of flaky croissants, fruity danishes, and glistening, glazed muffins, we cut them into wedges rather than the traditional bar shape. This allows us to bake the blondies in a round cake pan, ensuring that each piece has a chewy, toasted exterior and a soft center. This caramel-flavored treat demonstrates the powerful pairing of brown butter and barley. Macadamia nuts added at the end create a complete multitexture experience. Never leave them in the oven for too long; the key to a great blondie is baking it for the right amount of time. You will thank me for this recipe when the holiday season comes around. Because they're incredibly easy to make, keep for a few days, and travel extremely well, these blondies are an ideal homemade gift you can ship to friends and family all over the country.

MOTHER GRAINS | 48 | BARLEY

1. Place an oven rack in the middle position and preheat the oven to 350°F.

2. If using raw macadamia nuts, start by toasting them. Scatter the macadamia nuts on a baking sheet. Toast in the oven for 8 to 10 minutes or until golden. Let them cool completely.

3. Cut a 9-inch circle of parchment paper. Lightly coat the bottom of the cake pan with nonstick spray and line it with the parchment circle.

4. Put the butter in a medium pot. Split the vanilla bean lengthwise with a paring knife, use the back of the knife to scrape out the pulp, and put both pulp and pod into the pot. Cook over low heat until the butter starts to turn amber, about 8 minutes. Keep a watchful eye on your butter; it can go from blond to burned in a split second. When the butter is ready, pour it into a large heat-resistant bowl to stop the browning process. Make sure to use a rubber spatula to scrape all the flavorful milk solids at the bottom of the pot—much of the flavor of brown butter comes from these toasty bits. Carefully remove the vanilla bean with kitchen tongs and discard.

5. Sift the flours, baking powder, and salt into a bowl.

6. Add the brown sugar to the bowl of browned butter while the butter is still warm and stir to combine with a rubber spatula or wooden spoon. Add the eggs one by one, stirring after each addition. Add the flour mixture and the vanilla and stir just to combine. Finally, add the macadamia nuts and stir until they're evenly distributed throughout the batter. Transfer to the prepared pan and smooth the top with an offset spatula.

7. Bake for 20 minutes, until the edges are starting to brown but the center is still underdone. Then rotate the pan and bake for another 15 to 20 minutes, until the top is a rich golden brown and a toothpick inserted in the center comes out clean. Rotating the pan halfway through the baking process will ensure the blondies bake evenly. Remove from the oven and let cool completely, about 1 hour.

8. Invert the blondies onto a cutting board, peel off the parchment paper, and then flip so the crusty side is on top. Cut into 12 equal wedges. The blondies can be enjoyed on their own or alongside ice cream—I recommend vanilla or salted caramel. Stored in an airtight container, they will keep for up to 5 days.

Variation

Try making the blondies with einkorn flour instead of barley. Just substitute ¾ cup (80 g) einkorn flour for the barley flour. Einkorn performs well in recipes with a high butter ratio. Its wheat-forward flavor comes through and pairs very well with the depth of the brown butter. You will notice einkorn creates a chewier blondie. Learn more about einkorn flour on page 277.

Malt–Glazed Brownies

Equipment: 9-inch square cake pan

¾ cup plus 2 tablespoons (100 g) barley flour

¾ cup plus 2 tablespoons (115 g) all-purpose flour

1 teaspoon kosher salt

1 cup (2 sticks/225 g) unsalted butter, cut into 1-inch pieces

1⅓ cups (240 g) bittersweet chocolate chips

1½ cups (300 g) granulated sugar

½ cup packed (105 g) dark brown sugar

¼ cup (25 g) Dutch-processed cocoa powder, sifted

1 teaspoon vanilla extract

3 large eggs

For the malt-caramel glaze

8 tablespoons (1 stick/115 g) unsalted butter

¾ cup packed (160 g) dark brown sugar

⅓ cup (80 ml) barley malt syrup or barley extract

½ cup (120 ml) heavy cream

1 teaspoon kosher salt

½ cup (60 g) confectioners' sugar, sifted

Coarse sea salt such as Maldon or fleur de sel (optional)

Brownies are one of those chameleon treats that adopt different personalities depending on which ingredients you throw into the mixing bowl. This explains why you can see limitless variations across magazines, cookbooks, and food blogs. Brownies can be made with many of the mother grains covered in this book (see variations on page 52), acquiring unique profiles that range from fudgy and deeply chocolaty if made with rye to earthy and wheaty when made with spelt or Sonora wheat. Brownies made with barley flour are my favorite by far. The caramely flavor of barley flour is a great match for the assertive taste of chocolate. Barley also makes this a tender, chewy-edged brownie, which I prefer to those with a cakier structure. To achieve this texture, I incorporate as much barley flour as the batter can hold without making it dry or dense. Glazing brownies with malt-caramel sauce might sound over the top, and the stand-alone brownie is already great without it, but the glaze fulfills a dual purpose: it helps create a luscious confection while preserving the moisture of the brownie. Sprinkled with crunchy sea salt, these are dangerously addictive. The recipe for the Malt-Caramel Glaze makes more than you will need, about 2 cups. Save leftovers in the refrigerator and reheat to pour over ice cream for a quick homemade sundae.

RECIPE CONTINUES

1. Place an oven rack in the middle position and preheat the oven to 350°F.

2. Sift the flours and salt into a bowl.

3. Cut a 16-by-9-inch rectangle of parchment paper. Lightly coat the cake pan with nonstick spray, line it with the parchment paper rectangle, and fold the excess paper outward to the sides. This paper sling will make the step of unmolding the brownies much easier.

4. Place the butter and chocolate chips in a medium heat-resistant bowl. Fill a medium pot with water and place over low heat. When the water is barely simmering, place the bowl of butter and chocolate on top, making sure the bottom of the bowl doesn't touch the simmering water. Stir occasionally with a rubber spatula until completely melted. Remove the bowl from the heat. Mix in the sugars, cocoa, and vanilla. Add the eggs one by one, stirring vigorously with a rubber spatula after each addition. Finally, add the sifted flours and mix until thoroughly combined. Transfer the batter to the prepared cake pan and smooth out the top with an offset spatula.

5. Bake the brownies for 20 minutes, then rotate the pan and bake for another 20 to 25 minutes or until a toothpick inserted in the center comes out just a little bit moist. Rotating the pan halfway through the baking process will ensure that the brownies bake evenly. The edges should feel firm and pull slightly from the sides of the pan, while the center is soft and yields if pressed gently with your finger. Remove from the oven and let cool completely. Carefully run an offset spatula or paring knife along the sides of the pan and pull the sling of parchment paper from the pan to remove the brownies. Transfer to a cutting board and cut into sixteen 2¼-inch squares with a chef's knife. For a cleaner cut, I recommend wiping the blade of the knife with a wet towel after each cut.

6. To make the malt-caramel glaze, melt the butter in a small saucepan over medium heat, add the brown sugar, and stir to dissolve the sugar. Add the barley malt syrup and cream and continue to stir until the mixture comes to a simmer. Turn off the heat and whisk in the salt and confectioners' sugar. Pour the warm glaze into a small bowl. Carefully dip the tops of the brownies in the glaze and place them on a cooling rack to let the excess caramel drip down the sides. Sprinkle with sea salt and enjoy. The brownies will keep for up to 3 days stored in an airtight container at room temperature. The bare brownies can be frozen for up to 2 weeks. To finish them, let them thaw at room temperature and glaze as instructed.

Variations

Rye Brownies

For more fudgy and decadent brownies, use 1 cup (125 g) dark rye flour instead of the barley flour.

Spelt Brownies

For a more wholesome version, use 2 cups (260 g) whole-grain spelt flour instead of the barley and all-purpose flours.

Malted Almond Bars

Equipment: 9-inch square cake pan

For the shortbread crust

½ cup (45 g) sliced unblanched almonds

1 cup (140 g) all-purpose flour

1 cup (110 g) barley flour

⅓ cup (60 g) granulated sugar

¼ cup packed (55 g) dark brown sugar

1 teaspoon kosher salt

1 cup (2 sticks/225 grams) unsalted butter, cut into 8 pieces, at room temperature

1 teaspoon vanilla extract

1 teaspoon almond extract

For the caramel layer

½ cup (45 g) sliced unblanched almonds

⅓ cup (80 ml) heavy cream

2 tablespoons unsalted butter

3 tablespoons barley malt syrup

3 tablespoons granulated sugar

3 tablespoons all-purpose flour, sifted

1 teaspoon vanilla extract

½ teaspoon kosher salt

These bars may look elaborate, but they're actually really easy to make. Their most enticing feature is a soft yet chewy caramel layer covering a shortbreadlike bottom crust. A similar sweet, known as "millionaire's shortbread," is common in London bakeries. Imagine a sandy layer of buttery shortbread topped with a generous caramel layer and glazed with chocolate; no wonder it is so popular. This version is all about the barley malt, which is responsible for the caramel's pleasantly tacky texture and robust butterscotch flavor. I start by covering a pan with shortbread cookie dough made with ground almonds and barley flour, which has a delightful melt-in-your-mouth quality. The shortbread is then baked to perfection and topped with a stovetop barley caramel garnished with a good helping of toasted almonds. Once the caramel cools and hardens, the shortbread is cut into bars that are so rich and satisfying that you won't miss the customary chocolate. They can be served with afternoon tea or coffee or as a sweet finale for a casual lunch.

You might be tempted to use almond flour, but refrain from doing so—almond meal is too fine for this recipe.

1. Place an oven rack in the middle position and preheat the oven to 325°F.

2. Cut a 16-by-12-inch rectangle of aluminum foil and line the bottom of the cake pan with it. Fold the excess foil over the sides of the pan. This foil sling will help release the bars from the pan later. Coat the bottom and sides of the pan with nonstick spray.

RECIPE CONTINUES

3. To make the shortbread, put the almonds and the flours in the bowl of a food processor and grind to a fine meal. Add the sugars and salt and grind for another minute. Add the butter and pulse until the dough starts to come together. Remove the top of the food processor and scrape the sides of the bowl with a rubber spatula. Add the vanilla and almond extracts and continue pulsing until a uniform dough forms. Transfer this dough to the prepared pan and press down with your fingers or the flat bottom of a glass, until the dough is pressed into an even layer.

4. Bake the shortbread crust for 20 minutes, then rotate the pan and bake for another 20 to 25 minutes, until the top is a rich golden brown. Rotating the pan halfway through the baking process will ensure it bakes evenly. Remove from the oven and set aside while you prepare the caramel layer. Increase the oven temperature to 350°F.

5. To make the caramel layer, scatter the almonds on a baking sheet. Toast for 7 minutes or until golden. Let cool completely.

6. Warm the cream and butter in a medium saucepan. Add the barley malt syrup and sugar. Cook over medium heat, stirring constantly with a wooden spoon or a heat-resistant spatula. Bring the mixture to a boil and then continue to cook for 2 minutes, stirring vigorously. Reduce the heat to low, add the flour, vanilla, and salt all at once, and stir vigorously to combine. Add the toasted almonds and continue stirring for 2 minutes. At this point the caramel should be thicker and approximately 160°F.

Working quickly, pour the caramel over the baked shortbread layer and spread evenly. Let cool completely, at least 1 hour.

7. Use the excess foil to carefully transfer the bars from the pan to a cutting board. Cut into sixteen 2¼-inch squares with a large sharp knife. Wiping the blade with a kitchen towel between cuts will create a cleaner edge. Enjoy immediately or store the bars in a single layer in an airtight container for up to 2 days.

Persimmon Sticky Pudding

Equipment: 9-inch Bundt cake pan

For the pudding

2 large ripe Hachiya persimmons

¼ cup (60 ml) buttermilk

¾ cup (105 g) all-purpose flour, plus extra for dusting the pan

1 cup (110 g) whole-grain barley flour

1 teaspoon baking soda

1¼ teaspoons baking powder

¼ teaspoon kosher salt

8 tablespoons (1 stick/115 g) unsalted butter

1½ cups packed (320 g) dark brown sugar

2 large eggs

For the sticky sauce

8 tablespoons (1 stick/115 g) unsalted butter

½ vanilla bean

½ cup (120 ml) heavy cream

1 cup packed (215 g) dark brown sugar

¼ cup (60 ml) barley malt syrup

This dessert is an updated version of sticky toffee pudding, an English dessert consisting of a baked or steamed cake covered in caramel sauce and served with crème anglaise or vanilla ice cream. The fact that the pudding is actually a cake has prompted many to consider it a misnomer, but I prefer calling it pudding to pay homage to its British ancestry. Throughout the years I've made many versions of sticky pudding, adding fresh or dried fruits depending on the season. But this autumnal iteration with persimmons and barley flour will floor you. It's as if the two ingredients have always belonged together. The addition of tangy buttermilk to the cake batter strikes a balance with the deep, rich flavors of barley, brown sugar, and persimmon. If possible, use ripe Hachiya persimmons for this dessert, which can be mashed easily with a wooden spoon. Hachiyas are in season in the early fall and are typically available until midwinter. When ripe, Hachiyas are soft and suitable for baking like an overripe banana. If you can't find this variety, use overripe firm persimmons like Fuyu. As for the Malt-Glazed Brownies on page 51, barley malt syrup is the key ingredient in the sticky caramel sauce to bathe the pudding in. The sticky pudding can be made up to 2 days in advance since it keeps and reheats very well. And always, without exception, serve it piping hot, accompanied by unsweetened whipped cream or vanilla ice cream. For a beautiful presentation, I like baking the pudding in a 9-inch Bundt cake pan to be served family style. Save this dessert for large dinner parties; one pudding will serve up to 10 guests.

RECIPE CONTINUES

1. Place an oven rack in the middle position and preheat the oven to 350°F.

2. Remove any stems from the persimmons and mash in a bowl with a wooden spoon. Push through a fine-mesh sieve, using a rubber spatula to press as much of the pulp through as possible. Discard the skins and seeds. You should have approximately 1 cup (250 g) mashed fruit. Combine with the buttermilk.

3. Generously coat the surface of the Bundt pan with nonstick spray. Dust the pan with 2 to 3 tablespoons all-purpose flour, then invert the pan and tap out any excess flour.

4. Sift the flours, baking soda, baking powder, and salt into a bowl.

5. In a stand mixer fitted with the paddle attachment, beat the butter and brown sugar at medium speed to form a paste. Add the eggs one by one, mixing well after each addition. Add the sifted flours in two batches, alternating with the persimmon-buttermilk mixture. Stop the mixer after each addition to scrape the sides of the bowl with a rubber spatula. Transfer the batter to the prepared pan and bake for 20 minutes, then rotate the pan and bake for another 25 minutes, until a toothpick inserted in the center comes out clean. Rotating the pan halfway through the baking process will ensure that the pudding bakes evenly. Remove from the oven and let cool for 10 minutes.

6. While the pudding is baking, make the sticky sauce. Melt the butter in a medium saucepan over medium heat. Split the vanilla bean lengthwise with a paring knife, scrape out the pulp with the back of the knife, and put both pulp and pod into the pot. As soon as the butter melts completely but before it browns, add the cream, brown sugar, and barley malt syrup and bring to a boil, stirring constantly. Reduce the heat and let the sauce simmer for 1 minute. Remove the pot from the heat but hold in a warm spot.

7. Using oven mitts, carefully invert the Bundt pan onto a serving plate. Use a skewer or toothpick to gently poke a few holes across the pudding's surface. Pour about half of the warm sticky sauce over the plated pudding (if the sauce is no longer warm, reheat over medium heat for a few minutes while stirring to prevent it from burning). Wait for 5 minutes, allowing the sauce to be absorbed, and then pour the remaining sauce over the pudding. (Alternatively, you can reserve some sauce for guests to pour on their individual pudding portion.) Slice and serve immediately or reheat and serve later. If saving the pudding for another day, cool the bathed pudding and reserve the excess sauce that drips from it. Store the sauce in a container and refrigerate. Cover the pudding with plastic wrap and refrigerate up to a week. To reheat, preheat the oven to 350°F. Place the pudding on a baking sheet coated with pan spray and warm it for 15 to 20 minutes. In a saucepan, reheat the sauce over medium while stirring constantly. Bathe the pudding with the warm sauce.

Figgy and Purple Barley Cake

MAKES ONE 9-INCH CAKE, SERVING 8 TO 10

Equipment: 9-inch springform pan

For roasting the figs

12 ripe black figs (about 1 pound/450 g)

2 tablespoons unsalted butter, melted

1 tablespoon packed dark brown sugar

For the cake batter

¾ cup (85 g) purple barley flour

¾ cup (105 g) all-purpose flour

1 teaspoon baking powder

½ teaspoon baking soda

½ teaspoon kosher salt

8 tablespoons (1 stick/115 g) unsalted butter, at room temperature

1 cup (200 g) granulated sugar

3 large eggs

1 teaspoon vanilla extract

¼ cup (60 ml) buttermilk

6 ripe black figs (about 8 ounces/225 g), roughly chopped

When I began exploring the world of barley, I kept running into darker varietals that were used mainly by home brewers. While not as popular or widely available as regular barley, purple barley (along with brown and black barley) is rich in antioxidants and has a slightly smoky flavor. Its origins can be traced back to the Himalayas, and the Nile River valley before that. It may not be easy to find milled forms of purple barley, but it is possible to make flour out of it that is suitable for baking. My local mill, Grist & Toll, began grinding small amounts of purple barley a few years ago to encourage local bakers to use it in bread. And indeed, the first thing I made with purple barley was a dramatic loaf of bread packed with fresh and dried blueberries that accentuated its purple hue. Color was once again the inspiration for this satisfying cake made with Black Mission figs, which boast an intense, dark purple exterior. Black Missions are abundant in the late summer all over California, and they're my favorite variety to use in this cake, but any dark variety will do as long as they're very ripe. This dessert is visually striking; imagine a poetic, gray-violet cake topped with gorgeous roasted figs, halved so that you can appreciate their lustrous, juicy centers. To intensify the figgy flavor, I fold chopped figs into the batter.

If you can't find purple barley flour, you can substitute regular barley flour, but I dare you to seek this special ingredient and transform what would be a humble cake into a breathtaking and profoundly delicious dessert that celebrates the last few weeks of summer. Baking the cake in a 9-inch springform pan eliminates the need to invert it onto a plate to release it and keeps the top intact.

RECIPE CONTINUES

1. Place an oven rack in the middle position and preheat the oven to 350°F. Lightly coat the bottom and sides of the pan with nonstick spray.

2. To roast the figs, cut the 12 figs in half lengthwise and arrange them cut side up on a baking sheet or other shallow pan. Drizzle the melted butter over the figs, sprinkle with the brown sugar, and roast for 15 minutes. Remove from the oven and let cool completely.

3. Sift the flours, baking powder, baking soda, and salt into a bowl.

4. In a stand mixer fitted with the paddle attachment, cream the butter and granulated sugar at medium speed until light and creamy, about 2 minutes. Mix in the eggs one by one, scraping the sides of the bowl after each addition. Add half of the flour mixture and mix for 30 seconds. Add the vanilla and buttermilk and mix for 30 seconds. Add the remainder of the flour and mix until fully incorporated. Using a rubber spatula, fold in the chopped figs. Transfer the batter to the prepared pan and smooth out the top with an offset spatula. Arrange the roasted figs decoratively on top.

5. Bake for 25 minutes, then rotate the pan and bake for another 25 minutes, until a toothpick inserted in the center comes out clean. Rotating the pan halfway through the baking process will ensure that the cake bakes evenly. The top of the cake will be a rich golden brown and the figs should be juicy and slightly caramelized. Remove from the oven and let cool for at least 30 minutes. To unmold, run an offset spatula or paring knife along the side of the pan and loosen the springform lock. Transfer to a cake plate. Slice with a sharp knife. The cake will remain moist stored in an airtight container at room temperature for 2 days.

Above: Transfer the batter to the prepared pan and smooth out the top with an offset spatula. Arrange the roasted figs decoratively on top.
Opposite: The finished cake.

Potato Rolls

Equipment: 10-inch round cake pan

1 large russet potato (6 to 8 ounces/170 to 225 g)

1 cup (240 ml) whole milk

1¼ teaspoons instant yeast

4 tablespoons (½ stick/55 g) unsalted butter, at room temperature

1 large egg, plus 1 egg, beaten, for brushing

¾ cup (85 g) barley flour

2¼ cups (315 g) all-purpose flour, plus extra for rolling

3 tablespoons sugar

1 tablespoon kosher salt

1 to 2 tablespoons barley flakes, rolled oats, pepitas, flax, or other seeds for topping

I made these soft, squishy rolls for years before deciding to add barley flour, but ever since then I can't seem to make them any other way. Barley flour softens the dough's texture, and its subtle, earthy sweetness pairs well with the mild potato. The fact that barley's natural preserving qualities extend the rolls' shelf life is yet another asset. These rolls deserve a place at the Thanksgiving table, and whenever I bake them for this occasion I shape them into a pull-apart centerpiece. To highlight barley's contribution to the recipe, I decorate with a sprinkle of barley flakes, but feel free to use other garnishes. They are irresistible just after being baked. Split one in half and spread with butter, or do as I do and toast a day-old roll to make a Thanksgiving leftover sandwich for lunch.

You'll notice that this recipe calls for a higher ratio of all-purpose to barley flour. This is common in bread recipes containing barley, because barley flour's naturally low gluten content means it doesn't provide sufficient strength or structure to the crumb. Barley does, however, make the rolls moist, supple, and subtly sweet. The milk, mashed potato, and butter will make the dough soft and sticky, so a stand mixer is required to mix it.

1. Peel the potato and cut into 2-inch chunks. Put in a small saucepan and cover with water. Boil the potato for 25 to 30 minutes, or until very tender when poked with a fork. Drain, transfer to a bowl, and mash with the back of a fork while the potato is still warm. Let the mash cool completely before using. You can make the mash up to 2 days ahead and store it in an airtight container in the refrigerator. You will need 1 cup of the mash (about 140 g).

2. Warm the milk in a small saucepan until lukewarm (98° to 105°F), transfer to the bowl of a stand mixer fitted with the dough hook attachment, and sprinkle the yeast on top. Stir with a spoon to dissolve and let activate for 5 minutes.

3. Add the potato mash, butter, egg, flours, sugar, and salt and mix on low speed until the ingredients come together, about 2 minutes. Switch to the paddle attachment and mix on medium speed for another minute or until the dough looks smooth and uniform. Transfer the

dough to a floured surface and knead briefly into a ball. Lightly coat a medium bowl with nonstick spray and place the dough in it. Cover with a clean kitchen towel or plastic wrap and let the dough rise at room temperature for 2 hours, until doubled in size.

4. Gently transfer the risen dough to a lightly floured surface. Divide the dough into 12 equal portions (about 75 g each) and roll each one into a ball. If you wish to make pull-apart rolls, grease the sides of the cake pan and line the bottom of the pan with parchment paper. Arrange the buns in the pan. They should be almost touching with just ½ inch between them. They will stick to one another as they rise. If you wish to bake the rolls individually, place them at least 2 inches apart on a baking sheet lined with parchment paper. In both cases, let them rise again at room temperature for 30 to 45 minutes, until they no longer bounce back when you press them gently with a moistened index finger.

5. Place an oven rack in the middle position and preheat the oven to 350°F.

6. Gently brush the tops of the rolls with the beaten egg, garnish with barley flakes or seeds of your choice, and bake for 10 minutes. Then rotate the pan or baking sheet and bake for another 15 to 17 minutes, until the rolls are golden. Rotating the pan halfway through the baking process will ensure that the rolls bake evenly. Remove the rolls from the oven and carefully run an offset spatula or paring knife

along the sides of the cake pan. Let cool for 20 minutes. Gently invert the pan to release the buns from the pan. Serve while still warm or once they're completely cool. The rolls will keep well for another day if stored in an airtight container or sealed plastic bag. They also freeze well for a couple of weeks, but the thawed rolls will need to be reheated for a few minutes in a 350°F oven.

Kimchi Fried Barley

1 cup (200 g) hulled, hull-less, or pearled barley

1 tablespoon black or white sesame seeds

6 tablespoons (90 ml) vegetable oil such as avocado or grapeseed oil, plus extra for the fried eggs

2 slices bacon, cut into lardons or ½-inch strips (optional)

1 small yellow onion (about 85 g), cut into medium dice

1 cup mild or spicy kimchi (170 g), roughly chopped (I recommend King's or Mother in Law's, available in the Asian foods section of good grocery stores)

1 tablespoon soy sauce

1 teaspoon Asian sesame oil

4 large eggs (optional)

Kosher salt

1 scallion, thinly sliced on the diagonal

Los Angeles is home to the largest Korean population outside of Korea, and I happen to live and work within minutes of the city's bustling Koreatown. However, the first time I had this dish wasn't in one of the area's many great eateries. One day I was thinking aloud at work, wondering what I could make for dinner with only a jar of kimchi in my fridge, when a Korean American coworker suggested kimchi fried rice. Say what? I'd never heard of this. Upon arriving home, determined to put my kimchi to good use, I realized I had no rice. I decided to use a bag of barley I had in the pantry, and swapping one grain for another proved serendipitous.

When available, opt for hulled or hull-less barley (see page 40). Because of its higher fiber content, hulled and hull-less barley are the most flavorful. If you have trouble finding it, you can use the more common pearled barley. I like to add bacon to the recipe because its richness balances kimchi's intensity, but omit if you're cooking for vegetarians. This dish has so much texture and flavor that you truly won't miss it. I don't usually season with additional salt since the salt in the bacon, kimchi, and soy sauce seem to be enough. I always serve this with a fried egg on top, and, unless you're a vegan, you should too.

1. Place the barley in a medium pot and cover with 2 inches of water. Bring to a boil, reduce the heat so that the water simmers gently, and cook for 40 minutes, until the barley is tender but still toothsome in the center—similar to pasta cooked al dente. Drain in a colander and spread the barley on a baking sheet to prevent the grains from clumping as they cool.

2. Toast the sesame seeds in a small skillet over medium heat, stirring constantly to prevent them from burning. When the seeds start to smell toasty, after about 1 minute, transfer to a plate to cool.

3. Heat a large cast-iron skillet over medium-low heat, add 1 tablespoon of the vegetable oil, and sauté the bacon until it starts crisping up. Remove with a slotted spoon and transfer to a plate lined with paper towels to absorb the fat. Transfer the bacon fat in the skillet to a heat-resistant container and save for later use. In the same skillet, heat 3 tablespoons of the remaining vegetable oil and sauté the onion over medium heat until soft, about 2 minutes. Add the cooked barley and cook for another 2 minutes while stirring to combine. Add the kimchi and bacon and cook for 2 minutes, stirring occasionally to prevent it from sticking to the bottom of the pan. Turn off the heat. Stir in the soy sauce and sesame oil. Divide the kimchi fried barley among four plates.

4. Working quickly, fry the eggs one at a time: In a nonstick pan, heat about 2 teaspoons of vegetable oil over medium-high heat. Crack 1 egg into the pan and fry until the edges start to set. Season with salt. Carefully add about 1 tablespoon of water, immediately cover with a lid, and finish cooking for another minute, until the white is set but the yolk is still runny. Transfer to one of the plates, setting it on top of the kimchi fried barley. Wipe the pan with a paper towel and repeat the process until you've fried all the eggs. Sprinkle the toasted sesame seeds and sliced scallion on top and serve immediately.

Shiitake, Leek, and Toasted Barley Soup

1 cup (200 g) hull-less, hulled, or pearled barley

1 medium leek

4 cups loosely packed shiitake mushrooms (about 16 mushrooms)

4 to 6 tablespoons (60 to 90 ml) vegetable oil

Kosher salt

2 quarts (2 liters) mushroom or vegetable stock, homemade or store-bought

2 cups (60 g) baby spinach

2 tablespoons soy sauce or Bragg Liquid Aminos

Even though this is a vegetarian dish, there's something meaty about it. The richness of the browned mushrooms and depth of the toasted barley emulate the comforting flavors commonly found in a full-bodied beef stew. My husband, Daniel, and I try to eat minimal meat at home, so when craving beef barley soup one night he decided to concoct a version relying on the robust flavor of shiitake mushrooms. Another advantage to this soup is that, unlike its meaty relatives, it's ready in under an hour. The texture of cooked barley kernels is similar to that of brown rice, perhaps a bit chewy but still tender inside. In this soup, barley adds a satisfyingly toothsome bite. Besides browning the mushrooms to accentuate their earthiness, I lightly toast the barley to bring out its smoky, nutty tones. The smells emanating from this pot on the stove will make you swoon. Enjoy a bowlful as soon as the barley is tender, but make sure to save leftovers for the next day, when, like most soups, it will taste even better.

1. Place an oven rack in the middle position and preheat the oven to 350°F.

2. Scatter the barley on a baking sheet and toast in the oven for 10 minutes. Using oven mitts, carefully remove the sheet and give it a gentle shake to toss the barley around. Toast for another 5 minutes. You will know the barley is nicely toasted when the kernels look brown and start to smell like popcorn. Remove from the oven and set aside to cool.

3. Cut the leek in half lengthwise and slice each piece into half-moons about ⅛ inch thick. Put in a bowl and cover with cold water, swishing to remove any dirt. Drain. If the leeks are still gritty, repeat the rinsing process. When the leeks are clean, make sure to drain them well.

4. Use a damp paper towel to wipe each mushroom and remove any dirt. Do not rinse them, which would prevent them from browning. Remove and discard the mushroom stems and thinly slice the caps.

5. Heat 2 to 3 tablespoons of the vegetable oil in a stockpot over medium-high heat. Working in two batches, sauté the mushrooms until they start to brown, 3 to 4 minutes, adding more oil as necessary. Be careful not to overcrowd the pot, which can prevent the mushrooms from browning. Transfer the sautéed mushrooms to a plate.

6. Reduce the heat to low, add the remaining oil, and sauté the leeks until translucent, 4 to 5 minutes. Stir in the sautéed mushrooms and toasted barley. Season lightly with salt. Add the stock plus 1 quart of water. Adjust the heat so that the liquid simmers and cook for 35 to 40 minutes, or until the barley is plump and tender.

7. Add the spinach and simmer for another 2 minutes, until the spinach wilts. Mix in the soy sauce and serve immediately.

8. Allow the soup to cool completely before storing. Transfer it to a nonreactive container and store in the freezer for up to 1 month or in the refrigerator for up to 5 days.

Toasted Barley Tea

Toasted barley is the base for barley tea, an Asian beverage I've come to enjoy at local Korean restaurants. It is served chilled and is incredibly easy to make. Digestive benefits are often attributed to it, and while I have no proof of the veracity of these claims, I do feel a cup settles my stomach after a gargantuan dinner of Korean barbecue. At home I use whichever kernels I have on hand—hulled, hull-less, or pearled. As long as the barley is properly toasted, I can't tell the difference, but in Korea, only barley of the highest quality is used to prepare this tea. To make it, toast barley kernels in a dry sauté pan until the grains look golden brown and start to smell like popcorn. Really, they do smell like popcorn, and if you don't remove them from the stove soon enough, they will begin to pop. Let the toasted kernels cool. Place 1 tablespoon of toasted barley in a tea bag or infuser, and pour 1 cup of hot water over it. Alternatively, you can prepare a larger amount in a teapot, maintaining the proportion of 1 tablespoon toasted barley for every cup of water. Steep for 15 minutes and enjoy. For a cold preparation, refrigerate the steeped tea for a few hours. Pouring it directly over ice will dilute the flavor. Although it is traditionally served unsweetened, adding a bit of honey is delicious if desired.

buckwheat

FAGOPYRUM ESCULENTUM

Buckwheat, the little pseudocereal that could.

On France's wind-washed northwestern coast, buckwheat is known as *blé noir*, or "black flour," and it's used to make a dish so integral to Breton culture that a religious celebration—Virgin Mary's Blessing Day—was renamed *La Chandeleur*, or "Day of the Crepe." In Bhutan, buckwheat has been cultivated for generations and transformed into thick or thin pancakes served with spicy stews. Buckwheat became slippery soba noodles for the Japanese islanders in Shikoku and a hearty breakfast to buffer Russians against the bitter cold. Italians make a flat buckwheat pasta called *pizzoccheri*, while toasted buckwheat porridge, or kasha, is a staple across Eastern Europe. Jewish peasants in Poland used the crop to make a comforting noodle dish known as *varnishkes,* and in colonial North America early Amish settlers transformed it into griddle cakes. Almost every culture in the northern hemisphere has put its own spin on buckwheat cookery, where it has always exemplified working with what you have. Each regional dish is reflective of one thing: a resilient crop that thrives in challenging conditions.

It's important to clarify exactly what buckwheat is. Buckwheat is a pseudograin, like quinoa or amaranth, which means it comes from a leafy flowering bush or shrub rather than a grass. Technically, buckwheat is a dry fruit related to rhubarb and sorrel, but it can still be ground into flour like other cereals and grains.

Opposite: Buckwheat Banana Bread (page 73)

Buckwheat is naturally gluten-free, making it an excellent option for those with celiac disease or gluten intolerance. It's also remarkably healthful and high in zinc, copper, manganese, potassium, and protein. Buckwheat contains significantly more protein, fiber, and B vitamins than wheat or oats. One of buckwheat's most distinguishing features is its dark color, which comes from the rutin in its husks. If flavorful crepes and noodles weren't motivation enough, consider adding buckwheat to your diet for the anti-inflammatory and antioxidant properties of rutin.

In addition to being a powerful health staple, buckwheat is one of our oldest domesticated grains. It has coexisted with humankind for eight thousand years, most likely originating in southwest China and the Himalayan region. It's believed to have been first cultivated as a domestic crop in the Balkans, around 4000 BC, and can be traced specifically to the region surrounding Lake Baikal, in southern Siberia. Buckwheat prefers high altitudes and thrives in cool, moist conditions. Although sensitive to extreme weather, buckwheat can grow in acidic, underfertilized, and otherwise poor soil. This adaptability facilitated its propagation across Europe via historical trade and invasion routes. Eventually, early Dutch settlers brought it to America. They called it *bochweit*, or "beech wheat," because buckwheat's triangular fruit resembles beechnuts.

The grain was popular in early America—both Thomas Jefferson and George Washington grew it in Virginia—but eventually fell out of favor with the rise of industrialization. By the end of World War II, buckwheat was a niche crop, cultivated by Amish and Shaker communities. Between 1918 and 1954, the amount of buckwheat harvested in the United States fell from over a million acres to just 150,000. Thankfully, this trend began reversing in the 1970s, when health-conscious consumers became interested in buckwheat's nutritional value. Today, Washington State and the American Northeast are on their way to becoming vigorous buckwheat-growing regions.

Buckwheat is a powerful tool for field maintenance. It makes a great cover crop, choking out weeds that would otherwise rob crops of nutrition. Because of its versatility and short growth cycle, it's an excellent candidate for crop rotation, which involves alternating crops in specific fields to preserve and revitalize the soil. And as if these uses weren't enough, buckwheat creates no waste—its stalks can be used as straw to feed livestock.

Characterized by the slightly bitter, tannic taste of its hulls, buckwheat has a unique, lingering quality and distinct flavor profile—deeply earthy, like a garden after the rain, and nutty, like toasted sesame seeds, with subtle aromatic notes of green tea and rose. Although buckwheat is grown all year round, I think of it as a spring grain because of its short growing cycle and regenerative abilities. As such, I tend to pair it with spring flavors in dishes that embrace spring produce, such as the blini with an herbaceous Dungeness crab salad on page 95, the savory crepes stuffed with spring onions and asparagus on page 80, or my take on crepes Suzette, made with blood orange and mascarpone, on page 81. But truthfully, I bake with buckwheat often, regardless of the season. It gets along beautifully with the dark berries of summer, as in the Baked

Buckwheat Pancake with Berry Compote on page 83. In the fall, combine buckwheat with honey in the comforting Buckwheat Honey Cake on page 90, and in winter, pull your favorite dried fruits and nuts from the cupboard and make the Buckwheat Fruit-Nut Bread on page 99.

How to Purchase and Use

Groats and Kasha

You'll find several forms of buckwheat in the marketplace. The first, and simplest, is groats. They're triangular in shape and can be cooked into pilafs and hot cereals such as the legendary Eastern European porridge kasha. In kasha, the groats are roasted and partially broken. The resulting coarse meal is then cooked with water into a hearty mash. It's usually served with crispy onions and a dab of butter, or just like oatmeal with milk and sugar. Kasha is available in natural food markets, but I worry that the product doesn't rotate enough due to its lack of popularity. I recommend purchasing whole groats at retail mills or online specialty grain stores to guarantee freshness.

Flour

Buckwheat flour, one of my favorite pastry ingredients, is widely available. It's made by grinding groats and classified as light or dark depending on how much hull is left in the flour. I recommend purchasing whole-grain or dark buckwheat flour, which has more health benefits because the hull is left intact. When combined with moist ingredients, buckwheat flour develops a gluey texture. This rare binding property makes it a popular choice for gluten-free baking. I often mix it with all-purpose flour, which adds structure to breads and cakes and helps to tame buckwheat's assertive flavor. My go-to ratio is one part all-purpose flour to one part buckwheat flour. But as you will see in the following recipes, this isn't always the case. Bread requires a higher proportion of wheat flour, while pancake and waffle recipes can incorporate more buckwheat flour.

I buy freshly ground buckwheat flour at specialty mills such as Grist & Toll and Anson Mills whenever I can. The balanced flavor and attractive hue of fresh buckwheat flour always pays off. Popular suppliers like Bob's Red Mill and Arrowhead Mills are very consistent, and the recipes in this book have been made multiple times with each of those brands. Store flour in a cool pantry and try to use it within 3 months of purchase. To keep track, I recommend labeling the bag with the date of purchase.

Honey

Buckwheat's flowering bushes are an excellent source of pollen for honey bees. Just one acre can supply bees with enough pollen to make more than 150 pounds of honey. Buckwheat honey is usually a dark amber color and boasts a warm, robust flavor not unlike molasses. It packs a powerful punch that holds its own against other bold flavors. Rich in polyphenols, the antioxidant that creates its dark hue, buckwheat honey has higher nutritional and medicinal value than its counterparts. Whenever I feel a cold coming on, I have a tablespoon of buckwheat honey mixed with a few drops of lemon juice. Because it's stickier and more viscous than other honeys, it helps soothe my throat and suppress coughing. At home, I use buckwheat honey to sweeten baked goods made with buckwheat flour or even as a finishing touch to drizzle on top. It's the main ingredient in the Buckwheat Honey Cake on page 90 and can be used instead of regular honey, molasses, or barley malt syrup in any of the recipes in this book. Buckwheat honey isn't too expensive or hard to find, but you'll have to visit a store that offers a wide selection of honey. Honey stalls at farmers' markets often carry it as well.

Buckwheat Banana Bread

Equipment: 8½-by-4½-inch loaf pan or 8-mold mini loaf pan (3½-by-2¼-inch cavity size)

¾ cup (105 g) all-purpose flour

¾ cup (110 g) buckwheat flour

1½ teaspoons baking soda

¾ teaspoon kosher salt

⅔ cup packed (140 g) dark brown sugar

1½ cups (350 g) mashed ripe banana, plus 1 banana to decorate the top (about 4 bananas total)

¼ cup (60 ml) vegetable oil

2 tablespoons buttermilk

1½ teaspoons vanilla extract

2 large eggs

The buckwheat flour in this wholesome banana bread contributes a perfumed essence and delicate, silky crumb. Evocative of the baked goods in old-school macrobiotic shops, this banana bread is healthy and good for you, free of refined white sugar and high in fiber. But unlike those 1970s versions, this one is far from a hockey puck. Loaded with as many bananas as the batter can hold, my modern-day rendition is tender and moist. I often enjoy one piece with my morning coffee or as a late afternoon pick-me-up. We bake dozens of these daily at Friends & Family, and they're what I recommend to customers watching their caloric intake. We bake them as individual portions in small loaves (pictured on page 68), but a larger loaf pan works great too. If you like hiking, camping, and road tripping, I recommend you mark this page. Buckwheat banana bread will pack and travel very well, offering a source of energy and joy on your next adventure.

RECIPE CONTINUES

1. Place an oven rack in the middle position and preheat the oven to 350°F.

2. Cut a 12-by-7-inch rectangle of parchment paper. Lightly coat the loaf pan with nonstick spray, line it with the parchment paper rectangle, and fold the excess paper outward to the sides. This paper sling will make the step of unmolding the banana bread much easier. If you're making mini banana breads, coat the pan cavities with nonstick spray.

3. Combine the flours, baking soda, and salt in a medium bowl. Whisk the brown sugar, mashed banana, vegetable oil, buttermilk, vanilla, and eggs together in a separate bowl.

4. Make a well in the center of the dry ingredients with your hands. Pour the liquid mixture into the well and whisk to combine. The batter should be somewhat runny; this is what makes it such a moist cake. Transfer the batter to the prepared pan, dividing it evenly among the 8 cavities if you're using a mini loaf pan.

5. You can get creative decorating the top, which can be particularly fun, especially when baking with kids. For an impressive presentation, try slicing the additional banana in half lengthwise and placing it on top cut side up. You can also cut the banana into thin slices crosswise and arrange them in an overlapping pattern on top.

6. Bake for 30 minutes, then rotate the pan and bake for another 25 to 30 minutes, until a toothpick inserted in the center comes out clean. Rotating the pan halfway through the baking process will ensure that the banana bread bakes evenly. Let the baked banana bread rest for at least 1 hour before slicing. The banana bread will keep for 2 days in an airtight container at room temperature or up to a week in the refrigerator. It freezes well for up to 2 weeks if wrapped tightly with plastic wrap to prevent freezer burn.

Variation

Oat Banana Bread

For a more mildly flavored (yet equally delicious) banana bread, replace the buckwheat flour with ¾ cup (105 g) whole-grain oat flour.

Chocolate Buck Cake

MAKES ONE 9-INCH CAKE, SERVING 8 TO 10

Equipment: 9-inch springform pan

For the sponge

1 teaspoon instant yeast

¾ cup lukewarm (98° to 105°F) water

1 tablespoon buckwheat honey

½ cup (75 g) buckwheat flour

For the cake batter

¾ cup (135 g) bittersweet chocolate chips

8 tablespoons (1 stick/115 g) unsalted butter, cut into ½-inch cubes

¼ cup (25 g) Dutch-processed cocoa powder, sifted

½ cup (100 g) granulated sugar

1 tablespoon vanilla extract

Pinch of kosher salt

4 large eggs, separated

2 tablespoons confectioners' sugar for decorating

Made entirely with buckwheat flour, this is my favorite gluten-free cake. I always make it when I'm cooking for friends who avoid wheat. The crumb is light and airy, and its intense chocolate flavor shines alongside buckwheat's earthy tobacco undertones. The soufflélike texture comes from whipped egg whites and a prefermented spongelike batter of yeast and buckwheat that encourages the cake to rise in the oven while giving it a light and silky feel. The result is a moist, decadent cake that strikes a balance between rustic and elegant. I recommend this recipe to people who love entertaining but have hectic schedules; it's very easy to prepare and can be made up to 2 days in advance. Serve as a warm or room-temperature dessert with a sprinkle of confectioners' sugar and a generous dollop of whipped cream.

1. Start by making the sponge. Sprinkle the yeast over the warm water and stir. Whisk in the honey and buckwheat flour. Cover with a clean kitchen towel or plastic wrap. Let rest at room temperature for 1 hour. The sponge is ready when the surface looks frothy with large and small bubbles on top.

2. Place an oven rack in the middle position and preheat the oven to 350°F.

3. Coat the springform pan lightly with nonstick spray.

RECIPE CONTINUES

4. Place the chocolate and butter in a heat-resistant bowl. Fill a medium pot with water and place over low heat. When the water is barely simmering, place the bowl of chocolate and butter on top, making sure the bottom of the bowl doesn't touch the simmering water. Remove the bowl from the heat when the chocolate and butter are melted.

5. Working quickly, whisk in the cocoa powder, half of the granulated sugar, the vanilla, and the salt. Add the egg yolks, one at a time, whisking vigorously after each addition. Add the sponge and mix to combine. Set this mixture aside while you whip the egg whites.

6. In a stand mixer fitted with the whisk attachment, beat the egg whites with the remaining granulated sugar until soft peaks form; the egg whites should hold and form a soft peak that folds onto itself when the whisk attachment is turned upside down.

7. Gently fold the whipped whites into the chocolate mixture with a rubber spatula.

8. Transfer the batter to the prepared pan and bake for 25 minutes, then rotate the pan and bake for another 20 minutes, until a toothpick inserted in the middle comes out clean. Rotating the pan halfway through the baking process will ensure that the cake bakes evenly. Remove the cake from the oven and let it cool completely. To unmold, run an offset spatula or paring knife along the side of the pan and loosen the springform lock. Right before serving, put the confectioners' sugar in a sifter or fine strainer and shake it over the surface of the cake to create a thin, even layer. The cake will keep for 2 days at room temperature wrapped in plastic or up to a week in the refrigerator. It freezes very well for up to 2 weeks if wrapped tightly with plastic to prevent freezer burn.

Buckwheat Crepes Two Ways

After taking the time to panfry a respectable stack of buckwheat crepes, I would suggest making an occasion of it and inviting a few guests for brunch. Serve them a savory dish of crepes filled with sautéed spring onion, asparagus, and melted Brie (page 80) as a main course, followed by my riff on crepes Suzette with blood orange (page 81) as dessert.

Buckwheat Crepes

MAKES 15 CREPES

Equipment: 6-inch nonstick or cast-iron sauté pan or skillet

1 cup (240 ml) whole milk

2 tablespoons unsalted butter

2 teaspoons vegetable oil

1 cup (240 ml) water

½ cup plus 2 tablespoons (90 g) buckwheat flour

½ cup (70 g) all-purpose flour

¾ teaspoon kosher salt

1 large egg

1 large egg yolk

Most classically trained bakers and cooks, like me, were introduced to buckwheat by traditional dessert crepes, like crepes Suzette. Buckwheat crepes are hardly a novelty. In the French region of Brittany they're filled with various savory and sweet ingredients. In the Himalayas thin and thick crepes are a dietary staple, served as an accompaniment to spicy stews, and in Russia they're filled opulently with caviar and sour cream.

To the novice cook making crepes can be intimidating. But after a couple of trials most get the hang of it. Your crepes will be much better if the batter is rested in the refrigerator—no less than 2 hours and as long as 3 days. When making crepes, the size of the sauté pan is important since it determines the circumference of your crepes. I recommend a 6-inch nonstick pan. A cast-iron skillet also works well, but your wrist might grow weary from the repetitious movement of swirling a heavy pan. Crepes can be made a few days in advance, then stacked, wrapped, and stored in the fridge or freezer until ready to eat. With already-made crepes, it will be remarkably easy to whip up a quick breakfast of jam-filled crepes or even a midweek dinner of crepes filled with ham and Gruyère.

1. Heat the milk, butter, vegetable oil, and water in a small saucepan over medium-low-heat until the butter is completely melted, about 2 minutes. Remove from the heat and set aside.

2. Sift the flours and salt into a large mixing bowl. Make a well in the center with your hands.

3. Whisk the egg and egg yolk together in a separate bowl and slowly add the warm milk mixture while whisking vigorously. Pour the liquid mixture into the well in the dry ingredients. Slowly whisk from the center out to draw the dry ingredients into the liquids. Whisk well to work out any lumps. Let the batter rest in the refrigerator for at least 2 hours and up to 3 days. Check the batter after resting and before pan-frying the crepes. The mixture should be thinner than regular pancake batter.

4. To make the crepes, preheat the pan over medium-high heat. Lightly coat with nonstick spray or add a small amount of butter or oil and swirl to coat. Using a ladle, pour about ⅛ cup (2 tablespoons) the batter into the hot skillet, swirling immediately so a thin layer of batter coats the entire surface. Cook for 1 minute, then flip with a spatula. Cook for another minute and transfer to a plate. Repeat until all the batter has been used. If it's your first time making crepes, they won't be perfectly round or thin, but don't be discouraged; crepe making takes practice. Wrap the finished crepes in plastic until ready to fill so the edges don't dry out.

Buckwheat Crepes with Spring Onions, Asparagus, and Brie

SERVES 4 TO 6

Equipment: 13-by-9-inch baking dish

1 pound (455 g) asparagus, 2 inches trimmed off the bottom

4 tablespoons (½ stick/55 g) unsalted butter

½ cup (60 g) sliced spring onions

8 ounces (225 g) Brie, rind removed and cut into chunks

Finely grated zest of 1 small lemon

Kosher salt and freshly ground black pepper

Buckwheat Crepes (page 78)

Buckwheat's grounding flavor makes these crepes an ideal canvas for many fillings. Inspired by buckwheat's short growing season and deserved reputation as a regenerative crop, my first impulse is always to load them with spring vegetables. This crepe recipe, served with sautéed spring onions, asparagus, and melted Brie, makes a satisfying breakfast, lunch, or dinner. I like using Saint André, a Brielike soft cheese from Normandy, which is available in markets and cheese shops nationwide. But if you enjoy geeking out over cheese, feel free to experiment with other triple crèmes. This is an excellent dish to prepare ahead of time. Think of it as lasagna. You can fill and assemble the crepes in a baking dish, cover with aluminum foil, and reheat for a few minutes right before serving.

1. Place an oven rack in the middle position and preheat the oven to 350°F.

2. Slice the asparagus on a diagonal into 2-inch-long pieces. Melt the butter in a medium sauté pan over medium-low heat. Add the spring onions and cook until soft and translucent, 2 to 3 minutes. Add the asparagus and sauté until tender but still bright green, 3 to 4 minutes. Take care not to overcook them. Add the cheese, then stir with a wooden spoon to encourage it to melt over medium heat. Turn off the heat, stir in the lemon zest, and season with salt and pepper to taste.

3. To fill, spread about 2 tablespoons of filling on half of each crepe. You'll notice that every crepe has a prettier side, usually the first side to hit the pan. Make sure this side is face down and you're spreading the filling on the opposite side. Fold the crepe in half and then in half again to form a triangle. Place them, slightly overlapping, in the baking dish. Cover with aluminum foil and place in the oven to heat through, 15 to 20 minutes. Serve immediately.

Crepes Suzette with Blood Orange and Mascarpone

SERVES 4

1 cup (225 g) mascarpone

Buckwheat Crepes (page 78)

¼ cup (50 g) sugar

¼ cup (60 ml) water

½ vanilla bean

1 cup (240 ml) blood orange juice (from about 4 medium blood oranges)

4 tablespoons (½ stick/55 g) unsalted butter, cubed

This version of classic crepes Suzette—crepes sautéed in orange sauce and flambéed just before serving—is one of my favorite citrus-season desserts. I've diverged from the original by swapping blood oranges for regular navel oranges and filling the crepes with mascarpone. You will also notice, perhaps with a little disappointment, that I also skipped the step of setting the crepes aflame with brandy. But the intense color of the sauce made with the vibrant red juice of blood oranges will provide enough drama. The result is delicate and balanced, exemplifying how well a distinctive flour like buckwheat can take the backseat in support of brighter flavors.

1. Start by filling the crepes. Spread about 1 tablespoon of the mascarpone on half of each crepe. You'll notice that every crepe has a prettier side, usually the first side to hit the pan. Make sure this side is face down and you're spreading the mascarpone on the opposite side. Fold the crepe in half and then in half again to form a triangle. Place them, slightly overlapping, in a serving dish large enough to hold all the folded crepes.

2. Put the sugar in a small saucepan. Add the water to moisten the sugar, but do not stir. Split the vanilla bean lengthwise with a paring knife, scrape out the pulp with the back of the knife, and put both pulp and pod into the pot. Cook over high heat until the mixture comes to a boil, then lower the heat to medium and reduce to a thick syrup, 3 to 4 minutes. When the sugar starts to caramelize, add the blood orange juice and let it reduce in volume by half. Turn off the heat, remove the vanilla bean, and, working quickly, whisk the butter into the sauce one cube at a time to ensure proper emulsification. Pour the warm sauce over the filled crepes and serve immediately.

Baked Buckwheat Pancake
with Berry Compote

Equipment: 6- or 7-inch nonstick
sauté pan or cast-iron skillet

¼ cup (40 g) buckwheat flour

¼ cup (35 g) all-purpose flour

1 tablespoon granulated sugar

¾ teaspoon baking powder

½ teaspoon baking soda

¼ teaspoon kosher salt

½ cup (120 ml) buttermilk

1 large egg

½ teaspoon vanilla extract

3 tablespoons unsalted butter, melted and cooled
slightly, plus butter for frying and serving

Vegetable oil for frying

1 tablespoon confectioners' sugar

¼ cup (60 ml) maple syrup

Berry Compote (page 84) for serving

When I hear people say they don't like buck-wheat, I inevitably think, "That's because you've never had my buckwheat pancake." At Friends & Family, our baked buckwheat pancake is a fan favorite. We warn customers that their order will take up to 20 minutes, but the prospect of waiting doesn't deter them. Thicker and more filling than a regular flapjack, one buckwheat pancake is enough for me. You could make these entirely with buckwheat flour, but I use some all-purpose flour for a more balanced flavor profile. The pancake is finished in the oven, which imparts a dreamy fluffiness and a crispy exterior. Starting the pancake on the stove allows for an evenly brown, crispy layer, while finishing it in the oven promotes the batter in the center to rise and gel into a light and airy pancake. Once you get the hang of this technique, it's possible you won't make pancakes any other way.

You can certainly serve your pancake with the de rigueur butter and maple syrup, but I strongly recommend trying a berry compote made from scratch. Every effort spent on it will be well worth it. If available in your region, opt for huckleberries—the funky, wild cousin of cultivated blueberries—but in their absence, blueberries will do. Nothing complements the depth of buckwheat better than the bright tang of dark berries. But don't limit yourself when it comes to pancake toppings. Personally, I enjoy mine with a little bit of everything: a light sprinkle of confectioners' sugar, a lump of butter, warm maple syrup, and a side of berry compote. Pancake nirvana, indeed.

RECIPE CONTINUES

1. Place an oven rack in the middle position and preheat the oven to 350°F.

2. Sift the flours, granulated sugar, baking powder, baking soda, and salt into a mixing bowl. Make a well in the center with your hands. Whisk the buttermilk, egg, and vanilla together in a separate bowl. Pour the liquid mixture into the well in the dry ingredients. Whisk slowly from the center out to draw the dry ingredients into the liquids. Add the melted butter and whisk to combine. The mixture will be slightly thicker than regular pancake batter.

3. Preheat the pan over medium-high heat. Add about 1 teaspoon of butter and a drizzle of oil to the pan and swirl to coat. Using a rubber spatula, pour all of the batter into the pan; gently spread it over the entire surface. When the mixture starts to bubble around the edges (1 or 2 minutes), transfer the pan to the oven to bake for 5 minutes. Carefully remove the pan from the oven and flip the pancake with a wide flat spatula (like the one you use to flip burgers). Bake for another 1 or 2 minutes, until both sides have a brown and crispy exterior and a toothpick inserted in the fluffy center comes out clean. Transfer the pancake to a plate. Put the confectioners' sugar in a sifter or fine strainer and shake it over the surface of the pancake to create a thin, even layer. Serve immediately with butter, maple syrup, and berry compote.

Berry Compote

MAKES 2 CUPS

¾ cup (150 g) sugar

¾ cup (180 ml) water

½ vanilla bean

3 cups (1½ pints) blueberries, huckleberries, black currants, or blackberries

1 tablespoon cornstarch

Put the sugar in a heavy medium pot. Add ½ cup (120 ml) of the water to moisten the sugar, but do not stir. Split the vanilla bean lengthwise with a paring knife, scrape out the pulp with the back of the knife, and put the pulp and pod into the pot. Cook over high heat until the mixture comes to a boil. Lower the heat to medium and reduce to a thick syrup. Refrain from stirring at this point; it could cause the sugar to crystalize. Add the berries and stir with a wooden spoon, encouraging them to release their juices. Cook for 4 to 5 minutes, stirring occasionally, until all the sugar is dissolved and the fruit looks saucy. Dissolve the cornstarch in the remaining ¼ cup (60 ml) cold water and add to the pot. Cook while stirring constantly until the compote thickens, 1 to 2 minutes. Transfer to a heat-resistant glass jar and let cool completely. Remove the vanilla bean, cover, and refrigerate until ready to use. The compote will keep in the refrigerator for a week. It's great as an accompaniment for desserts such as the Ricotta Cornmeal Pound Cake on page 125 and the Corn Polenta Ice Cream on page 129, or served over the Rye Müesli on page 205.

Variation

Baked Cornmeal Pancake

In the summer, when I crave lighter flavors, I prefer making the baked pancake with cornmeal instead of buckwheat. Just replace the buckwheat flour with ¼ cup (40 g) yellow cornmeal and add 2 extra tablespoons all-purpose flour.

Buckwheat Cardamom Waffles
with Tangelo Curd

MAKES FOUR 7-INCH WAFFLES

Equipment: electric waffle iron

½ cup (70 g) all-purpose flour

⅔ cup (100 g) buckwheat flour

¼ cup (50 g) granulated sugar

¾ teaspoon baking powder

½ teaspoon baking soda

¼ teaspoon kosher salt

½ teaspoon ground cardamom

1 cup (240 ml) buttermilk

2 large eggs

½ teaspoon vanilla extract

1 tablespoon buckwheat honey

4 tablespoons (½ stick/55 g) unsalted butter, melted, plus extra for cooking the waffles and serving

⅓ cup sparkling water

2 tablespoons confectioners' sugar

Tangelo Curd (recipe follows) or maple syrup

I used to dismiss waffles as an overprocessed food confined to the frozen section of the grocery store, where they existed only to please customers with a practical desire for a quick and easy (yet flavorless) breakfast. That was until a fellow baker gifted me an electric waffle iron. A period of trial and error for the perfect waffle recipe ensued. In my research I discovered that waffles date from the Middle Ages, when bakers tried to mimic the technique used to make communion wafers by cooking batter in between hot plates. Over time, hand-forged plates with honeycomb or filigree patterns evolved into the tridimensional grid design modern waffles are known for.

Although many waffle lovers advocate for a yeast-risen batter, I prefer using baking powder and baking soda in mine. Many would argue that the yeast-based recipes yield a crispier waffle, but my side-by-side testers quickly debunked the theory.

In this recipe, buckwheat and cardamom demonstrate their strong affinity. A touch of sparkling water added to the batter right at the end helps create an airy interior with a crispy exterior. They're delicious served simply, with just a dusting of confectioners' sugar. The subtle spice of cardamom won't deter kids, especially when butter and maple syrup are in the picture. They can also be served with the Berry Compote on page 84, although my favorite accompaniment for these subtly aromatic waffles is a generous spoonful of citrus curd, like the tangelo one that follows.

RECIPE CONTINUES

1. Sift the flours, granulated sugar, baking powder, baking soda, salt, and cardamom into a mixing bowl and make a well in the center with your hands. Whisk the buttermilk, eggs, vanilla, and honey together in a separate bowl. Pour the combined wet ingredients into the well in the dry ingredients. Whisk slowly from the center out to draw the dry ingredients into the liquids. Mix well to work out any lumps. Stir in the melted butter followed by the sparkling water. The mixture will be slightly thicker than a regular waffle or pancake batter.

2. To make the waffles, preheat the waffle iron. Lightly brush the surface with melted butter. Pour in about ¾ cup (180 ml) of the batter and use a spatula to gently spread it over the entire surface. Close the lid and cook until golden. Make three more waffles with the remaining batter.

3. To keep them warm, line a plate with a clean kitchen towel, stash the waffles on top, and fold the kitchen towel over the waffles. Keep the plate in a warm spot such as beside the stove. Put the confectioners' sugar in a sifter or fine strainer and shake it over the surface of the waffles to create a thin, even layer. Top with butter, maple syrup, berry compote, tangelo curd, or as they are, dusted with the confectioners' sugar. Freeze leftovers up to 2 weeks, tightly wrapped in plastic, and reheat in the toaster oven for a quick midweek breakfast.

Variation

Cornmeal Waffles

I love making this variation every summer to serve with seasonal berries and whipped cream. Replace the all-purpose and buckwheat flours with ¾ cup (105 g) all-purpose flour and ⅔ cup (105 g) yellow cornmeal and omit the cardamom. When the batter is ready, let it sit for 20 minutes at room temperature to allow the cornmeal to hydrate and plump up.

Tangelo Curd

Grown all over Southern California and widely available in winter and spring, tangelos combine the sweet, tart flavor of tangerine with the flowery tang of pomelo grapefruit. Zesty and creamy tangelo curd goes hand in hand, flavor and texture wise, with a crispy cardamom-perfumed waffle. Citrus curd is a science project as much as a cooking one, but you shouldn't let it intimidate you. It requires only a few basic ingredients and a very simple technique. The magic of curd happens when acidic citrus juice causes egg yolks to coagulate into a homogeneous, thickened substance while cooked over low heat. Adding sugar makes it a delectable concoction and butter gives it a richer mouthfeel. If tangelos or tangerines aren't available, feel free to use Meyer lemons or regular lemons (see the variation).

MAKES ½ CUP

4 large egg yolks

½ cup (100 g) sugar

¼ cup (60 ml) fresh tangelo or tangerine juice

1 teaspoon finely grated tangelo or tangerine zest

2 tablespoons fresh lemon juice

4 tablespoons (½ stick/55 g) unsalted butter, cubed

Whisk the egg yolks and sugar vigorously in a nonreactive, heat-resistant bowl. Add the tangelo juice, zest, and lemon juice and whisk until well combined. Fill a medium pot with water and place over low heat. When the water is barely simmering, place the bowl on top, making sure the bottom of the bowl doesn't touch the simmering water. Cook for 20 minutes at very low heat, whisking occasionally, until the curd thickens. Remove the bowl from the heat. Whisk in the butter cubes. Strain into a nonreactive container and let cool completely. Store in a lidded jar in the refrigerator for up to 1 month.

Variation

To make classic lemon curd, replace the juices with ½ cup (120 ml) fresh lemon juice and use lemon zest instead of tangelo.

Buckwheat Honey Cake

Equipment: 9-inch springform pan

¾ cup (105 g) all-purpose flour

¾ cup (110 g) buckwheat flour

¾ teaspoon baking soda

1 teaspoon ground cinnamon

1 teaspoon kosher salt

¾ cup (150 g) sugar

2 large eggs

1¼ cups (300 ml) vegetable oil

¾ cup (180 ml) applesauce

½ cup (120 ml) buckwheat honey, plus 2 tablespoons for glazing the top

I've always felt this cake is full of good wishes. At Friends & Family we make it during the first few weeks of fall, when many of our customers celebrate Rosh Hashanah, the arrival of the Jewish new year. Rich with dark and full-flavored buckwheat honey, it represents new beginnings as much as it exemplifies the symbiotic relationship between the bees and the buckwheat flowers they pollinate to collect pollen and make their precious honey.

While not necessarily a traditional Jewish recipe, this cake made with fresh milled buckwheat flour and buckwheat honey leaves you wanting nothing more. The cake calls for a generous helping of applesauce, which is commonly used in baked goods more typical of this holiday. In spite of the symbolism of its origins and complexity of its flavors, this cake is very easy to prepare. The resulting cake is moist and aromatic, with hints of perfumed honey and cinnamon, and has the robust color of buckwheat. I like to brush the baked cake with a thin coat of additional buckwheat honey for a luscious appeal. As the winter holidays approach, you might feel compelled to prepare the variation on page 91 with rye flour instead of buckwheat and a smidge of warm spices. Regardless of which flour you use, do pay attention to the oven temperature; due to the recipe's high honey content, it must be baked at 300°F to prevent a burned honey aftertaste.

1. Place an oven rack in the middle position and preheat the oven to 300°F.

2. Lightly coat the bottom and sides of the springform pan with nonstick spray.

3. Sift the flours, baking soda, cinnamon, and salt into a medium bowl. Whisk the sugar, eggs, vegetable oil, applesauce, and the ½ cup (120 ml) honey together in a separate bowl. Make a well in the center of the dry ingredients with your hands. Pour the liquid mixture into the well and whisk to combine. Pour the batter into the prepared pan.

4. Bake for 30 minutes, then rotate the pan and bake for another 20 to 25 minutes, until a toothpick inserted in the center comes out clean. Rotating the pan halfway through the baking process will ensure that the cake bakes evenly. Remove from the oven and let cool for 1 hour. To unmold, run an offset spatula or paring knife along the side of the pan and loosen the springform lock. Transfer to a cake plate. Warm the remaining honey in a small sauté pan (or in the microwave) for about 1 minute and brush the top of the cake. The cake will keep for a couple of days in an airtight container at room temperature. It can also be frozen for up to 2 weeks—just make sure to wrap tightly with plastic to avoid freezer burn.

Variation

Rye Honey Cake

For a sober and elegant version, evocative of the traditional French spiced cake known as *pain d'épices*, substitute 1 cup (125 g) dark rye flour for the buckwheat flour and supplement the cinnamon with the following spices: ½ teaspoon ground cloves, ½ teaspoon ground cardamom, ½ teaspoon freshly grated nutmeg, and ½ teaspoon ground ginger.

Chocolate Raspberry Tart

MAKES ONE 9-INCH TART, SERVING 8 TO 10

Equipment: 9-inch tart pan

For the crust

8 tablespoons (1 stick/115 g) unsalted butter, at room temperature

⅓ cup (60 g) sugar

⅛ teaspoon baking soda

¼ teaspoon kosher salt

½ teaspoon vanilla extract

¼ cup plus 2 tablespoons (40 g) Dutch-processed cocoa powder

½ cup (70 g) all-purpose flour

½ cup (75 g) buckwheat flour

For the filling

½ cup (120 ml) homemade Raspberry Jam (page 94)

½ cup (90 g) bittersweet chocolate chips

2 large eggs

¼ cup (50 g) sugar

2 tablespoons buckwheat flour, sifted

I love chocolate. Oh, yes, I do. But, while one might be tempted to put chocolate in just about everything, not all fruits pair well with chocolate. Raspberries and chocolate are a classic, timeless combination. Nonetheless, it took me a while to bring the two together. When I was a young baker, dessert menus nationwide always had a take on chocolate mousse or soufflé with some raspberry element. Many of these desserts were made to look pretty and delicate but tasted unbalanced because the chocolate almost always overwhelmed the fruit. Most were also fussily plated with nonedible garnishes and gratuitous gold leaf adornments, a trend that never appealed to me. It took me a full decade to let go of my prejudice against the pairing. And it's a good thing I did, because it led to the birth of this chocolate raspberry tart. Unlike the overly sweet desserts of yesteryear, this rustic creation is beautifully balanced, doing justice to both tart raspberries and rich chocolate.

There are three parts to this tart: a cocoa buckwheat shortbread crust, a raspberry jam, and a soufflélike chocolate filling. I suggest you make the jam and unbaked tart shell up to 2 days in advance and keep them in the refrigerator. This way finishing the tart is very simple. Don't skip the step of making the jam. Store-bought versions tend to be sweeter, lacking the desired acidity that makes this a balanced dessert.

1. For the shortbread crust, lightly coat the tart pan with nonstick spray. In a stand mixer fitted with the paddle attachment, cream the butter and sugar on medium-high speed for about 2 minutes. Add the baking soda, salt, vanilla, and cocoa. Mix until homogeneous. Add the

flours and mix until thoroughly blended, 2 to 3 minutes. Turn the dough onto a clean work surface and knead into a ball. Flatten into a disk about 6 inches in diameter. Put the disk between two large pieces of parchment paper, about 16 by 12 inches each, and with a rolling pin, roll the dough into a circle about 10 inches in diameter and ¼ to ⅓ inch thick. Carefully transfer the circle to the prepared tart pan, pressing the dough up the pan's sides and removing any excess with a paring knife. If the dough rips while shaping the tart shell, patch it up with excess dough. Poke the bottom all over with a fork and freeze completely.

2. Place an oven rack in the middle position and preheat the oven to 350°F.

3. Put the tart pan on a baking sheet and bake for 10 minutes. Rotate the sheet and bake for another 10 minutes, until the surface of the crust resembles a baked cookie. Rotating the sheet halfway through the baking process will ensure that the tart shell bakes evenly. Make sure to bake the tart shell from frozen to prevent it from puffing and shrinking in the oven. Remove from the oven and let cool while you make the filling. Leave the oven on.

4. To fill the tart, spread the raspberry jam over the baked shell's surface. Put the chocolate in a heat-resistant bowl and set the bowl over a pot of barely simmering water, making sure the bottom of the bowl doesn't touch the water. Remove the bowl from the heat when the chocolate is melted. In a stand mixer fitted with the whisk attachment, whip the eggs and

sugar at high speed until pale yellow and the whisk leaves a trace as it beats the mixture, about 5 minutes. Fold in the melted chocolate with a rubber spatula, using gentle but assertive strokes. Similarly, fold in the buckwheat flour. The flour makes the filling more stable, helping it set in the oven. Spread the chocolate filling evenly over the jam in the tart shell. Bake for 30 minutes, until the top of the tart looks puffy with a matte finish. Avoid rotating the baking sheet to prevent the soufflé filling from dropping. Let cool completely, about 1 hour, and remove from the mold. Serve this delicious tart at room temperature, with unsweetened whipped cream if you like.

Raspberry Jam

MAKES 1 CUP

1 cup (200 g) sugar

½ cup (120 ml) water

½ vanilla bean

4 cups (480 g) raspberries, fresh or frozen

Put the sugar in a medium saucepan. Add the water to moisten the sugar, but do not stir. Split the vanilla bean lengthwise with a paring knife, scrape out the pulp with the back of the knife, and put both pulp and pod into the pot. Cook over high heat until the mixture comes to a boil. Lower the heat to medium and reduce to a thick syrup, 3 to 4 minutes. Add the raspberries and stir constantly with a wooden spoon for 10 minutes. Stirring is crucial because it breaks down the berries while preventing over-caramelization, which may cause the jam to stick to the bottom of the pot. To test the jam's readiness, chill a small plate in the freezer, spoon a bit of jam onto it, and run your finger through the jam. If your finger leaves a trace on the plate, the jam is ready. Transfer to a bowl and let cool completely. Remove the vanilla bean and discard. The jam can be stored in the refrigerator for up to 1 month.

Buckwheat Blini with Dungeness Crab Salad

Equipment: 9-inch nonstick or cast-iron sauté pan or skillet

1 cup (240 ml) whole milk

1 teaspoon instant yeast

½ cup (70 g) all-purpose flour

½ cup (80 g) buckwheat flour

1 tablespoon sugar

¾ teaspoon kosher salt

1 large egg, separated

3 tablespoons vegetable oil, plus extra to panfry the blini

1 avocado

Dungeness Crab Salad (recipe follows)

Blini hail from Russia, where buckwheat is a major dietary staple. They're a great vehicle for savory accompaniments, ranging from luxurious caviar to smoked fish, making them an ideal canapé. I like to veer from the traditional route, opting for fresh toppings like avocado and grated bottarga, a dollop of fromage blanc and rhubarb jam, or a smear of strained yogurt with dill and salted cucumber. When Dungeness crab is in season, I top blini with a simple crab salad. It's always a hit.

Making blini the correct way takes time. The first step of making a yeast-based sponge and waiting for it to ferment will add 2 hours to your cooking project, but it will be worth it. It is possible to make blini risen with artificial leaveners like baking powder and baking soda. But in my opinion, to make a soft and decadent blini, you must use yeast. Panfrying the blini is as easy as making silver dollar pancakes. Over the years, I've picked up a kitchen hack from fellow chefs to achieve perfectly round blini: put the batter in a squeeze bottle (available in restaurant supply stores) or an empty ketchup bottle and squeeze the batter directly onto the hot pan. Once cooked, they don't have a long shelf life, but you can prepare the batter ahead of time and make them right before serving. For larger parties I cook the entire batch the morning of, pack them between paper towels, and reheat in a low oven until they regain softness—it works every time.

RECIPE CONTINUES

1. Heat the milk in a small saucepan until lukewarm, between 98° and 105°F. Transfer to a heat-resistant container. Sprinkle the yeast over the warm milk. Stir with a spoon to help it dissolve and let sit for 5 minutes.

2. Meanwhile, sift the flours, sugar, and salt into a separate bowl and make a well in the center with your hands. Combine the egg yolk with the 3 tablespoons of oil and dissolved yeast mixture in a medium bowl. Pour the liquid mixture into the well in the dry ingredients and start whisking from the center out, slowly drawing in more flour while working out lumps. Once the mixture looks smooth, cover with a kitchen towel or plastic wrap and let rise at room temperature for 1½ to 2 hours, until doubled in size.

3. Beat the egg white until foamy in a separate bowl until soft peaks form. Fold the egg white into the batter. Cover and let it rest for 20 minutes.

4. Heat the pan over medium heat. (You could use a smaller pan, but when making a batch, a larger size will allow you to cook more blini at once. An electric griddle will also work well.) Coat the pan with a small amount of oil. If using a squeeze bottle, deposit dollops of batter into the skillet 1 inch apart, as if you were making silver dollar pancakes. Alternatively, you can pour dollops with a spoon onto the pan. The ideal blini is 2 to 2½ inches in diameter. It will take some attempts to make perfect blini, but practice makes perfect. Flip when small bubbles start to form on top, 1 minute, and continue to cook on the other side for 1 minute. Stash finished blini on a plate and cover with a clean kitchen towel to keep them warm. Wipe the skillet clean with a paper towel and repeat to make more blini.

5. To assemble the blini, halve the avocado and remove the pit. Scoop the flesh from the skin with a large spoon. On a cutting board, halve the avocado lengthwise and slice each quarter crosswise into thin slivers. Season lightly with salt and lemon juice. Top each blini with a dollop of crab salad and garnish with a thin slice of avocado. Alternatively, I like arranging the components on a tray so guests can help themselves and build their own blini.

Dungeness Crab Salad

This is my favorite topping to serve with blini. Dungeness crab live exclusively on the West Coast and are favored for their sweet, tender meat. If not available in your region, substitute the type of crab that is most common in your area. I recommend you buy crabmeat instead of whole crab or crab legs—it will save space in your refrigerator and time in the kitchen.

MAKES 2 CUPS

8 ounces (225 g) fresh lump crabmeat, preferably Dungeness

½ cup (120 g) sour cream

Finely grated zest of 1 small Meyer lemon

2 tablespoons minced chives

1 tablespoon minced dill

1 tablespoon fresh lemon juice, or to taste

½ teaspoon kosher salt, or to taste

Combine the crab, sour cream, lemon zest, chives, and dill in a nonreactive bowl. Season with lemon juice and salt to taste. Refrigerate until ready to use.

Buckwheat Fruit–Nut Bread

Equipment: 8-inch round banneton or 8½-by-4½-inch loaf pan, 4½-quart Dutch oven with lid, lame, digital thermometer

To feed the starter

2 tablespoons (20 g) bread flour

2 tablespoons (20 g) whole wheat flour

1 teaspoon (7 g) sourdough starter

3 tablespoons cold water (65° to 70°F)

For the dough

1½ cups (150 g) pecan halves

2 cups (270 g) bread flour, plus extra for dusting

½ cup (75 g) whole wheat flour

½ cup (75 g) buckwheat flour

1⅓ to 1½ cups (320 to 360 ml) warm (90° to 95°F) water

8 dried black figs, stemmed and chopped

1 cup (165 g) golden raisins

½ cup (75 g) dried black currants

A little less than ½ cup (100 g) sourdough starter fed in the morning

1 tablespoon kosher salt

1 tablespoon honey, preferably buckwheat

2 tablespoons Candied Kumquats (page 47) or other citrus peel

2 to 3 tablespoons flour, preferably rice flour, for dusting the banneton

Buckwheat lends flavor and texture to this festive loaf, studded with some of my favorite dried fruits and nuts. Even better the day after it's baked, it makes heavenly morning toast and the perfect accompaniment to cheese. The ingredients should be easy to find with the exception of kumquats, which I like to candy in sugar syrup (page 47). If kumquats prove difficult to come by, you can candy grapefruit, orange, or lemon peels instead. Hold on to the candying syrup, though—at Friends & Family, we use it to brush finished baked goods for its citrusy flavor and an eye-catching sheen.

This bread is leavened naturally with sourdough starter. If you've never made sourdough bread from scratch, read How to Start and Maintain Your Own Sourdough Starter on page 102. With starter on hand, you can follow the suggested Prep and Baking Schedule that follows. Even experienced home bakers are intimidated by the world of sourdough, but building a starter at home is far less confusing than you might think. It does require patience, plus precision when weighing ingredients. But the steps to keeping the starter healthy are simple and easy to follow, not to mention forgiving. Breads like this one, where add-ins are more integral to the flavor than the dough itself, are a good starting point for beginning bread bakers. The ratio of fruits and nuts is high in proportion to bread dough, and its inherently rustic appearance doesn't require fancy shaping techniques. The bread can be baked into a boule, into a free-form oval-shaped loaf, or in a loaf pan.

Remember that to make this bread you must make the dough the day before, so plan accordingly.

RECIPE CONTINUES

Prep and Baking Schedule

Prep Day (day prior to baking):

In the morning:

1. Feed the starter anytime between 6:00 and 10:00 a.m. The starter will be ready to use in 8 to 10 hours.

2. Candy your kumquats or other citrus peels and cool completely. This step can also be done a few days in advance.

3. Toast the pecans.

4. Weigh all fruits and flours.

Later that day (8 to 10 hours after feeding the starter):

1. Hydrate or autolyse the flours.

2. Soak the fruits and pecans.

3. Mix the starter, hydrated flours, and remaining ingredients into a dough. Let ferment for 3½ to 4 hours.

4. Shape the bread and put it in a banneton. Refrigerate overnight.

Baking Day:

In the morning:

1. Remove the bread from the refrigerator 1 hour before baking.

2. Preheat the oven and Dutch oven 30 minutes before baking.

3. Bake. Cool. Enjoy later that day.

Prep Day

1. In the morning of the day before you'd like to bake the bread, feed the starter by combining the flours and sourdough starter with the cold water. Cover and let the starter ferment at room temperature for 8 to 10 hours. You will know the starter is ready when it has increased in volume and bubbles have formed on the surface.

2. Candy the kumquats or other citrus peels following the method on page 47.

3. Place an oven rack in the middle position and preheat the oven to 350°F.

4. Scatter the pecans on a baking sheet and toast in the oven for 8 to 10 minutes, until a nut cut in half is golden inside.

5. About 8 hours after the starter was fed, hydrate, or autolyse, the flours: In a medium bowl, combine the flours with at least 1⅓ cups warm water (if too dry, add 1 to 2 tablespoons more) to create a wet, sticky dough. Cover and let rest for 1 hour. This resting phase, in which the flour is allowed to hydrate, is known as the *autolyse*. Autolysing the flour promotes elasticity as well as enzymatic activity and contributes to gluten development in the dough. Place the pecans and the dried fruits in a bowl, cover with cold water, let soak for 10 minutes, and strain through a fine-mesh sieve.

6. Add the starter to the autolysed flours and mix by hand until well combined. Add the salt, honey, soaked and drained nuts and fruits, and the candied kumquats and mix well by hand to

distribute them throughout the dough. Transfer to a clean bowl, wrap tightly with plastic, and let the dough proof at warm room temperature for 3½ to 4 hours, until it has risen by one-third.

7. To shape into a boule, transfer the dough to a floured surface. Gently flatten the dough into a rough rectangle and bring all four corners to the center. Pinch the corners together with your fingertips. Invert the boule on the work surface and, using your hands, gently rotate against the surface to tighten the boule further and seal the bottom where the corners connect. Generously flour the banneton and place the boule inside with the seam side up. Alternatively, to bake the bread in a loaf pan, place the boule seam side down in the loaf pan lightly coated with nonstick spray. Refrigerate uncovered overnight.

Baking Day

1. Remove the bread from the refrigerator 1 hour prior to baking. Let it sit at room temperature.

2. Place an oven rack in the lower position and place a lidded Dutch oven (if using) on it. Preheat the oven to 450°F for 30 minutes.

3. If baking in a Dutch oven, cut a piece of parchment paper a few inches wider than the boule. Invert the banneton on the parchment paper to release the bread. Using a lame or a sharp paring knife, cut an X about ½ inch deep on the surface of the boule. These cuts will serve as steam release vents when the bread expands in the oven.

4. Using oven mitts, carefully put the hot Dutch oven on a heat-resistant surface and remove the lid. Lift the parchment paper from the sides to help you transfer the bread to the Dutch oven. Put the lid back on and place the Dutch oven back in the oven. Bake for 30 minutes; the lid will help retain enough steam to allow the surface of the bread to remain supple and expand. Remove the lid and bake for another 15 to 20 minutes; removing the lid will help the bread's exterior caramelize and bake into a chewy crust. The bread is ready when the crust is a dark mahogany brown and a digital thermometer inserted in the center reads 200°F. Using oven mitts, carefully remove the Dutch oven from the oven. Gently invert it over a cooling rack to release the bread. Let cool completely before slicing.

5. If baking in a loaf pan, cut an X about ½ inch deep on the surface of the loaf. Cover the bread with aluminum foil. Bake for 30 minutes. Then remove the foil and bake for another 15 to 20 minutes or until the top is a dark mahogany brown and a digital thermometer inserted in the center reads 200°F. Cool for 30 minutes before removing from the pan and wait at least 1 hour before slicing. Once baked, this bread will keep for a week at room temperature in a paper bag or wrapped tightly with plastic. If you plan to keep it for longer, place the bread in the refrigerator to prevent molding. It freezes well for up to 2 weeks, but wrap it tightly first to avoid freezer burn.

How to Start and Maintain Your Own Sourdough Starter

A sourdough starter (also known as a *sourdough culture* or *leaven*) is a fermented dough or batter used to flavor and leaven bread doughs without the use of commercial yeast. It allowed humans to make bread for millennia, long before we understood the science behind it. When put under the microscope, a sourdough starter is a culture of yeasts and bacteria known as *lactobacilli* that feed on the carbohydrates present in the flour in a moist environment, generating ethanol and carbon dioxide as by-products. Creating your own sourdough culture—or starter—is one of those things that can seem intimidating until you actually do it. If you can read a scale, you can make a sourdough starter. The key is to stick to the schedule, making sure to feed the starter regularly so the colony that makes up your culture never runs out of carbohydrates to metabolize. Regardless of what kind of bread you want to prepare, start your culture with rye flour, which is rich in fast-acting enzymes, laying the foundation for a successful starter. I have gone over the process of building a sourdough starter several times over the years. I find the following 8-day schedule pretty reliable. For maximum accuracy, use a digital scale over the volume measurements provided below. Filtered water is also recommended, although not required. Preferably, all feedings should happen at the same time every day. Choose a week when you plan to be home early in the morning and in the early evening—think of it as being home for breakfast and dinner—and brace yourself to witness how the simple combination of flour and water bubbles up into a living being that's infinitely more than the sum of its parts.

Before you begin, make sure you have on hand a digital scale, a handful of dark rye flour, plenty of bread flour and whole wheat flour, and a clean 2-quart glass jar with a lid.

Note: The container you keep your starter in should have plenty of room, as the starter will grow and expand exponentially, which is why you need a 2-quart jar.

Day 1

Start your culture by combining 125 g (1 cup) dark rye flour with 180 g (about ¾ cup) filtered water at room temperature. Mix thoroughly until no flour streaks remain. Cover and store at room temperature.

Day 2

Combine the culture from Day 1 with 60 g (about ¼ cup plus 3 tablespoons) bread flour, 60 g (about ¼ cup plus 2 tablespoons) whole wheat flour, and 112 g (½ cup) water. Cover and store at room temperature.

Day 3

Combine 115 g culture from Day 2 with 60 g (about ¼ cup plus 3 tablespoons) bread flour, 60 g (about ¼ cup plus 2 tablespoons) whole wheat flour, and 112 g (½ cup) water. Discard the rest of the Day 2 culture. Cover and store at room temperature.

Day 4

Combine 115 g culture from Day 3 with 60 g (about ¼ cup plus 3 tablespoons) bread flour, 60 g (about ¼ cup plus 2 tablespoons) whole wheat flour, and 112 g (½ cup) water. Discard the rest of the Day 3 culture. Cover and store at room temperature.

Day 5

Start feeding the starter twice a day. Feedings should be 8 to 12 hours apart. Think of them as breakfast and dinner. For each feeding: Combine 30 g (about 2 tablespoons) culture with 75 g (½ cup plus 1 tablespoon) bread flour, 75 g (½ cup) whole wheat flour, and 150 g (about ½ cup plus 3 tablespoons) water. Discard the remaining culture. Cover and store at room temperature.

Days 6 and 7

Feed the starter twice a day, per instructions for Day 5.

Day 8

Your starter is mature and ready to use on the morning of Day 8. The surface should be bubbly, almost frothy, with a pleasantly sour smell. To use, reserve the amount you need for your desired recipe, feed the starter per the instructions for Day 5, and discard the remaining culture.

Refrigerating Your Starter

Refrigerating your starter will retard its activity level by slowing down its metabolic rate. If you bake bread less frequently than once a week, I recommend refrigerating in between bakes. In my experience, a starter can withstand 2 weeks unfed in the refrigerator without deteriorating. To do so, refrigerate the starter on the day you used it last. A few days later, to bring it back to speed, resume feeding twice a day per the instructions for Day 5. It will take 2 days of regular feedings at room temperature for the starter to regain its activity level. You can bake with it as usual then.

Glazed Meyer Lemon Cornmeal Muffins · Blueberry Blue Cornmeal Scones ·
Hatch Chile and Cotija Corn Bread · White Cheddar Cornmeal Biscuits · Corn Linzer Cookies ·
Ricotta Cornmeal Pound Cake · Olive Oil Polenta Cake · Corn Polenta Ice Cream ·
Vegan Pozole Verde · Savory Chickpea Pancake

corn

ZEA MAYS

Corn, as American as apple pie.

Corn is undoubtedly the most defining food crop in the history of the Americas. It was revered by the Mayans thousands of years ago, and it was integral to nearly every aspect of their daily life, from cooking and commerce to religion and politics. As related in the Popol Vuh (the Mayan "Book of the People"), early men were created from yellow and white corn purposely to tell the story of how the world was made. Through the centuries, corn hasn't lost its relevance and remains as important to our society as it once was to the Mayans. Today corn is one of the most widely grown crops in the United States, used to fuel our bodies, our livestock, and even our cars. In many ways our society runs on this grain.

The crop we call corn is more widely known as *maize*—a word derived from the Arahuacan *mahisi*, meaning "that which sustains us." The name *corn* came from the generic English word for "kernel" and its Germanic root, *Korn*, which means small pieces.

Teosinte, the earliest known form of maize, was domesticated in Mexico's Central Balsas River valley, some nine thousand years ago. Modern corn can be traced back to this ancestor. By about AD 600 it had spread prolifically and was grown by various indigenous tribes. The only grain native to North America, corn has defined American history since its very beginning. Before European colonizers arrived at the continent, corn was already an indelible foundation in the lives of indigenous people across North and Central America. Many Native Americans, the original corn farmers, developed rituals and ceremonies around the corn harvest and extended its uses far beyond food. Later, when the English and other Europeans arrived in the New World, Native Americans taught early settlers to grow corn so they wouldn't starve. Fast forward to 1492, when Christopher Columbus introduced it to Spain. By the seventeenth century it was a major European crop. The Portuguese took it to East Africa and Asia, and Silk Road traders carried the crop to India.

With such widespread proliferation, it's no surprise that corn provides around 20 percent of human nutrition worldwide. However, corn grown in North America is fed mostly to animals or used in industrial products like ethanol, cosmetics, ink, glue, laundry starch, medicine, and fabric, to name a few. U.S. agricultural policy and global trade markets now perceive corn as a marketplace commodity, rather than a nutritious grain. These politics stem from the Great Depression, when corn subsidies were employed to augment American agriculture. These subsidies, which remain a fixture of U.S. agricultural policy, sent corn production into overdrive. With more corn than Americans could eat, surplus flooded foreign markets. Suddenly it was cheaper for other countries to purchase subsidized American corn than grow it themselves. Corn subsidies are a point of contention in food policy to this day. In contrast to vilified commodity corn, a small segment of farmers nationwide is drawing attention to another side of the crop, growing heirloom varieties rich in flavor, color, nutrients, and history.

According to the Whole Grains Council, corn contains ten times more vitamin A than other grains, is high in antioxidants and carotenoids associated with optic health, and often plays a key role in gluten-free foods. The combination of corn and beans, a centuries-old culinary practice across Mesoamerica, creates a nutritious, high-protein meal that many cultures enjoy together, including my Costa Rican ancestors. Corn is regularly nixtamalized—a process in which it's soaked in an alkaline solution and then drained to make masa flour for tortillas and other foods, helping nutrients become more available for absorption.

The vast majority of common corn varieties belong to three categories: sweet corn (a sugar-rich vegetable generally consumed by humans), dent or field corn (used for livestock feed and industrial products), and flint corn, which is ground to make corn flour, cornmeal, polenta, and grits. Popcorn and the colorful cobs emblematic of Thanksgiving are flint corn.

How to Purchase and Use

Corn, the Vegetable

Fresh corn is typically classified as a vegetable, while dried corn, including popcorn, is considered a grain. Fresh corn is a summertime staple—sweet, sunny, and fresh. It's best prepared simply: grilled with a pat of butter, served as raw kernels in a crisp salad, or sautéed alongside zucchini, peppers, and other summer veg. Here in Southern California, corn shoots into vivacious ears all summer long. When in season, I buy heirloom corn at my local farmers' market. Varieties range in color from cream white to bright yellow. I find the yellow varieties to be sweeter, but to me fresh corn is always a treat and I don't have a preference. Buy corn at the height of the summer season and through early fall. To pick the right ears, inspect what's underneath the husks—you should find tight rows of plump kernels that look as if they're about to burst. In fact, if you were to stab a kernel with your fingernail, it should snap and release a bit of juice. Fresh corn is highly perishable, so purchase just before eating and always store in the refrigerator. To make space in the refrigerator, peel the ears and place in a freezer bag or a container with a lid to retain its moisture.

Cornstarch

As its name indicates, this is a starch derived from corn. It's extracted by a process called "wet milling," in which corn is steeped and milled to collect any starch that washes off. The starch is dried and modified for its designated purpose. It's commonly used as a thickener and anticaking agent and has many uses outside the kitchen—think laundry starch and baby powder. Cornstarch is often vilified as overprocessed, but it has immense value in cooking. Used in moderation, it can add a sandy texture to cookies or thicken sauces and fruit compotes. It's a standardized product that behaves similarly across brands. Non-GMO cornstarch is available in upscale supermarkets, but I typically use the brands offered in regular grocery stores.

Cornmeal

Although the yellow and white varieties are readily available in most supermarkets, cornmeal actually comes in a plethora of colors. Hopi Pink Corn and Hopi Blue Corn, both heirloom varieties grown by the Hopi People of northern Arizona, yield rosy-pink and bluish-purple cornmeal, respectively, while the emerald kernels of Oaxacan Green Corn take on a mossy hue when ground.

In addition to being visually striking, colorful cornmeal has a higher nutrient density. Beta-carotene is the naturally occurring pigment responsible for yellow and orange cornmeal. When digested, this pigment becomes vitamin A, which is beneficial to our vision and immune system. Black, red, and blue cornmeal get their rich coloring from anthocyanin—a pigment with impressive antioxidant properties. Blue, yellow, and white cornmeal can be found in grocery stores, health food stores, or online. Cornmeal is typically labeled fine, medium, or coarse. You can swap colors freely, but pay attention to the specified grind; fine cornmeal is more compact than coarse cornmeal and therefore different in both weight and volume, which can affect the texture of your baked goods, making them tougher and dense. If you visit a local mill or granary, you can often find heirloom varieties worth trying, such as Bloody Butcher (for Hatch Chile and Cotija Corn Bread, page 117). Heirloom varieties are unique in their own ways and offer flavor and texture nuances specific to each variety. The recipes in this chapter are a good start.

Corn Flour

Corn flour is superfine cornmeal, and it imparts the same sweet, earthy flavor as cornmeal with a less grainy texture. I always use it in combination with all-purpose flour, observing a ratio of one part corn flour to one part all-purpose flour to prepare anything from cookies to cakes. I've tried using corn flour exclusively, but because it doesn't contain any gluten, baked goods made with it need the additional structure that all-purpose flour provides. I don't recommend exchanging corn flour for cornmeal in recipes, because corn flour is finer and more compact and therefore yields different results. In a pinch, you may pulse cornmeal in a coffee or spice grinder to obtain a smaller particle. I recommend Bob's Red Mill's corn flour, which is easy to find in grocery stores and online. Store flour in a cool pantry and try to use it within 3 months of purchase. To keep track, I recommend labeling the bag with the date of purchase.

Polenta

Polenta is a coarse cornmeal that comes from flint corn. It's also the name of a common dish in Italy, Switzerland, Slovenia, and Croatia, cooked low and slow in milk, stock, or water and finished with butter and cheese. Once considered peasant food, polenta is now featured on upscale restaurant menus worldwide. In my baking I use it like cornmeal. It adds an earthy, sweet, grounding flavor to cakes, cookies, and biscuits. When buying polenta, ensure it's labeled "whole corn" or "whole-grain corn" for a higher nutritional value. I purchase polenta from my local independent miller, Grist & Toll, but Bob's Red Mill offers a decent grocery store alternative. A personal favorite is buckwheat polenta from Anson Mills, an elegant cereal enhanced by the addition of freshly ground buckwheat. In Italy this polenta and buckwheat blend is known as *taragna*.

Grits

Like polenta, grits are a coarse cornmeal often prepared as warm porridge. They're ground from a variety known as dent corn. Grits are a staple in the American South, where settlers adopted the dish from Muskogee Natives in the sixteenth century. Shrimp and grits is a delicious and well-known dish featuring this form of corn. You can replace grits for polenta when making porridge, but keep in mind that the grind of grits tends to be slightly coarser than that of polenta, which may affect the cooking time. Avoid using grits instead of cornmeal in baking—it will affect the texture of your baked goods.

Hominy and Masa

Hominy is field corn that is dried and then soaked or cooked in an alkaline solution, like lye or lime water. The alkali loosens each kernel's exterior to soften the grain. Hominy can be prepared as a dish at this point or allowed to dry again. It's the base of pozole, a popular Mexican stew made with red or green chiles and chicken or pork, and garnished with shredded cabbage, radish, and lime (see Vegan Pozole Verde, page 131). In Meso-american cooking, freshly cooked hominy is mashed into a paste to make masa, a key ingredient in tortillas and tamales. Fresh masa is also dried and sold in powder form, known as instant masa, but true tortilla makers always prefer fresh masa.

Popcorn

Popcorn is an all-American snack prepared with certain corn varieties; namely, those that have strong hulls and starchy endosperms with 14 to 20 percent moisture. When heated, this moisture becomes steam and causes the kernel to pop. On average, Americans consume 52 quarts of popcorn a year. Although typically coated in copious amounts of melted butter, salt, or sugary caramel, popcorn can be considered a whole grain and a healthy food. When prepared mindfully (such as with olive oil and a sprinkle of sea salt), popcorn can constitute a healthy snack.

Glazed Meyer Lemon Cornmeal Muffins

Equipment: muffin tin

For the muffin batter

1⅓ cups (185 g) all-purpose flour

1⅓ cups (215 g) coarse yellow cornmeal

1 cup (200 g) granulated sugar

2 teaspoons baking powder

½ teaspoon kosher salt

½ cup (115 g) sour cream

¼ cup (60 ml) Meyer lemon juice (from about 1 large lemon)

Finely grated zest of 1 Meyer lemon

Finely grated zest of 1 tangerine

¼ cup (60 ml) vegetable oil

2 large eggs

For the Meyer lemon glaze

1¼ cups (155 g) confectioners' sugar, sifted

3 tablespoons Meyer lemon juice

1 tablespoon whole milk

2 tablespoons melted butter

Finely grated zest of 1 Meyer lemon

Finely grated zest of 1 tangerine

I'm an avowed member of the Meyer lemon cult, and it's not hard to see, smell, or taste why. Meyers are sweeter and more fragrant than regular lemons, revealing their ancestral link to oranges and tangerines. They have a long growing season in Southern California, where we enjoy them from fall until late spring or early summer. The floral, slightly spiced perfume of Meyer lemon really comes through in this recipe, and the cornmeal adds a satisfying texture and subtle sweetness. Never forgo the zest. Much of the Meyer's spellbinding powers are in its zest. I also use the zest from a tangerine here, in homage to Meyer lemons' early citric ancestors. The muffins are moist and delicious by themselves, but I can't resist finishing them with a tart glaze to give them an additional hit of Meyer lemon magic while making them delectably shiny. Serve for brunch or as a midafternoon treat to be enjoyed with a cup of Earl Grey tea.

If life gives you regular lemons, make muffins regardless! They're also great made exclusively with tangerine juice and zest, and one of our recipe testers claims she's gotten great results using only oranges. You get the idea—keep the ratio of juice to zest, but use your citrus fruit of choice.

1. Place an oven rack in the middle position and preheat the oven to 350°F.

2. For the muffin batter, combine the flour, cornmeal, granulated sugar, baking powder, and salt in a mixing bowl. Make a well in the center with your hands. Whisk the sour cream, juice, zests, vegetable oil, and eggs together in a separate bowl. Pour this liquid mixture into the well in the dry ingredients. Mix to combine with a rubber spatula. The muffin batter should be very thick.

3. Coat 10 cups of the muffin tin lightly with nonstick spray.

4. Evenly distribute the muffin batter among the 10 muffin cups, about ⅓ cup (80 ml) of batter per muffin. Bake for 15 minutes. Then rotate the muffin tin and bake for another 10 minutes, until a toothpick inserted in the center comes out clean. Rotating the muffin tin halfway through the baking process will ensure that the muffins bake evenly. Remove from the oven and cool for 20 minutes before removing the muffins from the tin.

5. Meanwhile, make the glaze. Whisk the confectioners' sugar, lemon juice, milk, and melted butter together in a mixing bowl until smooth. Add the zests and stir to combine. Put the glaze in a small, deep bowl, where you can comfortably dip the tops of the muffins.

6. Place a cooling rack over a baking sheet. Glaze the muffins one at a time by dipping top down into the glaze and place them back on the rack to let excess glaze drip onto the baking sheet underneath. Wait 5 minutes and dip the tops again. The double dunk will ensure well-coated muffins. Alternatively, you can leave the muffins on the cooling rack and spoon the glaze over their tops. Let the glaze set completely. The muffins will keep for a couple days stored in an airtight container at room temperature.

A Citrus Wonderland

At the turn of the twentieth century, when California was still a Western adventure, land developers sold its virtues by promising fresh oranges to be picked in your own backyard. Indeed, the state's reputation as a land of plenty, with bountiful produce, fresh flavors, and vibrant food, stems in part from its abundance of citrus. An entire county, Orange County in Southern California, had more orange trees than people before it began its rapid urbanization in the 1950s. Like southern Europe, California's climate is well suited for citrus trees, and hundreds of varieties are grown across the state, from the southern coast to the northern valleys and even the desert regions. Citrus season typically extends from fall to spring, though many varieties are available year round. As a result, it's possible to incorporate fresh, flavorful California citrus into cooking and baking almost anytime you want.

Everything from pomelos to tangerines are grown in the state, but certain citrus varieties are emblematic of California cuisine and agriculture. Perhaps none more so than the Meyer lemon, a round golden variety with a sweet flavor and low acidity unmatched by other lemons. As for limes, Bearss limes (also known as Tahitian or Persian limes) stand out in particular. They are a natural hybrid of Mexican limes and citron, available all year with a peak harvest in summer. Cara Cara oranges, a seedless variety with vibrant pink flesh and a sweet candy flavor with strawberry notes, are sought by parents for being kid friendly. Californians have grown so accustomed to the availability of extraordinary fruit that few may realize how surreal blood oranges like Moro or grapefruits like Oro Blanco are. One of my favorites, Pixie tangerines, a niche variety grown in the Ojai Valley, comes to market in spring and is perfect for eating out of hand, with easily peelable skin. At the beginning of winter, when we do most of our holiday baking, Satsuma tangerines provide a welcome respite from the spice-forward flavors of the season. Rarer citrus fruits like kumquats, finger limes, and Buddha's hand can be found in farmers' markets across the state. Even as a trained chef with decades in the business, I'm in constant awe of the sheer variety of citrus fruits within my reach. If I were to write a slogan for the state of California, it would be "Come for the weather; stay for the Pixies."

Blueberry Blue Cornmeal Scones

MAKES 6 SCONES

1½ cups (210 g) all-purpose flour, plus extra for dusting

¾ cup (120 g) coarse or medium blue cornmeal

⅓ cup (65 g) sugar, plus extra for dusting

1 tablespoon baking powder

¼ teaspoon kosher salt

12 tablespoons (1½ sticks/170 g) cold unsalted butter, cut into ½-inch cubes

¾ cup (130 g) frozen blueberries

⅓ cup plus 1 tablespoon (90 ml) buttermilk

1 large egg

While writing this cookbook, when I shared with fellow bakers my desire to feature as many cornmeal varieties as possible, they would often look at me with an epiphanous grin, followed by the suggestion that I include a blueberry and blue cornmeal pairing. All bakers must think alike, because this was one of the first recipes I developed for the book, long before any of my clever friends proposed the blue-on-blue combination.

Blue corn describes varieties that produce blue, gray, red, or purple kernels. Many blue corn varieties come from heirloom Native American sources, dating back to pre-Columbian times. Blue corn kernels are initially white and darken as they dry. Cornmeal ground from such kernels has a deep indigo hue and strong, fresh corn flavor. The nutrient content and attractive color of blue corn have made it a desired ingredient in cereal, tortillas, and corn chips, thus increasing its popularity among farmers.

I recommend freezing the blueberries before adding them to your dough; otherwise they'll become mushy and hard to work with as you mix and shape the scones. Make sure to use the entire amount of berries, even if it seems like a lot. Thanks to their high pectin content, the blueberries will cook into mini jam pockets throughout the scones.

Opposite: Ginger Scones (page 245), Chocolate Cherry Scones (page 209), Blueberry Blue Cornmeal Scones (page 115), Granola Scones (page 153)

RECIPE CONTINUES

1. Line a baking sheet with parchment paper and set aside.

2. Combine the flour, cornmeal, sugar, baking powder, and salt in a mixing bowl. Toss the cold butter cubes into the dry ingredients. Quickly cut the cold butter cubes into the dry ingredients by progressively pinching it with your fingertips, until the mixture resembles a coarse meal with hazelnut-size pieces of butter. Add the blueberries and toss gently to combine. Make a well in the center with your hands. Whisk the buttermilk and egg together in a small bowl, then pour the mixture into the well in the dry ingredients. Toss gently with both hands (as if tossing a salad) until a shaggy dough is formed. (If the dough is too dry to come together into a ball, mix in an additional tablespoon of buttermilk). To shape the scones, transfer the dough to a floured surface. Pat it down into a disk, about 7 inches in diameter and 1 inch thick. Using a large chef's knife, slice the disk in half, then slice it into 6 equal wedges total (as you would a cake or pie). Transfer each individual scone to the prepared baking sheet, placing them at least 2 inches apart. Put uncovered in the freezer for 30 minutes. Freezing the scones will encourage them to hold their shape while baking.

3. Place an oven rack in the middle position and preheat the oven to 400°F.

4. Remove the scones from the freezer, brush each with a bit of water, and dust generously with sugar. Bake for 10 minutes. Rotate the baking sheet and bake for another 10 to 15 minutes, until the edges of the scones are golden. Rotating the sheet halfway through the baking process will ensure that the scones bake evenly. Let cool completely before serving. Scones should be eaten fresh, but leftovers can be stored in an airtight container to reheat the next day. They won't be quite as good as a fresh batch, but serve them with a spoonful of crème fraîche and nobody will complain.

Hatch Chile and Cotija Corn Bread

Equipment: 9-inch cast-iron skillet

1¼ cups (190 g) coarse cornmeal, preferably an heirloom cornmeal such as Bloody Butcher

¾ cup (105 g) all-purpose flour

½ teaspoon kosher salt

2 teaspoons baking soda

¾ cup (150 g) sugar

1¼ cups (300 ml) buttermilk

2 large eggs

⅓ cup (80 ml) vegetable oil

3 tablespoons butter, melted and cooled slightly, plus extra for greasing the pan

¾ cup (90 g) crumbled Cotija cheese

One 4-ounce can diced Hatch chiles, drained

Just when I thought I knew all I needed to know about cornmeal, my local miller introduced me to the heirloom varietal Bloody Butcher. It was developed commercially around 1845 in Virginia, where it was well established among Native Americans. Named for its reddish tint and not some macabre myth, Bloody Butcher is incredibly flavorful and deeply evocative of Mexican cookery. This corn bread recipe deviates from the traditional southern approach (characterized for its simplicity and lack of adornments) and incorporates Cotija cheese and Hatch chiles, giving the corn bread a southwestern flair. Hatch chiles are a flavorful green variety cultivated in the summer from New Mexico to California. I chose Hatch chiles because they add a savory smoky kick without the heat, but if you prefer hotter chiles you may use jalapeños instead. They can be found fresh only for a short period of time in certain regions of the country, but are available canned in well-stocked grocery stores year round. Cotija, a crumbly semihard cow's milk cheese hailing from Michoacán, Mexico, further emphasizes the southwestern bent of this corn bread. Don't go crazy looking for Bloody Butcher—despite its popularity among grain geeks, it can be hard to find. I've often made this recipe with the more common coarse yellow cornmeal, and it works every time.

The best baking vessel for this corn bread is a 9-inch cast-iron skillet. Before serving I score the corn bread into wedges, then present it in the skillet so guests can help themselves—talk about a lovely staple for your next brunch or picnic!

RECIPE CONTINUES

1. Place the cornmeal, flour, salt, baking soda, and sugar in a mixing bowl and make a well in the center with your hands. Combine the buttermilk, eggs, and oil in a separate bowl. Pour the liquid mixture into the well in the dry ingredients. Using a whisk, mix until well combined. Add the melted butter and mix just to combine. Stir in the Cotija cheese and Hatch chiles and let the batter sit for 20 minutes. The cornmeal will absorb the liquid and swell up, making the batter slightly thicker.

2. Place an oven rack in the middle position and preheat the oven to 350°F.

3. Brush the skillet with melted butter. Transfer the batter to the prepared skillet, using a spatula to even out the top. Bake for 30 minutes, then rotate the skillet and bake for another 15 minutes, until the top is golden brown and a toothpick inserted in the center comes out clean. Rotating the skillet halfway through the baking process will ensure that the corn bread bakes evenly. Place the skillet on a cooling rack and wait at least 30 minutes before serving, still warm or at room temperature. The corn bread can be wrapped tightly in plastic and stored in the refrigerator for 2 days or the freezer for 2 weeks. Individual wedges reheat very well in a toaster oven.

White Cheddar Cornmeal Biscuits

Equipment: 2½-inch plain biscuit cutter

2 cups (280 g) all-purpose flour

2 cups (320 g) fine white cornmeal

2 tablespoons sugar

1 tablespoon baking powder

1½ teaspoons baking soda

2 teaspoons kosher salt

1 cup (2 sticks/225 g) cold unsalted butter, cut into ½-inch cubes

1½ cups (360 ml) buttermilk

4 ounces (115 g) white Cheddar, grated

2 tablespoons thyme leaves

Biscuit experts are wholly convinced that self-rising flour is a prerequisite for tender, fluffy biscuits. And they're right. Self-rising flours blend softer wheats with leavening agents to achieve incredible heights and billowy softness. Serious southern biscuit bakers have used White Lily Flour, a well-loved self-rising flour brand, to make biscuits for generations. But self-rising flour is the antithesis of everything a whole-grain enthusiast like me favors. As a refined and manufactured product, self-rising flour has been stripped of all fiber and nutritional value. In the process, it has been rendered flavor neutral—a perfect canvas for butter, lard, or buttermilk that contributes no flavor from the grain itself. But it turns out, it's totally possible to bake a buttery whole-grain biscuit filled with flaky layers. Whole-grain biscuits may feel a degree denser than white flour counterparts, but they're packed with flavor, texture, and nutrition. I especially enjoy making biscuits with yellow or white cornmeal, which makes them wholesome without compromising the biscuits' quintessential lightness. I've always found traditional biscuits a bit doughy in the middle, and cornmeal remedies this, while creating a crunchy exterior. If this sounds enticing, use equal parts cornmeal and all-purpose flour, as given in the ingredients list. For a lighter biscuit, use a higher percentage of all-purpose flour. Use 2½ cups (350 g) all-purpose flour and 1½ cups (240 g) fine cornmeal instead.

I top these biscuits with shredded white Cheddar and fresh thyme, so I like using white cornmeal. You could try a variation with yellow cornmeal, yellow Cheddar, and minced

RECIPE CONTINUES

chives or serve the bare biscuits alongside butter and jam or with gravy.

It's important to use a biscuit cutter, which is easy to find in cooking supply stores. Biscuits with clean-cut sides will rise better. As an alternative, you can cut the dough into 2½-inch squares with a sharp chef's knife, making sure to wipe the blade clean after each cut.

1. Place an oven rack in the middle position and preheat the oven to 350°F.

2. Line a baking sheet with parchment paper.

3. Sift the flour, cornmeal, sugar, baking powder, baking soda, and salt into a mixing bowl. Toss the cold butter cubes into the dry ingredients. Quickly cut the cold butter cubes into the dry ingredients by progressively pinching it with your fingertips, until the mixture resembles a coarse meal with hazelnut-size crumbs. Make a well in the center with your hands. Pour the buttermilk into the well in the dry ingredients. Toss gently with both hands (as if tossing a salad), until a shaggy dough forms. Transfer to a floured surface and shape by hand into a 10-by-5-inch rectangle about 1 inch thick. Fold the dough onto itself as if you were closing a book (this step helps create layers) and flatten by hand or using a rolling pin until the rectangle is 1 inch thick. Cut with a 2½-inch plain biscuit cutter. Gather scraps to cut a few additional biscuits. Discard anything left afterward; the dough is overworked and will yield tough biscuits. Transfer the biscuits to the prepared baking sheet. Top each biscuit with white Cheddar and a sprinkle of thyme.

4. Bake for 10 minutes. Rotate the baking sheet and bake for another 10 to 15 minutes, until the biscuits are golden. Rotating the sheet halfway through the baking process will ensure that the biscuits bake evenly. The biscuits are delicious 20 to 30 minutes after coming out of the oven, but they will reheat very well the next day. Store leftovers in an airtight container and reheat in a toaster oven at 350°F for 6 to 8 minutes.

Corn Linzer Cookies

Equipment: 2½-inch and ½-inch fluted or plain round cookie cutters

8 tablespoons (1 stick/115 g) unsalted butter, at room temperature

2 tablespoons granulated sugar

2 tablespoons confectioners' sugar, plus extra, sifted, for decorating

1 large egg white

½ teaspoon kosher salt

½ teaspoon vanilla extract

¼ cup plus 2 tablespoons (55 g) fine yellow corn flour

¾ cup (105 g) all-purpose flour

½ cup (160 g) homemade Raspberry Jam (page 94), Tangelo Curd (page 89), or Lemon Curd (page 89), or store-bought

Corn flour, the superfine relative of cornmeal, is one of my favorite corn-based ingredients. Like cornmeal, corn flour is milled from the whole kernel—hull, germ, and endosperm—so it's as nutrient dense as its coarser counterparts polenta, grits, and cornmeal. I buy corn flour in specialty markets and health food stores, but if it proves elusive there are online retailers that offer it such as Bob's Red Mill.

Linzer cookies typically describe a berry-jam-filled nut-based shortbread cookie sandwich. While classic European linzer dough uses almonds or hazelnuts to add texture and flavor, this New World version calls on corn flour. The sweetness of corn pairs well with fruity fillings like strawberry-rhubarb jam, lemon curd, or blood orange marmalade. In the summer I opt for a raspberry jam like the one on page 94, but in the winter I prefer these filled with lemon, tangelo, or tangerine curd (page 89).

Do pay attention to the oven temperature. Because corn flour caramelizes at a lower temperature than all-purpose flour, the cookies should be baked at 300°F.

1. In a stand mixer fitted with the paddle attachment, cream the butter and sugars, about 2 minutes. Add the egg white, salt, and vanilla and mix for another 2 minutes. Stop the mixer and scrape down the sides of the bowl with a rubber spatula. Add the flours and mix until well combined.

RECIPE CONTINUES

2. Turn the dough onto a clean, lightly floured work surface and flatten into a disk about 6 inches in diameter. Cut two sheets of parchment paper, about 16 by 12 inches each. Place the disk of dough between the parchment sheets and, with a rolling pin, roll as evenly as possible until $\frac{1}{8}$ inch thick. Carefully put the flattened dough on a tray and refrigerate for 30 minutes.

3. Place two oven racks in the middle positions and preheat the oven to 300°F.

4. Remove the cookie dough from the refrigerator and put on a work surface. Peel off the top layer of parchment, invert the dough rectangle directly onto your clean work surface, and remove the remaining parchment. Cut cookies with a 2½-inch round cutter. Divide the cookies evenly between the two baking sheets. Leave one sheet of cookies as is (these will be the bottoms). To make the tops, use a ½-inch round cookie cutter to cut out the center of each cookie on the other sheet to form doughnut-shaped tops. Gather leftover scraps and reroll in between sheets of parchment, just as you did before, to get a few extra cookies.

5. Bake for 15 minutes. Rotate the sheets and switch their positions in the oven and bake for another 10 to 15 minutes or until the cookies' edges are golden. Rotating and switching the sheets halfway through the baking process will ensure that the cookies bake evenly. Keep a watchful eye—these thin cookies can brown quickly. Remove from the oven and let cool completely.

6. To finish the linzer cookies, dust the tops with sifted confectioners' sugar. Spread about 1 teaspoon of jam or curd in the middle of each bottom cookie and top with the dusted doughnut-shaped cookie. The cookies will soften within a few hours of being filled. If you don't plan to serve them all at once, reserve the baked cookies in an airtight container and fill as needed—the baked cookies will stay crisp for 2 days unfilled.

Ricotta Cornmeal Pound Cake

Equipment: 8½-by-4½-inch loaf pan

1 cup (140 g) all-purpose flour

1 cup (160 g) fine white cornmeal

1¾ teaspoons baking powder

¾ teaspoon kosher salt

10 tablespoons (1¼ sticks/140 g) unsalted butter

1 cup (200 g) granulated sugar

2 large eggs

1 large egg yolk

¼ cup (60 g) sour cream

1 cup (240 g) whole-milk ricotta

2 teaspoons vanilla extract

I wouldn't be surprised if this recipe ends up in your regular rotation. It hits all the marks: easy to make, ideal for multiple occasions, keeps for a few days, can be made in advance, indulgent without feeling excessive, incredible baking smells, readily accessible ingredients, and kids love it. In Spanish, this cake is called *queque seco*, or "dried cake," because it isn't iced, glazed, or frosted. My grandmother, Yenita, made many versions of this cake—rum raisin, lime zest, plain with vanilla extract—and this recipe triggers some of my sweetest memories. She never put ricotta in hers, but as a trained pastry chef I couldn't help incorporating this enriching adornment. Ricotta, a fresh Italian cheese made from cow's or sheep's milk, is available in most supermarkets and adds a buttery richness and desirable tang to the batter. If you can't find it, substitute full-fat cottage cheese. I prefer the subtlety of white cornmeal in this recipe, but you can use yellow too. This comforting, craving-worthy pound cake can be served for breakfast with a little jam, for dessert alongside lightly whipped cream and fresh fruit, or as is, to accompany afternoon coffee.

RECIPE CONTINUES

1. Place an oven rack in the middle position and preheat the oven to 325°F.

2. Cut a 7-by-12-inch rectangle out of parchment paper. Lightly coat the loaf pan with nonstick spray, line it with the parchment paper rectangle, and fold the excess paper outward to the sides. This paper sling will make the step of unmolding the pound cake much easier.

3. Sift the flour, cornmeal, baking powder, and salt into a bowl.

4. In a stand mixer fitted with the paddle attachment, cream the butter and sugar until lightened, about 5 minutes. Add the eggs and egg yolk one by one. Stop the mixer and scrape the sides of the bowl with a rubber spatula. Add half of the dry ingredients and mix just to combine. Add the sour cream followed by the rest of the dry ingredients and mix for 1 minute. Scrape the sides of the bowl one more time, add the ricotta and vanilla, and mix till well combined.

5. Transfer the batter to the prepared loaf pan. Smooth the top with a spatula.

6. Bake for 40 minutes. Then rotate the loaf pan and bake for another 20 to 30 minutes or until a toothpick inserted in the center comes out clean. Rotating the pan halfway through the baking process will ensure that the pound cake bakes evenly. Don't be surprised if the cake takes a long time in the oven. Baking it low and slow will yield a tender and creamy crumb and prevent it from drying out. Let cool for at least 1 hour.

7. Carefully run an offset spatula or paring knife along the sides of the pan and pull the excess parchment paper to lift the cake from the pan. The pound cake will keep in an airtight container for 2 days at room temperature. It also freezes well for up to 2 weeks, but wrap it tightly in plastic to prevent freezer burn.

Variation

Ricotta Semolina Pound Cake

Replace the cornmeal with 1 cup (165 g) semolina (for more on semolina, see page 278–79), then flavor the batter with the finely grated zest of one lemon instead of the vanilla extract and brush the top with a generous layer of Meyer Lemon Glaze (see page 110).

Olive Oil Polenta Cake

Equipment: 9-inch springform pan

1 cup (160 g) polenta

1 cup (240 ml) buttermilk

1 cup (140 g) all-purpose flour

1½ cups (300 g) sugar

½ teaspoon baking soda

1 teaspoon baking powder

½ teaspoon kosher salt

3 large eggs

1 cup (240 ml) extra virgin olive oil

½ cup (120 ml) fresh orange juice

Finely grated zest of 1 orange

Not long ago, olive oil and polenta were considered fancy, imported foods; today they're common pantry staples. This cake beautifully blends these two Old World ingredients into a New World aromatic concoction. Like grits and cornmeal, polenta is stone-ground from whole corn kernels. The main difference is that polenta is ground from flint corn, which holds up in the cooking process without becoming too mushy. In polenta's ancestral home, Italy, it is a quintessential comfort food comparable to mashed potatoes. It's usually served as a hot porridge alongside braised meats or vegetable stews, but polenta is quite versatile and can be used in both savory and sweet recipes.

Use the best olive oil you can find for this cake. My go-to is Arbequina extra virgin olive oil, produced here in California. Besides adding richness and a velvety mouthfeel, it brings bright citrusy notes to the batter. To further accentuate these flavors, the cake is enriched with orange juice and zest. For a softer crumb, hydrate the polenta by soaking it overnight in buttermilk. If you enjoy a crunchier texture, you can certainly skip this step.

1. Place the polenta in a 2-quart nonreactive container and add the buttermilk. Cover with plastic wrap and let soak in the refrigerator overnight.

2. The next day, place an oven rack in the middle position and preheat the oven to 350°F. Lightly coat the pan with nonstick spray.

RECIPE CONTINUES

3. Sift the flour, sugar, baking soda, baking powder, and salt into a bowl and make a well in the center with your hands. Combine the soaked polenta with the eggs, olive oil, orange juice, and orange zest in a separate bowl. Pour this mixture into the well in the dry ingredients and whisk to combine.

4. Transfer the batter to the prepared pan and bake for 30 minutes. Then rotate the pan and bake for another 20 to 25 minutes, until a toothpick inserted in the middle comes out clean. Rotating the pan halfway through the baking process will ensure that the cake bakes evenly. Remove from the oven and let cool completely before serving. To unmold, run an offset spatula or paring knife along the side of the pan and loosen the springform lock. Transfer to a cake plate. Thanks to its high oil content, this cake will stay moist for days on your kitchen counter. Just make sure it stays covered.

Clockwise from top: Carrot Snack Cake (page 266), Olive Oil Polenta Cake (page 127), Buckwheat Honey Cake (page 90), Sorghum Gingerbread (page 264)

Corn Polenta Ice Cream

MAKES 1½ QUARTS

Equipment: ice cream maker

3 cups (720 ml) whole milk

3 cups (720 ml) heavy cream

¼ cup (40 g) polenta

1 cup (200 g) sugar

2 tablespoons honey

2 ears fresh corn

6 large egg yolks

I first made this ice cream a few years ago, when one of my favorite farmers had a beautiful crop of an heirloom corn variety called Valencia. I steeped milk and cream with a generous cup of freshly grated corn, but the resulting flavor was a bit faint. In a second attempt, I added both grated kernels and cobs to the infusion. The corn flavor improved but still needed something. I decided to throw in some polenta and was amazed by the results. The polenta thickened the ice cream base slightly, making it even creamier, and added the flavor kick I'd been searching for.

Corn may not be a flavor you find at the local ice cream parlor, but there's nothing challenging about it. Reminiscent of the milk left behind from a bowl of cornflakes, it's bound to become your favorite frozen treat. Serve topped with the Berry Compote on page 84 or alongside the Corn Linzer Cookies on page 123.

1. Combine the milk and cream with the polenta, sugar, and honey in a medium nonreactive saucepan and stir to combine. Grate the kernels from the ears of corn on the large holes of a box grater into a bowl. Add the cobs and kernels, with all their milky juices, to the milk mixture. Cook over medium-low heat, stirring occasionally to prevent the mixture from sticking to the bottom of the pot. Once the mixture comes to a boil, turn off the heat and let rest for 30 minutes.

2. Carefully remove the cobs with kitchen tongs. Bring the liquid mixture back to a boil over medium heat. Place the egg yolks in a mixing bowl and whisk to break them up. Temper the egg yolks with the hot mixture: Add a ladleful of the heated liquid while whisking the yolks vigorously. Continue until all liquid has been added. Strain through a fine-mesh sieve into a separate container. Discard the polenta and corn kernels collected in the sieve and strain the ice cream base one more time. Chill over a bowl of ice.

3. Once the ice cream base is cool, churn it in your ice cream machine following the manufacturer's instructions. Place the finished ice cream in the freezer to firm up completely, at least 4 hours.

Vegan Pozole Verde

SERVES 4 TO 6

2 cups (170 g) dried hominy

2 poblano peppers

1 jalapeño pepper

2 teaspoons cumin seeds

3 tablespoons extra virgin olive oil

1 small yellow onion, sliced

2 garlic cloves, sliced

½ cup (30 g) chopped cilantro leaves and stems

One 14-ounce can tomatillos, drained

3 cups (720 ml) water

1 tablespoon kosher salt or as needed

For garnish

1 cup (75 g) shredded green cabbage

4 to 6 radishes, shaved into thin slivers with a mandoline

¼ cup (15 g) cilantro leaves

2 limes, cut into wedges

One rainy evening, after a long day at the bakery, I rushed home eager to rest my feet, pet my cat, and enjoy some soup for dinner. My husband—a hardworking chef but infrequent home cook—had prepared a version of this pozole-esque stew. I opened the door and was overwhelmed with the intoxicating aromas of cumin, green chile, and cilantro. I had two back-to-back bowlfuls, swooning over every spoonful of this savory dish. The flavors in the stew are familiar yet complex, deep, and satisfying. Cooking the hominy takes a little time and forethought, but preparing this dish is fairly simple. For the vegan version, which is my personal favorite, garnish with shredded cabbage, cilantro leaves, shaved radishes, and a squeeze of lime. For a vegetarian take, I like to add crumbled Cotija cheese. Omnivores can include shredded chicken or pork.

Hominy is made through nixtamalization, a process in which dried corn kernels are soaked and cooked in alkalized liquid, typically water with lime. Nixtamalized grain is the key component of masa—the mash used to make tortillas and tamales. The hominy you buy at a grocery store is dried, nixtamalized corn kernels (my favorite brand is Rancho Gordo). Hominy can take up to an hour to cook, so I strongly recommend you soak it overnight to reduce the cooking time.

This recipe calls for canned tomatillos, but if you have access to fresh tomatillos, use one pound of those instead. To prepare them, remove the husks, put the tomatillos on a baking sheet, drizzle with about 1 tablespoon olive oil, and roast in a preheated 400°F oven for 15 to 20 minutes or until they start to blister.

RECIPE CONTINUES

1. The night before preparing this dish, put the hominy in a stockpot with 2 quarts cold water. Cover and let soak at room temperature overnight.

2. The next day, drain the hominy and cover with fresh water by 3 inches. Bring to a boil over high heat, decrease the temperature, and simmer for 50 to 60 minutes or until tender. Drain and set aside.

3. Over an open flame, like a gas burner, char the skins of the poblano and jalapeño peppers, turning them every so often to blacken evenly. Put the charred peppers in a bowl and cover with plastic wrap to let them steam for 20 to 30 minutes. Peel and seed the peppers, then slice them roughly.

4. Toast the cumin seeds in a skillet over medium-low heat until they begin releasing their aroma; this will be quick, about 1 minute. Make sure to swirl the skillet nonstop, which will prevent them from burning. Let the seeds cool before pounding them with a mortar and pestle or grinding to a powder using a spice grinder. The flavor and aroma of freshly toasted cumin seeds is central to this dish. I recommend toasting and grinding your own whole cumin seeds over using store-bought ground cumin for this recipe.

5. In a medium saucepan, heat the oil over medium heat and sauté the onion, garlic, chopped cilantro, and peppers until translucent, about 5 minutes. Add the tomatillos and cook for 2 minutes. Add the water, season with the salt and cumin, and simmer for 10 to 15 minutes. Cool briefly. Puree in a blender, return to the pot, and simmer for another 5 minutes. Add the cooked hominy and simmer for 10 to 15 minutes. Check the seasoning and add more salt if necessary. Serve in bowls, garnished with cabbage, radishes, and cilantro on top and a few lime wedges on the side. Leftovers will keep for up to 5 days in the refrigerator, but you may have to add a little water to thin it when reheating.

Savory Chickpea Pancake with Bitter Green Salad and Cumin Yogurt

Equipment: 9-inch nonstick skillet or cast-iron pan

For the pancake

1 small butternut squash (1¼ pounds/565 g), peeled, seeded, and cut into ½-inch cubes

¼ cup (60 ml) extra virgin olive oil, plus extra for panfrying the pancake

Kosher salt

1 shallot, thinly sliced

1 cup (160 g) canned chickpeas

½ cup (30 g) chopped cilantro leaves and stems

½ cup plus 2 tablespoons (90 g) fine yellow corn flour

½ cup plus 2 tablespoons (90 g) all-purpose flour

1 teaspoon baking powder

½ teaspoon baking soda

3 large eggs

1 cup (240 ml) buttermilk

For the cumin yogurt

1 teaspoon cumin seeds

½ cup (145 g) Greek yogurt

For the bitter green salad

3 cups (100 g) bitter greens such as arugula, frisée, radicchio, dandelion greens, or any combination

2 teaspoons harissa

3 tablespoons sherry vinegar

¼ cup plus 2 tablespoons (90 ml) extra virgin olive oil

Kosher salt

This is one of my all-time favorite vegetarian dishes. Imagine bites of roasted squash and whole chickpeas woven into a zesty corn flour batter. A schmear of cumin yogurt and bitter greens dressed with harissa vinaigrette make this a complete meal. My husband, Daniel, developed the dish as the chef of a small restaurant in West Hollywood. The pancake was very popular and put many line cooks to the test. Making six of these on a small stovetop, at once, in the middle of a very busy dinner service, is no easy feat. For a stress-free experience I recommend making a family-style pancake in a larger skillet for everyone to share. Make your garnishes ahead of time and then just mix the batter and panfry the pancake with ease right before serving. I prefer using a nonstick skillet, but a well-seasoned cast-iron pan works really well.

The flavor and aroma of freshly toasted cumin seeds is central to the cumin yogurt. I recommend toasting and grinding your own whole cumin seeds over using store-bought ground cumin for this recipe.

To make the vinaigrette for the bitter green salad, you will need harissa, a popular North African condiment available in well-stocked grocery stores or Middle Eastern markets.

RECIPE CONTINUES

1. Place an oven rack in the middle position and preheat the oven to 375°F.

2. Toss the squash with 2 tablespoons of the olive oil in a small mixing bowl. Season with a little salt and transfer to a baking sheet. Roast in the oven until tender, 20 to 25 minutes. Remove from the oven, leaving the oven on.

3. Put 2 tablespoons of the remaining olive oil in a skillet and sauté the shallot over medium heat until soft, about 2 minutes. Add the chickpeas and cilantro and sauté for 1 minute. Stir in the roasted squash. Transfer to a separate dish and let cool completely.

4. To prepare the cumin yogurt, toast the cumin seeds in a skillet over medium-low heat until they begin releasing their aroma; this will be quick, about 1 minute. Make sure to swirl the skillet nonstop, which will prevent them from burning. Let the seeds cool before pounding them with a mortar and pestle or grinding in a spice grinder. Combine the freshly ground cumin with the Greek yogurt and set aside until the pancake is ready to serve.

5. To prepare the salad, place the bitter greens in a bowl. Whisk the harissa and vinegar together in a separate bowl. Add the olive oil in a steady stream while whisking vigorously until the vinaigrette emulsifies. Season with kosher salt to taste. Keep the vinaigrette and greens separate but ready to be tossed together just before serving.

6. To make the batter, sift the flours, baking powder, baking soda, and ½ teaspoon salt in a mixing bowl. Make a well in the center with your hands. Whisk the buttermilk, eggs, and olive oil together in a separate bowl. Pour the liquids into the well in the dry ingredients. Using a whisk, slowly mix from the center out to draw the dry ingredients into the liquid ingredients. Whisk well to work out any lumps. Add the sautéed vegetable mixture and stir to combine.

7. To panfry the pancake, preheat the pan over medium heat. Add a generous drizzle of olive oil and swirl to coat. Pour in the batter, then use the back of a spoon to spread it gently over the entire hot surface. Cook until you see bubbles forming on top of the pancake. Transfer the skillet to the preheated oven for 5 minutes or until the surface is just firm to the touch. Carefully flip with a wide flat spatula (like the one you use to flip burgers), bake for another 2 minutes, and remove from the pan. If flipping a large pancake feels intimidating, you can try this kitchen hack: Slide the pancake onto a plate, keeping the cooked side at the bottom. Using oven mitts, invert the pan or skillet over the plate with the pancake, hold the sides of the plate and skillet with both hands (as you would a sandwich or a burger), and then invert so the uncooked side of the pancake lands on the bottom of the pan. Cook for another 2 minutes on the stovetop.

8. To serve, place the pancake on a large plate. Dress the salad with the harissa vinaigrette and season with kosher salt to taste. Spread the cumin yogurt over the pancake and top with the dressed bitter greens. You could also set all the components on a table so your guests can help themselves.

oats

AVENA SATIVA

Oats—more than gruel.

There's something humble about oats. They're never the flashiest grain, never used to make the sexiest dish. They evoke times of hardship and are forever linked to Dickensian images of a famished Oliver Twist, pleading for a second bowl of gruel. Oatmeal, after all, is a notoriously mundane breakfast. But don't be mistaken—oats have fueled civilizations, celebrated the supernatural, and in modern times even replaced milk. Our tendency to relegate oats to a microwave porridge overlooks the myriad ways in which they can be consumed. In Ireland oats are a common flavoring component when distilling whiskey or brewing ale. In China oats are ground into flour to make rolls or noodles known as *youmian*. In Latin America oats form the base of avena, a sweet, milky drink similar to horchata.

The exact timeline of their introduction to the human diet is murky, but ancient civilizations in the Near East were clearly cultivating oats ten thousand years ago. In fact, excavators found wild oats stored in an ancient building near Jericho, in the West Bank. Oats were domesticated relatively late in comparison to wheat and barley—most likely during the Bronze Age in central Europe, shortly before spreading to the Mediterranean. They eventually made their way to northern Europe, including the northernmost British Isles, where their low heat requirement and high rain tolerance allowed them to thrive.

Opposite: Oat Graham Crackers (page 164)

Legend claims the English author Samuel Johnson described oats as "eaten by people in Scotland, but fit only for horses in England," to which a Scotsman replied, "That's why England has such good horses, and Scotland has such fine men!" Many of his country-men shared this sentiment. The notable Scottish physician Sir James Crichton-Browne credited oats for producing "big-boned, well-developed and mentally energetic" Scots. His words aren't surprising. Even then, oats were associated with sustenance—a nutri-tious grain that can be mixed with nothing but water to make a meal fit for energizing empires. Oats are intimately attached to the folklore of the region. For example, the Celtic dish fuarag—essentially oatmeal with cream—celebrated Samhain, a night when deceased loved ones returned to roam the earth as fairies and spirits. Fuarag was served in a communal bowl, with objects like a ring, coin, or thimble hidden inside. Whichever item you were served signaled your fortune for the coming year.

Scottish settlers brought oats to North America in 1602. They were a major crop in the United States until the 1920s, when machines began replacing horsepower. Because oats had been grown to feed horses and livestock, their acreage declined and oat grow-ing land was repurposed. Thankfully, domestic oats have seen a resurgence in recent decades, largely due to their reputation as a healthy cereal with superfood status. Because their husk and germ are almost never removed, oats retain many health ben-efits when we eat them. Compared to most whole grains, oats are high in protein and healthy fat, but low in carbohydrates. Also, their strong antioxidant, anti-inflammatory, and anti-itching abilities make oats a powerful ingredient in skin care products.

Oats' warm, comforting flavor is perfect for fall and winter dishes but also shines in spring and summer sweets alongside seasonal fruit. Oats come in several forms, from whole groats to the steel-cut and rolled oats we use in morning oatmeal. I incorporate all oat forms in my baking, including oat flour, which is wonderfully delicate considering it comes from a hearty grain associated with sustenance and hardship.

How to Purchase and Use

Oat Groats

Oat groats comprise the entire kernel, including bran, germ, and endosperm. They're very nutritious but aren't as popular as steel-cut or rolled oats because they take a long time to cook. Even if soaked overnight and simmered for 45 to 50 minutes, they remain toothy. I prefer steel-cut oats; they're almost identical, but broken into smaller pieces so they don't require as lengthy a preparation. They're not particularly difficult to find. Many markets with bulk sections, such as Whole Foods and Sprouts, carry them.

Steel-Cut Oats

Steel-cut oats are groats cut into smaller segments with steel blades. The resulting pieces are somewhat irregular in shape but cook twice as fast as whole groats. Porridge made with steel-cut oats has an earthy, wholesome taste and a pleasantly chewy texture. Steel-cut oatmeal is very popular in Ireland and Scotland, where it's often garnished with dried black currants and a drizzle of buttermilk. Imported cans of McCann's Irish Oatmeal are easy to find, but I recommend Bob's Red Mill organic steel-cut oats, which is produced domestically and therefore has a lesser eco footprint.

Rolled Oats

This is the most common oat product on the market. To make rolled oats, groats are steamed until soft and pressed between steel rollers; hence the name *rolled oats*. Oats rolled even thinner to reduce cooking time are known as *instant* or *quick oats*. Whole rolled oats or old-fashioned rolled oats are thicker and therefore slightly chewier. They're also considered more wholesome and nutritious. They can be prepared as porridge or incorporated into many recipes, both sweet and savory. Baked goods containing rolled oats have an enhanced cereal flavor and desirable texture. In savory dishes like force-meats or stews oats can act as a thickener, without adding any pronounced flavor. Keep in mind that not all oats can be considered gluten-free unless the label indicates it. Oats may have been in contact with flours containing gluten if processed in the same facility.

Oat Flour

Ground from whole oat groats, oat flour has a subtle, sweet cereal flavor. I prefer toasted oat flour to plain for its intense nuttiness. Many vendors offer toasted and untoasted oat flour—Bob's Red Mill, King Arthur, and Arrowhead Mills, to name a few. But my go-to online source is Anson Mills. Their whole-grain oat flour is well suited for a wide range of recipes. You could use oat flour without the addition of all-purpose flour when making cakes or pancakes, but thin, crisp cookies like Swedish Pepparkakor (page 158) and Oat Graham Crackers (page 164) require equal parts oat and all-purpose flour. Store flour in a cool pantry and try to use it within 3 months of purchase.

Oat Milk

Oat milk has become an incredibly popular dairy alternative, taking coffee shops and grocery aisles by storm. Milking oats may sound strange, but it works because they contain a globulin protein called *avenalin*. Globulins are water soluble, which is why oats yield milky liquid. The flavor is pleasant and malty, not unlike the milk left at the bottom of your cereal bowl. I enjoy it in an oat milk latte or poured over granola. It can replace milk in vegan recipes. but skip it in dessert recipes like custard, which require the viscosity, density, and richness of dairy. To make your own, see page 140.

Make Your Own Oat Milk

Upgrade your morning coffee with a splash of this affordable and nutritious dairy-free milk alternative. If you own a blender and a strainer, you are 5 minutes away from a fresh batch of creamy oat milk. I like to add a couple of dates for a touch of sweetness and body. Use as a cold milk replacement and avoid warming it up beyond lukewarm—because it's rich in starch, it will thicken when exposed to high heat. If you store it in in the refrigerator, be sure to shake the jar before pouring.

MAKES 1 QUART

1 cup (105 g) old-fashioned rolled oats

3 cups water

2 large dates such as Medjool, pitted

Pinch of kosher salt

Put the oats in a strainer and rinse under cold running water. Shake the strainer to remove excess water. Blend the rinsed oats with the water, dates, and salt until smooth. Strain through a fine-mesh sieve into a container. Store in a glass jar for up to a week in the refrigerator.

Sticky Oat Doughnuts

Equipment: 3-inch doughnut cutter or 3-inch round and ¾-inch cookie or biscuit cutters

For the dough

½ cup (120 ml) whole milk

1½ teaspoons instant yeast

3 cups (420 g) all-purpose flour, plus extra for dusting

1¼ cups (175 g) oat flour

1 teaspoon kosher salt

¾ cup (170 g) sour cream

2 large eggs

1 large egg yolk

⅓ cup (65 g) granulated sugar, plus extra for rolling

6 tablespoons (¾ stick/85 g) unsalted butter, at room temperature

½ teaspoon vanilla extract

Vegetable oil for frying (about 1 quart)

For the sticky caramel sauce

8 tablespoons (1 stick/115 g) unsalted butter

1 cup packed (215 g) dark brown sugar

½ cup (120 ml) heavy cream

½ teaspoon kosher salt

½ cup (55 g) pecans

For the doughnut holes

½ teaspoon ground cinnamon

½ cup (100 g) granulated sugar

One of my all-time favorite ingredients is Anson Mills' toasted oat flour (see Sourcing on page 336), which we use extensively at the bakery. Oat flour, with its high bran content, often translates into tender and moist baked goods. Its nutty taste and soft feel are similar to that of whole wheat, without the added gluten. In this case the right combination of oat and all-purpose flours creates a wholesome yet light doughnut.

I suggest making the dough the night before and refrigerating overnight, which makes it fairly easy to roll, cut, and fry the doughnuts the following morning. Dipped in sticky caramel sauce and sprinkled with toasted pecans, these doughnuts are my ultimate fall breakfast. Never discard the doughnut holes; instead, fry, then toss in cinnamon sugar.

RECIPE CONTINUES

1. Start with the doughnut dough. Warm the milk in a small saucepan over medium heat until lukewarm, 98° to 105°F, about 2 minutes. You can use a digital thermometer to check the temperature. Higher temperatures could ruin the yeast. Transfer the warm milk to the bowl of a stand mixer, then sprinkle the yeast over the liquid. Stir to dissolve and let sit for 5 minutes.

2. Add the remaining dough ingredients except the oil for frying to the yeast mixture. Fit the mixer with the dough hook attachment and combine on low speed for 1 to 2 minutes or until the ingredients just come together. Stop the mixer, scrape down the sides of the bowl with a rubber spatula, and beat on medium speed for 2 minutes.

3. Transfer the dough to a bowl lightly coated with nonstick spray—the bowl should be large enough to let the dough double in size. Cover the bowl loosely with plastic wrap and let rest at room temperature for 2 hours or until the dough doubles in volume. Gently punch the dough in the middle to release its gases, wrap the bowl tightly with plastic, and refrigerate overnight.

4. The next morning, remove the dough from the refrigerator and turn it out onto a lightly floured work surface. Line a baking sheet with parchment paper and dust it generously with flour. Roll the dough with a rolling pin until it is ½ to ¾ inch thick. Cut 12 rounds with a 3-inch doughnut cutter or a round cookie or biscuit cutter. If using a cookie cutter, cut a smaller inner circle on each doughnut with a cutter about ¾ inch in diameter. Place the doughnuts and holes on the prepared baking sheet, cover with a kitchen towel, and let rise for 1 hour. You

can discard the scraps or, if you wish, gather them into a ball, let it rest for 30 minutes, and cut a few more doughnuts and holes.

5. While the doughnuts are rising, prepare the sticky caramel sauce. Combine the butter, brown sugar, cream, and salt in a small saucepan over medium heat and stir until the liquid comes to a boil. Remove from the heat.

6. Place an oven rack in the middle position and preheat the oven to 350°F. Scatter the pecans on a baking sheet and toast in the oven for 8 to 10 minutes, until toasted and fragrant and a nut cut in half is golden inside. Let them cool and chop them coarsely with a chef's knife. Add to the sticky sauce. Put the sauce aside in a warm spot of the kitchen until ready to use.

7. Fill a large heavy pot with vegetable oil (such as canola, sunflower, or peanut), about 3 inches deep, and place over medium heat until the oil reaches 360°F on a digital thermometer. Line a baking sheet with paper towels.

8. Working in batches, carefully drop a few doughnuts into the hot oil, one at a time. Fry until the doughnuts are golden brown, 1 to 2 minutes, then flip over and fry the other side, 1 more minute. To test for doneness, choose a sacrificial doughnut and cut in the middle to ensure it's cooked through. If it seems dry, it's overcooked and will have a shorter shelf life, so cut down on the cooking time for the rest of the doughnuts. When the doughnuts are done, remove them from the oil with a slotted spoon and place on the paper-lined baking sheet. Repeat until all the doughnuts are fried. Carefully put all the holes in the fryer at once, stir continuously so they fry evenly, and remove

RECIPE CONTINUES

from the hot oil when they're golden brown. The holes will fry much faster than the doughnuts. Drain on paper towels. Combine the cinnamon and sugar in a small bowl and toss the holes in the cinnamon-sugar mixture.

9. While the doughnuts are still a bit warm, gently dip their tops in the sticky caramel sauce, one at a time. Transfer the doughnuts to a separate baking sheet. If the sticky caramel has cooled down and become too thick, warm it over low heat on the stovetop. Feel free to spoon leftover sauce over the finished doughnuts, making sure that each one gets a few pecan pieces on top. Enjoy them the day they're prepared; once glazed they'll keep well for 6 to 8 hours at room temperature.

Power Oat Bars

Equipment: 8-mold mini loaf pan (3½-by-2¼-inch cavity size)

10 to 12 large (150 g) Medjool dates, pitted

1 teaspoon flaxseed

2 tablespoons unsalted almond butter

2 tablespoons coconut oil

¾ teaspoon vanilla extract

½ cup (60 g) almond flour

½ cup (50 g) old-fashioned rolled oats

¼ teaspoon kosher salt

¼ teaspoon baking powder

½ cup (35 g) unsweetened shredded coconut

⅔ cup (85 g) dried apricots, chopped into ¼-inch pieces

¼ cup (30 g) raw cashews, chopped

¼ cup (20 g) raw walnuts, chopped

¼ cup (25 g) sliced almonds

A few years ago I started running. My hobby quickly became a habit, and while my times are nothing to boast about, I've stuck with it. Determined to make a portable snack to refuel when I go out on a run, I began testing my own power bars. Nuts were a win, but small seeds like chia and poppy were scrapped early on because they didn't add much. A binding substance free of refined sugar and capable of holding the bars together proved difficult to find, until my friend Sarah Lange, a fellow baker and runner, suggested date paste.

With that in mind, my sous-chef at the time, Sarah Hirata, concocted one final attempt. She nixed anything without a purpose and added shredded coconut and dried apricot bits to up the bar's flavor and energizing abilities. In addition to date paste, Sarah soaked a small amount of flaxseed in hot water, forming a viscous solution to bind the nuts and fruits. The result is this hearty combination of healthy nuts, oats, and dried fruits.

I prefer baking them in mini loaf pans as opposed to a whole sheet to be cut once baked. This allows the bars' entire exterior to brown and become sturdy, so they won't fall apart on the go. They're so satisfying that it's hard to wait until my next run to eat one. And if I were a parent, I'd pack one of these in my kid's lunch box every day.

RECIPE CONTINUES

1. Place an oven rack in the middle position and preheat the oven to 300°F.

2. Put half of the dates in a small bowl and pour about 1 cup boiling water over them. Let soak for 10 minutes. Drain and puree in a food processor until smooth. Chop the remaining dates into ¼-inch pieces.

3. Place the flaxseed in a small dish, add 1 tablespoon of hot water, and let sit for a few minutes.

4. In a stand mixer fitted with the paddle attachment, cream the almond butter with the coconut oil until smooth, about 2 minutes. Add the date puree, flaxseed mixture, and vanilla and beat at medium speed for 1 minute. Add the almond flour, oats, salt, and baking powder and mix to combine. Add the coconut, apricots, cashews, walnuts, and sliced almonds. Mix until a compact, sticky mixture forms. If necessary, knead briefly by hand to ensure the mixture is fully bound together.

5. Divide the mixture into eight equal portions, about 3 ounces (85 g) each. Coat mini loaf pans lightly with nonstick spray. Press the fruit-and-nut mixture into the pan as tightly as possible, using your fingertips. Bake for 15 minutes. Rotate the pan and bake for another 15 minutes. Rotating the pan halfway through the baking process will ensure that the bars bake evenly. The bars should brown lightly around the edges and puff slightly. The surface will be soft to the touch, but it will firm up as they cool. Let cool completely. Invert the pan and tap on the table to release the bars. Bars will keep for up to 2 weeks at room temperature tightly wrapped in plastic or in an airtight container.

Oatmeal Date Cookies

8 tablespoons (1 stick/115 g) unsalted butter, at room temperature

¼ cup (50 g) granulated sugar

½ cup packed (105 g) dark brown sugar

½ teaspoon kosher salt

1 teaspoon baking soda

½ teaspoon ground cinnamon

1 large egg

¾ cup (100 g) Sonora wheat flour, or any other heirloom wheat flour (for more on heirloom wheats, see page 279)

¾ cup (80 g) old-fashioned rolled oats

1 cup (145 g) chopped pitted Medjool dates (about 16)

Oatmeal cookies often rank second to chocolate chip, but if there were ever a recipe to convert the toughest skeptics this would be it. Classic oatmeal cookies are made with raisins or dried black currants, but I decided to try substituting chopped dates in a moment of appreciation for all things California. Fortunately for me, dates thrive in the desert regions surrounding Los Angeles. I've become addicted to the diverse varieties grown by local farmers, and there's rarely a day I don't eat a date. They're a flavorful snack on their own and make a great addition to dishes savory and sweet.

Dates contribute a satisfying chew and rich butterscotch flavor to these cookies, but you can use any dried fruit that suits your palate. Dried apricots, cranberries, or blueberries also make a delectable oatmeal cookie. Old-fashioned rolled oats are favored by most bakers, and for these cookies I agree. Avoid quick rolled oats, which lack the texture of thicker varieties. You'd be hard pressed to find a better oatmeal cookie, if I may say so myself.

1. In a stand mixer fitted with a paddle attachment, cream the butter and both sugars at medium speed until smooth, about 3 minutes. Add the salt, baking soda, and cinnamon and mix until well combined, 1 minute. Add the egg and mix for another minute. Add the flour and oats and mix on low speed until combined. Finally, add the dates in two additions to make sure they're distributed evenly throughout. The dough will be very soft at this point.

RECIPE CONTINUES

2. Transfer the dough to a sheet of parchment paper or plastic wrap. Flatten into a disk with your hands, then wrap tightly and refrigerate for at least 30 minutes (and up to 2 days)—chilled dough will be much easier to handle.

3. Place two racks in the middle positions and preheat the oven to 350°F. Line two baking sheets with parchment paper.

4. Divide the dough into 15 equal portions, about 1½ ounces (45 g) each. Working quickly so that the dough doesn't warm up, shape each portion into a ball with your hands. You can freeze the cookie dough balls for up to 2 weeks in a freezer bag to be baked from frozen at a later time. Place cookies on the prepared baking sheets, at least 3 inches apart to prevent the cookies from touching as they spread when they bake. Bake for 10 minutes, rotate the baking sheets and switch their positions in the oven, and bake for another 6 to 8 minutes, until the edges are brown and the middle is golden. Rotating and switching the sheets halfway through the baking process will ensure that the cookies bake evenly. Let the cookies cool completely on the baking sheets. The cookies keep well for a couple of days stored in an airtight container.

Friends & Family Granola

1½ cups (160 g) old-fashioned rolled oats

¼ cup (40 g) raw whole almonds

¼ cup (20 g) raw walnut halves

¼ cup (35 g) raw or dry-roasted whole cashews

¼ cup (40 g) pumpkin seeds (pepitas)

¼ cup (35 g) shelled sunflower seeds

2 tablespoons sesame seeds

2 tablespoons flaxseed

⅔ cup (45 g) unsweetened shredded coconut

2 tablespoons dehydrated coconut milk or powdered milk

¼ cup (25 g) almond flour

1½ teaspoons ground cinnamon

⅛ teaspoon freshly grated nutmeg

⅛ teaspoon ground cloves

¼ cup (60 ml) honey

¼ cup (60 ml) maple syrup

¼ cup (60 ml) applesauce (homemade or store-bought)

¼ cup (60 ml) vegetable oil

1 tablespoon vanilla extract

½ teaspoon kosher salt

1 cup (150 g) dried blueberries, golden raisins, chopped dried apricots, or a blend of your favorite dried fruits

What's so unique about this combination of oats, nuts, and seeds? Honestly, not very much. And yet, I dare say, this is the best granola I've ever tasted. I spent years perfecting the recipe and proudly serve it every day at the bakery.

I love when granola forms crunchy clusters, and to achieve that I make the mixture somewhat sticky. This requires longer baking at a lower temperature, but it's very effective. Also, adding whole nuts helps create tasty, nut-filled morsels. I use honey, maple syrup, and applesauce to sweeten instead of refined white sugar, and spice it with cinnamon, nutmeg, and clove. As for shelf life, 45 minutes of baking at a low temperature makes the granola dry and crunchy enough to last 2 weeks, maybe longer, but we always finish it before then. Feel free to add dried fruit at the end, stirring it into the granola as soon as it comes out of the oven. Golden raisins, dried black currants, dried blueberries, and cranberries are all great additions. If using dried apricots or figs, chop them into smaller pieces.

The recipe also includes dehydrated coconut powder, which adds a hint of coconut flavor and prevents the granola from getting soggy. You can buy it at Thai markets or online, but powdered milk produces the same effect.

RECIPE CONTINUES

1. Place an oven rack in the middle position and preheat the oven to 325°F. Coat a rimmed baking sheet lightly with nonstick spray.

2. Combine the oats, almonds, walnuts, cashews, pumpkin seeds, sunflower seeds, sesame seeds, flaxseed, coconut, dehydrated coconut milk, almond flour, and spices in a medium bowl.

3. In a small saucepan, combine the honey, maple syrup, applesauce, oil, vanilla, and salt and heat while stirring constantly, until the mixture is lukewarm. Add the warm liquids to the oat mixture and combine with a rubber spatula until all the seeds and nuts are nicely coated.

4. Spread on the prepared baking sheet and toast for 45 minutes, stirring with a wooden spoon or heat-resistant spatula every 15 minutes so that the granola toasts evenly.

5. Remove the toasted granola from the oven and stir in the dried fruit. Line a work surface with a sheet of parchment paper, about 16 by 12 inches, spread the warm granola over it, and let it cool completely. Transfer to an airtight container and store in a dark, dry place for 2 weeks or longer.

Granola Scones

¼ cup plus 2 tablespoons (50 g) all-purpose flour

¼ cup plus 2 tablespoons (60 g) whole wheat flour

2 tablespoons turbinado sugar, plus extra for sprinkling

½ cup plus 1 tablespoon (65 g) old-fashioned rolled oats

½ teaspoon baking powder

¼ teaspoon baking soda

⅛ teaspoon kosher salt

½ teaspoon ground cinnamon

6 tablespoons (¾ stick/85 g) cold unsalted butter, cut into ½-inch cubes

½ cup (45 g) sliced almonds

⅓ cup (30 g) unsweetened shredded coconut

5 tablespoons (50 g) pumpkin seeds (pepitas)

½ cup (80 g) flaxseed

6 tablespoons (55 g) dried black currants

1 cup (145 g) chopped pitted Medjool dates (about 16)

1 cup (145 g) golden raisins

Finely grated zest of 1 orange

⅓ cup (80 ml) heavy cream, plus extra for brushing

From a very young age I've loved all things sweet. I've never met an ice cream pint I didn't like, and I doubt I'll ever be able to stop eating chocolates before the box is empty. It may come as a surprise, but I'm equally drawn to healthy things. I love candy but appreciate kale in equal proportion.

These granola scones are a compromise between the two sides of my dietary psyche. They're neither terribly sweet nor what a nutritionist would recommend. Landing somewhere in the middle, these scones are an opportunity to satisfy both hungers. They're rich in fiber, omega-3s, antioxidants, and protein, with a sweet kick from copious dried fruit and a sprinkle of raw sugar. Unlike classic, fluffy scones, these are compact and full of flavors and textures reminiscent of a granola bar. They don't need to be served with clotted cream or jam and are best enjoyed as a midday snack or an accompaniment to morning coffee. They're also one of the few instances in which my Dr. Jekyll and Mr. Hyde coexist in perfect harmony.

RECIPE CONTINUES

1. Place an oven rack in the middle position and preheat the oven to 350°F. Line a baking sheet with parchment paper.

2. Combine the flours, sugar, oats, baking powder, baking soda, salt, cinnamon, and cold butter cubes in the bowl of a food processor. Pulse until the butter is cut into pea-size pieces. Transfer to a large bowl and mix in the sliced almonds, coconut, pepitas, flaxseed, currants, chopped dates, golden raisins, and orange zest. Toss by hand until well combined and make a well in the center. Pour the cream into the well in the dry ingredients. Toss vigorously with both hands (as if you were tossing a salad) until the mixture comes together to form a dough.

3. To shape the scones, transfer the dough to a clean floured surface. Pat down until it forms a disk about 6 inches in diameter and 1 inch tall. Using a large chef's knife, cut the disk into six equal wedges (as if you were cutting a cake). Transfer each individual scone to the prepared baking sheet, spaced at least 2 inches apart. Brush each top with approximately 1 teaspoon cream and sprinkle with turbinado sugar. Bake for 15 minutes, then rotate the baking sheet and bake for another 10 to 15 minutes, until the scones are light golden. Rotating the sheet halfway through the baking process will ensure that the scones bake evenly. Let cool completely before serving. Most scones should be eaten shortly after being baked, but these granola scones keep for 2 to 3 days in an airtight container.

Nectarine and Blackberry Crisp

MAKES ONE 9-INCH CRISP, SERVING 6 TO 8

Equipment: 9-inch round or square glass or ceramic baking dish

For the filling

½ cup plus 2 tablespoons (125 g) granulated sugar

¼ cup plus 2 tablespoons (90 ml) water

1 pint blackberries

2 tablespoons cornstarch

1 pound (455 g) nectarines

¼ cup (60 g) sour cream

For the topping

4 tablespoons (½ stick/55 g) cold unsalted butter, cut into ½-inch cubes

¾ cup (55 g) old-fashioned rolled oats

½ cup packed (105 g) dark brown sugar

The temptation to throw multiple stone fruits and berries into a crisp or cobbler always looms at the height of summer. However, narrowing it down to one or two fruits lets you understand each in a more intimate way, hopefully sparking ideas for future creations.

Of all the stone fruits, I find that nectarines have a more complex flavor profile than others, varying from slightly acidic to heady with a tropical funk, or explosively citric, depending on the crop. They're delicious on their own but bake beautifully without losing their seductive nuance. Combining them with blackberries creates the perfect stage for both fruits to shine.

In this recipe nectarines are seasoned simply with sour cream and sugar. I ask that you do a bit more with the blackberries, cooking them into a quick compote. This might seem like extra effort, but it allows the tart, seedy berries to become saucy and tender. Adding the berries without prior cooking can cause a soggy mess—the berries will break down and bleed their juices without thickening sufficiently in the baking process.

Now that we've discussed fruit, let's talk about topping—arguably the most important part of a crisp. A simple crumble of oats, brown sugar, and butter is the best pairing for these fruits. Because cooked nectarines and blackberries aren't very textured, toasty oats also lend a wonderful chew.

RECIPE CONTINUES

1. Place an oven rack in the middle position and preheat the oven to 350°F.

2. Begin with the filling. In a small saucepan, combine ½ cup (100 g) of the granulated sugar with ¼ cup (60 ml) of the water. Cook over high heat until the sugar dissolves and becomes a thick syrup, about 5 minutes. Add the blackberries and cook, stirring with a wooden spoon, to release their juices, about 5 minutes. Dissolve 1 tablespoon of the cornstarch in the remaining 2 tablespoons of water and add to the berries. Stir constantly until the compote has thickened, about 5 minutes. Transfer to a separate container and let cool completely.

3. While the compote cools, cut each nectarine into eight equal wedges, discarding the pits. Toss them in a large mixing bowl with the remaining 2 tablespoons (25 g) of sugar, the remaining 1 tablespoon of cornstarch, and the sour cream. Let the nectarines macerate at room temperature while you make the topping.

4. To make the topping, pulse the cold butter, oats, and brown sugar in a food processor until a coarse, irregular meal with pea-size butter pieces forms.

5. To assemble the crisp, gently combine the cooled berry compote with the nectarine mixture using a spatula. Transfer the fruit filling to the baking dish and top with a generous layer of oat crumble. Put the baking dish on a rimmed baking sheet to catch the drips and bake for 30 minutes. Rotate the baking sheet and bake for another 20 to 30 minutes, until the top is golden brown and the juices start to form thick bubbles. Don't be alarmed if the thick juices spill over and drip a little on the sides of the baking dish—this is a sign of a jammy filling. Rotating the baking sheet halfway through the baking process will ensure that the crisp bakes evenly. The crisp will benefit from cooling for 20 minutes before digging in. Serve warm with a scoop of vanilla ice cream. This crisp reheats very well, so if you plan to serve it later, let cool completely and reheat in a preheated 350°F oven for 10 to 15 minutes.

Swedish Pepparkakor

MAKES 3 TO 4 DOZEN COOKIES,
DEPENDING ON THE SIZE OF YOUR COOKIE CUTTERS

Equipment: holiday cookie cutters

1¼ cups (170 g) oat flour

1½ cups (210 g) all-purpose flour, plus extra for dusting the dough

2¼ teaspoons ground cinnamon

2¼ teaspoons ground cloves

2¼ teaspoons freshly grated nutmeg

1¼ teaspoons ground cardamom

1½ teaspoons baking soda

½ teaspoon kosher salt

12 tablespoons (1½ sticks/170 g) unsalted butter

1 cup plus 2 tablespoons (225 g) granulated sugar

1 large egg

1 tablespoon honey

Swedish pearl sugar (see page 160)

At Friends & Family, Christmas season doesn't officially start until we make our first batch of Swedish pepparkakor. These crisp Scandinavian wafers are known for their decorative shape and spice-forward flavor. The recipe has been in my husband's family for generations. Come Christmastime, his Swedish grandmother always made pepparkakor, packing them in cookie tins to keep all season long. I kept the recipe intact for some time, following each instruction to the letter. But when I started incorporating more whole grains into my repertoire, I added oat flour to the mix. Oats are a hugely important cereal in Nordic countries, and the silky flour didn't compromise the cookie's texture or detract from the spices—it actually complemented them.

It's crucial to roll the dough thin to extend the cookies' shelf life and keep them snappy. The pepparkakor will keep for a long time in an airtight container.

Pepparkakor offers the opportunity to use every Christmas cutter you own, and decorating the cookies with pearl sugar is a fun activity for younger bakers.

1. Sift the flours, spices, baking soda, and salt into a bowl.

2. In a stand mixer fitted with the paddle attachment, cream the butter and granulated sugar for about 2 minutes. Add the egg and honey and mix for another minute. Scrape the sides of the bowl with a rubber spatula, add the sifted flour mixture, and mix on low speed until thoroughly combined, about 2 more minutes.

3. Divide the dough into two equal portions. Place one portion in between two sheets of 16-by-12-inch parchment paper and flatten as thin as possible with a rolling pin. The rolled dough should be no thicker than ⅛ inch. Repeat with the remaining dough. Refrigerate or freeze for at least 30 minutes.

4. Place two oven racks in the middle positions and preheat the oven to 325°F. Line two baking sheets with parchment paper.

5. Working with one dough portion at a time, peel off the top parchment sheet, dust lightly with flour, invert the dough, and peel off the

RECIPE CONTINUES

other sheet of parchment. Cut the cookies with your preferred cutters. Using an offset spatula, transfer the cut cookies to the prepared sheets, spacing them at least 1 inch apart. If the dough warms up and becomes hard to manipulate, put it back in the refrigerator for 10 minutes and then resume cutting. Gather the scraps into a ball and repeat the previous steps to get a few more extra cookies. Sprinkle each cookie with Swedish pearl sugar. Bake for 6 minutes, then rotate the sheets and switch their positions in the oven. Bake for another 6 to 7 minutes, until the cookies are evenly mahogany brown in color. Rotating and switching the sheets halfway through the baking process will ensure that the cookies bake evenly. Remove the cookies from the oven and let cool completely before enjoying. Store in an airtight container or tin for up to 2 weeks.

Variation

Rye Pepparkakor

When made with dark rye flour, the pepparkakor are a touch crispier and slightly darker in color with a subtle rye flavor. I can't decide which version is my favorite. Give it a try and decide for yourself. To make, replace the oat flour with 1 cup (125 g) dark rye flour.

What Is Swedish Pearl Sugar?

Swedish pearl sugar is a common baking garnish used throughout Scandinavia, particularly in—you guessed it!—Sweden. Fittingly, I use it to decorate Swedish Pepparkakor (page 158) and Cardamom Buns (page 300). It is also used across the Midwest, where descendants of Norwegian, Finnish, Danish, and Swedish immigrants continue making traditional recipes finished with a sprinkle of pearl sugar. Also known as *pärlsocker* (or *raesokeri*, meaning "hailstone sugar," in Finland), Swedish pearl sugar is made from sugar that has been compressed to form large white sugar granules, like oversized sprinkles.

Because of the size of the granules, they don't melt at high oven temperatures, retaining their shape, appearance, and texture. As a result, pearl sugar makes the perfect adornment to baked goods for added texture and decoration. You can use it to top almost any pastry, including sweet yeasted buns like cinnamon rolls, French chouquettes, braided decorative sweet breads, or even sugar cookies. You can find Swedish pearl sugar in the United States from Lars Own, a maker and importer of traditional specialty food products from Scandinavia and northern Europe. (See Sourcing on page 336.)

Digestive Biscuits

Equipment: fluted or plain pastry wheel cutter

½ cup (70 g) all-purpose flour, plus extra for dusting

½ cup (70 g) oat flour, plus extra for dusting

1½ cups (155 g) old-fashioned rolled oats

1 tablespoon turbinado sugar

¾ teaspoon baking soda

¾ teaspoon kosher salt

2 teaspoons ground psyllium husks

8 tablespoons (1 stick/115 g) cold unsalted butter, cut into ½-inch cubes

2 tablespoons minced fresh sage

2 tablespoons barley malt syrup

1 large egg

Digestive biscuits, or "oatcakes," are delicious, slightly savory cookies with toothsome texture and wholesome flavor. They aren't actually biscuits, at least not in the American sense, but I call them biscuits regardless as a nod to their country of origin. The whole-grain concoction was developed in 1939 by two Scottish doctors. Today they're industrially produced and sold worldwide, most notably by the popular brand McVitie's.

Originally created to promote good digestion, they included baking soda, added to act as an antacid, and malt extract to aid starch digestion—both notions that modern nutrition science dismisses. One element that does contribute to good digestion is "brown meal," or whole-grain flour, which is rich in fiber. And while the biscuit's "digestive" properties are questionable, the cookie hasn't lost its mass appeal.

In an effort to restore the digestive biscuit's original intent, I made a version with whole-grain flours, oats, minced sage leaves, and psyllium husks, all of which have proven digestive properties. Whole-grain flours and oats are high in fiber, sage is popular in naturopathy for its cleansing powers, and psyllium husks, a popular dietary supplement derived from seeds that produce a gluey substance, act as a lubricating dietary fiber that promotes colon health. Psyllium husks in powdered form are a common staple in health food stores. The biscuits are easy to prepare and can be enjoyed on their own or with cheese, such as a sharp Cheddar or crumbly blue. I may not be a doctor, but I can confirm that you'll surely find yourself eating more than a few, and in doing so will ingest plenty of fiber, thus improving your digestion.

RECIPE CONTINUES

1. Place two oven racks in the middle positions and preheat the oven to 350°F. Line two baking sheets with parchment paper.

2. Pulse the flours, oats, sugar, baking soda, salt, psyllium husks, and butter in a food processor until all the butter is cut into pea-size pieces. Add the sage, barley malt syrup, and egg. Pulse until the dough comes together.

3. Turn the dough out onto a clean, lightly floured work surface and flatten into a disk. Place the disk between two 16-by-12-inch sheets of parchment paper, making sure to flour the parchment lightly so the dough doesn't stick to it. With a rolling pin, roll the dough as evenly as possible until it's ¼ inch thick.

4. Peel off the top sheet of parchment, invert the dough rectangle directly onto the work surface, and peel off the other sheet of parchment. Use a fluted or plain pastry wheel cutter to cut 3-inch squares. You can also cut round biscuits using a 3-inch round cookie cutter. Place the biscuits on the baking sheets, spaced at least 1 inch apart. You can gather the dough scraps and roll once more to get a few extra biscuits.

5. Bake the biscuits for 8 minutes, then rotate the baking sheets and switch their positions in the oven. Bake for another 8 to 10 minutes, until the biscuits are light golden. Rotating and switching the sheets will ensure that the biscuits bake evenly. Remove from the oven and let cool completely on the baking sheets. They'll keep for up to 3 days in an airtight container at room temperature.

4. Remove the dough from the refrigerator and put on a clean, lightly floured surface. Peel off the top sheet of parchment, invert the dough rectangle directly onto the work surface, and peel off the other sheet of parchment. Use a fluted or plain pastry wheel cutter to cut the dough into 3-inch squares. Place the crackers on the prepared baking sheet, spaced at least 2 inches apart. Gather the dough scraps and roll out to get a few extra crackers. You should get 10 to 12 graham crackers. Sprinkle lightly with sugar and bake for 8 minutes. Then rotate the baking sheet and bake for another 8 to 10 minutes, until the cookies are golden brown on the edges. Rotating the baking sheet halfway through the baking process will ensure the cookies bake evenly. Remove from the oven and let cool completely. The graham crackers or crumbs made from them will keep for up to 3 days at room temperature in an airtight container.

Tangerine Dream Pie

MAKES ONE 9-INCH PIE, SERVING 6 TO 8

Equipment: 9-inch glass pie pan

For the crust

10 Oat Graham Crackers (page 164)

6 tablespoons (¾ stick/85 g) unsalted butter, melted

1 tablespoon sugar

¼ teaspoon kosher salt

For the tangerine filling

One 14-ounce can sweetened condensed milk

7 large egg yolks

½ cup (120 ml) fresh tangerine juice (from 3 to 4 tangerines)

2 tablespoons fresh lemon juice

Finely grated zest of 1 tangerine

1 cup (240 ml) heavy cream, whipped to soft peaks, for serving

Using the building blocks of Key lime pie, I created this recipe to spotlight the explosive Pixie tangerines grown in the Ojai Valley, a few hours north of Los Angeles. You can substitute other citrus for the juice and zest in the filling or even passion fruit, which is just as acidic—acidity is key here.

Don't cut corners with store-bought graham crackers; instead, make my Oat Graham Crackers from the preceding recipe, in which the flavor of oat shines, standing up wonderfully to the intense, bright tangerines. A dream pie indeed! A few of my bakers like this pie at room temperature, but I think it's best chilled, straight from the fridge, with unsweetened whipped cream. We'll let you decide.

1. Place an oven rack in the middle position and preheat the oven to 350°F. Lightly coat the pie pan with nonstick spray.

2. To make the crust, pulse the graham crackers in a food processor until ground to crumbs with no pieces larger than a small pebble. Measure 1½ cups (about 225 g) crumbs and put in a bowl. Add the melted butter, sugar, and salt and stir with your hands until the crumbs are well coated with butter. Transfer the crumb mixture to the pie pan and use the bottom of a glass to press the crumbs into a crust, making sure the crust evenly covers the pan's entire bottom and sides. Put the pie pan on a baking sheet and bake for 10 minutes. Then rotate the baking sheet and bake for another 5 minutes, until the crust smells toasty. Rotating the baking sheet

about halfway through the baking process will ensure that the crust bakes evenly. Remove the pie pan from the oven, place on a wire rack, and let cool completely.

3. Lower the oven temperature to 325°F.

4. While the crust cools, prepare the filling. Whisk the condensed milk and egg yolks together in a nonreactive bowl. Add the citrus juices and whisk until smooth. Strain the mixture through a fine-mesh sieve into a clean container, add the zest, and stir to combine. Place the pie pan back on the baking sheet and carefully pour in the filling. Bake until the filling is set, about 30 minutes. To test for readiness, shake the sheet gently; if the filling is no longer jiggly in the middle, the pie is ready. Remove from the oven and allow to cool completely. Serve at room temperature or refrigerate for a few hours and serve chilled, with a dollop of the whipped cream.

Leah's Overnight Oats

MAKES ONE 12-OUNCE JAR, ENOUGH FOR 1 SERVING

For the overnight oats

⅓ cup (35 g) old-fashioned rolled oats

1 tablespoon raw pumpkin seeds (pepitas)

1 teaspoon flaxseed

1 teaspoon chia seeds

1 tablespoon unsweetened shredded coconut

Pinch of kosher salt

Pinch of ground cinnamon

Pinch of ground cardamom

1 Medjool date, pitted and chopped

½ cup (120 ml) oat milk, homemade (page 140) or store-bought, or enough to cover

For garnish

1 to 2 tablespoons Greek yogurt (optional)

1 to 2 tablespoons maple syrup

Almond butter (optional)

Banana slices, mango pieces, berries, or other fresh fruits (optional)

A year after opening Friends & Family, our business had grown enough to necessitate hiring more bakers. At the time, Los Angeles was experiencing a bakery growth spurt; new shops were popping up all over town. Despite being great for the city, this made finding experienced bakers much harder. After a week of interviewing candidates, I read a résumé from Leah Stinson. Leah had studied psychology before shifting her focus to farming. She loved to cook and bake at home but had never worked in a serious bakery. Regardless, there was something irresistible about Leah. Trusting my gut, I offered her a job.

She quickly learned to make bread, becoming one of our fastest and most precise shapers. We soon realized she was also a meticulous organizer, and when Thanksgiving came around she designed the ordering, packaging, and delivery system we still use today. We marveled at Leah's cool head and Zen-like energy, joking that it must be the overnight oats she ate daily. Soon the staff wanted to try making oats like Leah's. We tested a few versions under Leah's tutelage, and this one was an absolute winner.

Unlike oatmeal porridge, overnight oats absorb liquid from one day to the next, no cooking involved. They swell up, becoming softer and more palatable, and providing a perfect canvas for fruits, seeds, and nuts. When Leah left the bakery to go back to school, I developed a list of small projects so she could keep working with us in her free time—including creating the conversion chart for this book! We eventually ran out of tasks, but her contributions are still palpable, top among them her recipe for overnight oats. We don't serve these at Friends & Family, but if you walk into the bakeshop around 6:00 a.m. you'll likely catch a baker or two eating Leah's overnight oats from a jar.

Combine the oats, seeds, coconut, salt, spices, and date in a 12-ounce glass jar. Add enough oat milk to cover the oat mixture. Cover the jar with its lid and refrigerate overnight. The next morning, add 1 tablespoon Greek yogurt (if using) and 1 tablespoon maple syrup and give it a good stir. Taste and add more to taste. Finish with almond butter and fresh fruit if desired. Eat immediately. Tasty, right? You could make a habit of overnight oats. Later in the day, don't forget to prep your oats for the following morning.

Oatmeal Two Ways

Transforming mundane morning oatmeal into a transcendent breakfast is easier than you might think. It's fun to unleash your creativity on a bowl of oatmeal or porridge, an old label that has made a coolness-coated come-back. Steel-Cut Oatmeal Porridge (left; page 170) and Classic Oatmeal (page 171) are two options illustrating ways you can evolve your oatmeal.

Steel–Cut Oatmeal Porridge with Ghee, Garam Masala, and Black Currants

SERVES 4

5 cups (1.2 liters) water, plus ½ cup (120 ml) if needed

2 tablespoons ghee

1 cup (200 g) steel-cut oats

Pinch of kosher salt

1 cup (240 ml) buttermilk, plus extra for serving (optional)

1 tablespoon turbinado sugar, plus extra for serving (optional)

¼ to ½ teaspoon garam masala

¼ cup (35 g) dried black currants

Steel-cut oats take the longest to cook, so making porridge with them is often considered cumbersome. Porridge aficionados suggest soaking the oats overnight or cooking over a double boiler, but I doubt these methods make the process much simpler. Given their lengthy preparation, I think of steel-cut oats the way I think about brown rice, barley, or wheat berries—a delicious but worthwhile culinary commitment requiring about 40 minutes of my time.

Thanks to their hearty bite and pronounced grain flavor, steel-cut oats stand up well to assertive ingredients. I start this porridge by toasting oats in ghee (clarified Indian butter), for a roasted, nutty flavor, then I add liquid in a five-to-one water-to-dairy ratio. I use buttermilk to give the porridge a pleasant tang, but you can use milk if you prefer. Garam masala (an Indian spice blend that includes black and white pepper, coriander, cinnamon, and cardamom) adds the perfect amount of warmth. Finally, I add turbinado sugar and dried black currants for sweetness and texture.

1. Bring the water to a boil in a medium pot.

2. Melt the ghee in a medium saucepan and add the oats. Toast, stirring, over medium-high heat for 2 minutes. Add the boiling water, salt, and buttermilk. Simmer, stirring occasionally, over low heat for 30 to 35 minutes. Taste and check for doneness. The oats should be tender but still have a little bite. Think of them as risotto cooked al dente. If the porridge has become too thick, add the extra water.

3. Add the sugar, garam masala, and black currants. Stir gently and cook for another 2 minutes. Spoon into a serving bowl and top with additional buttermilk and turbinado sugar if desired.

Classic Oatmeal with Roasted Apple Compote

SERVES 4

For the roasted apple compote

2 firm apples, such as Fuji, Pink Lady, Cox, or Spitzenburg, peeled, cored, and diced into ½-inch pieces

3 tablespoons granulated sugar

3 tablespoons packed dark brown sugar

⅛ teaspoon kosher salt

3 tablespoons unsalted butter, melted

½ teaspoon ground cinnamon

2 teaspoons cornstarch

¼ cup (60 ml) water

For the oatmeal

1 quart (1 liter) water

2 cups (210 g) old-fashioned rolled oats

Pinch of kosher salt

½ cup (120 ml) whole milk or lactose-free milk such as oat, almond, or coconut milk

2 to 4 tablespoons turbinado sugar

¼ teaspoon ground cinnamon

I typically garnish my oatmeal simply, with brown sugar and raisins. If preparing porridge for others, I serve it with this roasted apple compote. It elevates the humble porridge to a level of soul-soothing goodness. We don't have snow days here in Los Angeles, but if you live in an area with harsher winters, I suggest keeping this recipe clipped to your fridge. The comforting aromas of apple, cinnamon, and oat make this porridge the ultimate cold-weather breakfast.

1. Place an oven rack in the middle position and preheat the oven to 350°F.

2. For the compote, combine the apples with the granulated and brown sugars, salt, butter, and cinnamon in a roasting pan. In a small bowl, dissolve the cornstarch in the water. Add the cornstarch slurry to the apple mixture and toss until combined. Cover the pan with aluminum foil, roast for 15 minutes, remove from the oven, and stir with a heat-resistant spatula. Roast, uncovered, for another 15 minutes. The compote is ready when the apples are tender but not mushy. If you're making the compote in advance, let it cool before transferring to a container. Store in the refrigerator for up to 2 weeks. Reheat the compote in a double boiler or the microwave.

3. To make the oatmeal, bring the water to a boil in a medium saucepan and rain the oats into the boiling water. Add the salt. Lower the heat and simmer for 3 minutes, stirring occasionally. Turn off the heat, cover the pot, and let rest for 5 minutes. Stir in the milk, turbinado sugar, and cinnamon. Serve immediately with additional milk, turbinado sugar, and apple compote on top.

rice

ORYZA SATIVA

The mundane food of the mystics.

Rice is the grain most consumed by humans. It's a nutritious staple that has long sustained global populations, grown on every continent except Antarctica. Entire regional economies depend on its production; in fact, over one billion people are actively involved in rice cultivation across varied climates and conditions. Accessible, familiar, and nutritious, rice is a crucial part of myriad cuisines worldwide.

And yet rice toes the line between mundane and mystical, between material needs and spiritual practices. Perhaps its central role in many cultures' diets explains the grain's ties to myth and legend. In Buddhism, for example, rice is a common offering left on altars, as much as a part of virtually every meal. According to a Malaysian legend, the rice spirit is personified by a little girl who is affectionately called "flower princess." The Japanese have Inari, the patron saint of rice, while Indonesians have Dewi Sri, the goddess of rice and fertility. In Indonesian mythology there's also the Rice Mother, who provides rice as her version of milk, considered the soul-stuff of every living thing. This legend is mirrored by Chinese goddess Guan Yin, who saves her people by retrieving rice from the heavens.

But Asia isn't the only rice-revering continent. Almost every culture has a unique rice dish—think paella in Spain, congee in China, gallo pinto in Central America, chirashi in

Opposite: Tres Leches (page 194) made with brown rice flour

Japan, and dirty rice in the American South. Tahdig, a staple composed of the golden, crispy crust of rice that forms at the bottom of the cooking dish, can make or break a Persian chef's culinary reputation.

Rice can grow in diverse climates, which is a major reason for its widespread influence. Typically grown as an annual crop, rice plants are flooded throughout their lives to prevent weed and pest propagation. The plant can grow from 3 to 6 feet tall and thrive in multiple terrains, from flatlands to steep mountainsides. Worldwide, it's second in production to corn, and Thailand, Vietnam, India, and the United States are the world's top rice exporting countries.

Rice originated over ten thousand years ago in China's Yangtze River valley. From there it spread west to India and south to Sri Lanka. It's believed to have arrived in Europe with Alexander the Great's soldiers, who brought the grain to Greece after an expedition in India. The Moors of North Africa introduced it to southern Europe via the coasts of Spain and Italy. Many centuries later the Portuguese and Spanish brought rice to Central and South America, and, in the early years of the newly founded United States, Thomas Jefferson supposedly smuggled Italian rice seed into the country after a diplomatic mission.

Rice flourished in the American South's damp, marshy lowlands and soon became a staple trade crop. But its cultivation relied on the knowledge and innovation of enslaved West Africans and their descendants. These individuals introduced complex agricultural technology needed to grow rice prosperously in America. In fact, many enslaved men sold at Charleston's port garnered higher prices for their knowledge of rice production. Unsurprisingly, Carolina Gold, the most predominant strain grown in the Carolinas, originated in West Africa.

A deceptively complex ingredient, rice is a grain of great biodiversity. With the plant kingdom's largest gene bank by a long shot, rice has over 120,000 varieties. It's classified by size—hence the labels *long-*, *medium-*, and *short-grain rice*—as well as by texture, like glutinous rice, which gets its characteristic texture from a higher starch content. Rice varieties can also be distinguished by their aromatic qualities, as for basmati and Ambemohar rice, which have their own distinct scents and flavors.

Rice varieties play an important role in cooking and baking. Arborio rice, for example, is a short-grain, high-starch variety, making it perfect for risotto. You couldn't achieve its signature, creamy texture with jasmine rice. And the trick to great sushi lies not only in the fish—the correct style of short-grain rice with a proper starch balance is also crucial.

Another key distinguisher of rice varieties is their color. We typically think of rice as white or brown, but it comes in multiple tones. For instance, Himalayan red rice is a red-brown Indian variety with a complex nutty flavor. Purple Thai rice, a slightly sweet grain with a reddish-blue blush, is traditionally used in dessert. Chinese black rice, known by the ominous moniker "forbidden rice," is a deep purple.

All varieties of rice offer a number of health benefits. Brown rice is considered a whole grain because the bran and germ are intact. It's accordingly much higher in vitamins and nutrients. It's an excellent source of manganese, selenium, thiamine, niacin, riboflavin, iron, and calcium, and like many other whole grains, it will help you feel fuller longer.

How to Purchase and Use

Brown or Whole-Grain Rice

Whole-grain rice (more commonly known as "brown rice") is categorized by size: long, medium, and short grain. Every variety of white rice in the market, regardless of size, was once whole-grain rice. It contains every part of the rice kernel—bran, germ and starch—minus the inedible hull, and is therefore higher in fiber than its white counterpart. Long-grain rice varieties tend to hold their shape during cooking, while medium- and short-grain varieties often clump together. When purchasing rice, I first ensure that it's whole-grain. Then I look for a variety best suited to the recipe I'm preparing. For example, if making rice pudding I go for a short- or medium-grain rice to yield a creamier dessert. But if I'm preparing a pilaf-style dish, such as the Gallo Pinto on page 198, I prefer a long-grain variety that will remain intact after cooking. As with other whole grains, brown rice takes longer to cook than white rice. To shorten the cooking process, it can be soaked overnight or for a few hours in cold water.

There are many reputable producers of heirloom rice across the United States. One of my favorites is Koda Farms (see Sourcing on page 336), a third-generation producer in central California, for their diverse offering of organic Japanese varieties. Anson Mills sells its regional Carolina Gold rice online, and larger operations with broad distribution like Lundberg Family Farms offer multiple rice varieties in grocery stores across the country.

White Rice

Refined or white rice is brown rice without its bran. Even without its outer fibrous layer, white rice is considered a nutritious and important food across regions. The majority of rice consumed around the world is white rice, and iconic dishes everywhere are based on it, from refined basmati rice in tahdig to pearled bomba rice in paella and short-grain Koshihikari in chirashi rice. White rice is recommended in dishes where the desired outcome is subtlety in flavor and texture. I seldom buy white rice, but if you do, seek organic varieties with aromatic flavor profiles and interesting textures such as jasmine or Arborio rice.

Brown Rice Flour

Brown rice flour is often bone white, despite containing the rice kernel's bran and germ. It's very fine with a slightly gritty texture and a mild, toasty flavor. It contains no gluten and cannot be utilized in the traditional ways we use wheat flour. However, it can enhance crispness in cookies or lightness in cakes. It's also useful in savory dishes. I like to use it in place of all-purpose flour to make gluten-free fried chicken or tempura. The flavor of rice flour ranges from clean and creamy to rich and nutty. I favor organic heirloom brown rice flour from artisan producers like Anson Mills (see Sourcing on page 336) or Koda Farms, which can specify the variety used, but procuring it requires planning ahead. Luckily, easier-to-find options like Bob's Red Mill and Authentic Foods are available nationwide. Store flour in a cool pantry and try to use it within 3 months of purchase. To keep track, I recommend labeling the bag with the date of purchase.

Rice Grits

Rice grits are a by-product of rice milling. When the long grain is put through the strain of removing the hull, the fragile kernel can split or break. The broken pieces are then collected and sold as grits or cream of rice. They can be cooked just like corn grits, with water, milk, or broth, to produce a creamy porridge not unlike risotto. Most rice grits sold in the United States are produced and consumed in the South, and grits are still considered a niche product. Although I don't run into grits often, I do like to make rice pudding with them. They can also be prepared as a morning porridge and served with a pat of butter and a soft-boiled egg or more creative garnishes like toasted sesame seeds, fried shallots, and bacon bits.

Aromatic Rice Pudding

SERVES 4

For the rice

1 cup (200 g) brown short-grain rice

2 cups (480 ml) water

1 cinnamon stick

For the cream

One 14-ounce can Thai coconut milk such as Mae Ploy or Thai Kitchen

¼ cup plus 2 tablespoons (75 g) sugar

1½ teaspoons kosher salt

8 green cardamom pods

Finely grated zest of 1 lime

A porridge of rice, milk, sugar, and aromatic herbs or spices tops the list of universal comfort foods. Whether it's served for breakfast or dessert, every culture seems to have a take on rice pudding. I grew up eating arroz con leche, white medium-grain rice cooked in sweet, cinnamony milk. But living in Los Angeles has introduced me to many variations—Thai mango sticky rice, Indian basmati rice pudding with cardamom and saffron, Persian jeweled rice with pistachio and candied orange zest. This eclectic version of the dessert made with heirloom short-grain rice, soft-bark Mexican cinnamon, lime zest, Thai coconut milk, and cardamom is informed by them all. It's a multicultural mosaic, built with elements from different regions.

I prepare the rice and cream separately to reduce overall cooking time, then simmer them together for a few minutes. The grains should be tender but still toothy. If you prefer a softer texture, you can certainly cook them longer. I love eating the pudding warm, but it's also delicious chilled. If you decide to serve this cold, cook the rice until soft and almost mushy—the kernels will firm up as they cool.

1. Put the rice in a bowl, cover with water, and soak for 2 hours or overnight.

2. Drain the soaked rice and transfer to a medium saucepan. Add the water and the cinnamon stick and simmer over medium heat for 30 to 35 minutes, until the rice is tender yet toothy (think pasta cooked al dente) and almost all the water has dried out. If the water

RECIPE CONTINUES

evaporates before the rice has softened, add an extra ½ cup (120 ml) water and continue cooking.

3. While the rice is cooking, make the cream. Combine the coconut milk, sugar, and salt in a small nonreactive pot. Stir with a wooden spoon to encourage the sugar to dissolve. Crush the cardamom pods in a mortar and pestle. Add the crushed pods and the black cardamom seeds that will spill out of them to the pot. Bring the mixture to a simmer over medium heat. Cook until the cream has thickened a bit and is infused with cardamom flavor, stirring often to prevent it from sticking to the bottom of the pot, about 5 minutes. Remove from the heat and strain through a fine-mesh sieve into a container. Discard the solids.

4. When the rice is tender, add the cream and simmer for 5 minutes over low heat while stirring constantly. Don't step away from your pudding; all that starchy rice can stick to the bottom of the pot and burn easily. Transfer the pudding to individual cups while still warm, grating the lime directly over each portion. You can also serve the pudding at room temperature or chilled. If you plan to do so, cook the rice until very soft, anticipating that, as they cool, the rice kernels will be firmer in texture. Store leftovers in an airtight container in the refrigerator, and enjoy within a couple of days.

Peach Cobbler with Brown Rice Drop Biscuits

Equipment: 9-inch glass pie dish

For the peach filling

6 medium to large ripe peaches

2 tablespoons sugar

2 tablespoons honey

½ cup (120 ml) homemade Peach Jam (page 181)

2 tablespoons cornstarch

1 tablespoon unsalted butter, melted

For the drop biscuits

½ cup (70 g) brown rice flour

½ cup (70 g) all-purpose flour

½ teaspoon kosher salt

1¼ teaspoons baking powder

2 tablespoons sugar, plus extra for dusting

¾ cup (180 ml) heavy cream

Cobbler is the kind of dessert I prepare on a whim, when fruit is abundant and I don't feel like investing time in an elaborate pie or tart. Sometimes you just want to toss fruit with a bit of sugar and make a simple topping. One I often opt for is drop biscuits, and something magical happens when rice flour enters the mix. It creates an impossibly tender biscuit with a crispy exterior and soft center. It's imperative to use a light touch, mixing ingredients just until they come together. This prevents the dough from becoming tight and compact.

Peaches are common in summer cobblers, but feel free to substitute other stone fruit or berries at peak ripeness. In this recipe I toss wedges of fresh peach in a bit of homemade peach jam, but other jam flavors like apricot or raspberry also work well, contrasting the sweetness of the peach. Taste your fruit for sweetness and adjust the filling's sugar accordingly. Hold some sugar back if the fruit is very sweet and add more if it's on the tart side. I like to serve this while still warm with a scoop of vanilla ice cream.

1. Start by prepping the peaches for the filling. Fill a medium pot with water and bring to a boil over high heat. With a paring knife, score an X on the skin of each peach. Gently drop a few peaches at a time into the boiling water. Blanch for 1 minute, remove with a slotted spoon, and place in a separate container until you've finished all the peaches. Once cool enough to handle, remove the peach skins—they should come off easily.

2. To make the filling, slice the peeled peaches into wedges, about 8 wedges per peach, and discard the pits. Put the peach wedges in a bowl and macerate with the sugar and honey for 30 minutes. Add the peach jam and the cornstarch and toss until well combined.

3. Place an oven rack in the middle position and preheat the oven to 375°F.

RECIPE CONTINUES

4. Lightly coat the pie dish with the melted butter, transfer the peach filling to the pie dish, and place on a rimmed baking sheet to catch any drips.

5. To make the drop biscuits, sift the flours, salt, baking powder, and sugar into a mixing bowl. Pour in the heavy cream. Mix gently by hand until the mixture comes together to form a dough.

6. Using a spoon, scoop the dough into 8 lumps equal in size. Place each lump atop the peach filling, making sure they're at least 1 inch apart. As they bake, the biscuits will expand and touch each other. Dust each biscuit generously with sugar.

7. Bake for 25 minutes. Then rotate the baking sheet and bake the cobbler for 25 to 30 minutes more, until the biscuits are golden and the fruit is juicy and bubbly. Rotating the sheet halfway through the baking process will ensure that the cobbler bakes evenly. Let cool for just 10 to 15 minutes—it's always a good idea to let the bubbly filling settle before serving to allow the juices to thicken and prevent any burned tongues. Enjoy while still warm with a scoop of vanilla ice cream. Refrigerate leftovers. Reheat in a preheated 350°F oven.

Peach Jam

MAKES 1 CUP

4 medium to large ripe peaches

1 cup (200 g) sugar

½ cup (120 ml) water

½ vanilla bean

1. Fill a medium pot with water and bring to a boil over high heat. With a paring knife, score an X on the skin of each peach. Gently drop the peaches into the boiling water. Blanch for 1 minute, remove with a slotted spoon, and place in a separate container. Once cool enough to handle, remove the peach skins—they should come off easily. Chop into 1-inch pieces.

2. Put the sugar in a medium saucepan. Add ½ cup of water to moisten the sugar, but do not stir. Split the vanilla bean lengthwise with a paring knife, scrape out the pulp with the back of the knife, and put both pulp and pod into the pot. Cook over high heat until the mixture comes to a boil. Lower the heat to medium and reduce the mixture to a thick syrup, 3 to 5 minutes. Add the chopped peaches and cook for 8 to 10 minutes while stirring constantly. Stirring is crucial, because it breaks down the peaches while preventing overcaramelization, which may cause the jam to stick to the bottom of the pot. To test the jam's readiness: chill a small plate in the freezer, spoon a bit of jam onto it, and run your finger through the jam. If your finger leaves a trace on the plate, the jam is ready. Transfer to a separate bowl and let cool completely. Remove the vanilla bean and discard. The jam can be stored in the refrigerator for up to 1 month.

Banoffee Tart with Rice Shortbread Crust

Equipment: 9-inch tart pan

For the tart shell

7 tablespoons (100 g) cold unsalted butter, cut into ½-inch cubes

3 tablespoons granulated sugar

¼ cup plus 2 tablespoons (55 g) brown rice flour

½ cup plus 2 tablespoons (90 g) all-purpose flour, plus extra for dusting

¼ teaspoon kosher salt

2 large egg yolks

2 tablespoons ice water

Scant ¼ cup (45 g) bittersweet chocolate chips

For the banoffee filling

4 tablespoons (½ stick/55 g) unsalted butter

¼ cup packed (55 g) dark brown sugar

¼ cup plus 2 tablespoons (90 ml) sweetened condensed milk

¼ cup plus 2 tablespoons (90 ml) dulce de leche, homemade (page 185) or store-bought

½ teaspoon kosher salt

2 ripe bananas

1 cup (240 ml) heavy cream, whipped to soft peaks

Cocoa powder or chocolate shavings to decorate (optional)

As hinted by its name, banoffee tart is a dessert filled with bananas, cream, and toffee. My friend and colleague Michelle Smith was obsessed with creating a version of this English classic. She had tried it as a child, while traveling with her family in England, and as a grown-up and professional baker became determined to re-create the banoffee tart of yore.

We tried both a piecrust and a tart shell for side-by-side comparison. The fork-tender piecrust was delicious, but we worried it would take too much toffee cream to fill it up, making it unbearably sweet. In contrast, we loved how buttery shortbread paired with a thin layer of flavorsome filling. I decided to incorporate rice flour when the creamy filling turned our tart shell soggy. Rice flour, with its fine and gritty texture, is ideal for adding a crispy texture to baked goods. This quickly resolved the problem. We painted a tiny amount of melted dark chocolate across the shell's bottom, adding a flirtatious hint of bitterness to contrast with the toffee's sweetness. A solid layer of thinly sliced banana followed. Then we topped the finished tart with unsweetened whipped cream. When we cut into the tart, we marveled as each slice revealed layers of each component, and once we ate a forkful we knew we had a hit. This was one chic dessert! I never asked Michelle how our rendition compared to her first banoffee, but I can confirm that many happy customers claimed it was the best they'd ever had.

I suggest you hold on to the tart dough recipe for all your tart purposes. The flavor is neutral and pairs well with a variety of fillings.

1. Lightly coat the tart pan with nonstick spray.

2. In a stand mixer fitted with the paddle attachment, combine the butter, sugar, flours, and salt. Mix on low speed until the mixture resembles a coarse meal, about 2 minutes. Add the egg yolks and ice water and mix until the dough comes together.

3. Turn the dough out onto a floured surface and shape into a disk.

4. With a rolling pin, flatten the dough into a circle about 10 inches in diameter and ⅛ inch thick, dusting with flour as necessary to prevent sticking. Carefully transfer the dough circle to the tart pan, gently pressing the dough up the sides of the pan and removing any excess dough. If the dough rips while shaping the tart shell, patch it with a lump of additional dough. Using a fork, poke the surface of the tart shell all over. Chill the tart shell for 30 minutes.

5. Place an oven rack in the middle position and preheat the oven to 350°F.

6. Put the tart pan on a baking sheet, cut a parchment paper circle about 12 inches in diameter, and line the inside of the tart shell with it. Fill with beans or pie weights and bake for 20 minutes. Then rotate the pan and bake for another 20 to 25 minutes, until the crust is golden. Rotating the pan halfway through the baking process will ensure that the tart shell bakes evenly. Remove from the oven and carefully lift out the parchment circle with the pie weights. Sprinkle the chocolate chips over the warm shell. Wait 2 minutes, or until the chocolate melts, and using a pastry brush, paint the surface of the tart shell with the melted chocolate. Let cool completely.

7. For the filling, combine the butter, brown sugar, condensed milk, dulce de leche, and salt in a medium saucepan over low heat. Cook for 3 to 4 minutes or until the mixture has thickened, stirring nonstop with a wooden spoon to prevent it from sticking to the bottom of the pan. Immediately pour the caramel filling into the tart shell. Using an offset spatula, spread it out in an even layer. Let cool completely.

8. Slice the bananas into thin coins. Cover the caramel layer with the banana slices. If needed, you can do a double layer of bananas—just make sure you use all the fruit.

9. Cover the top with the whipped cream. Refrigerate the tart until ready to serve. If you wish, sprinkle the top lightly with sifted cocoa powder or chocolate shavings. Enjoy within 2 days.

Dulce de Leche

To make the toffee cream, you will need dulce de leche (also known as *milk jam* in the United Kingdom and *confiture de lait* in France), which can be found in the Latin American section of the grocery store. It's usually made by manufacturers of sweetened condensed milk such as Borden and Nestlé. You can also make your own: Pour one 14-ounce can of condensed milk into a glass baking dish such as a 9-inch pie dish. Set the baking dish inside a larger vessel, such as a roasting pan, and add hot water until it reaches halfway up the sides of the pie dish. Cover with a lid or aluminum foil and bake in a preheated 400°F oven for 60 to 75 minutes or until the condensed milk has caramelized and is the color and consistency of peanut butter.

Strawberry Fool with Rice Ladyfingers

Equipment: 6 goblets (wineglasses or mason jars will also work well) or one 9- or 10-inch trifle dish, pastry bag fitted with a plain round tip with a ½-inch mouth

For the ladyfingers

½ cup (70 g) all-purpose flour

½ cup (70 g) brown rice flour

3 large eggs, separated

¼ teaspoon kosher salt

¼ teaspoon cream of tartar

½ cup (100 g) granulated sugar

½ teaspoon vanilla extract

2 tablespoons confectioners' sugar

For the fool

¼ cup (60 g) sour cream

1½ cups (360 ml) heavy cream

4 large egg whites

¼ cup plus 2 tablespoons (75 g) granulated sugar

1 cup (240 ml) homemade Strawberry Jam (page 188)

½ cup (70 g) shelled pistachios, chopped, plus a little extra for garnish

A fool is a traditional English dessert, made by folding stewed fruit into sweet pastry cream. Classic gooseberry fool can be traced back to the Middle Ages, but today blueberry, black currant, and rhubarb are more common. Updated versions substitute whipped cream for pastry cream, yielding a lighter, fluffier dessert. I also fold in meringue, adding volume and stability to the base.

To add some substance, I weave ladyfingers between the layers of flavored cream. Ladyfingers are sweet, spongy cookies, shaped roughly like a large thumb. They have a subtle vanilla flavor and delectable foamy texture. Laced in the fool, ladyfingers enrich the cream's character without taking over. Made by whipping eggs to full volume, much like a sponge cake, ladyfingers typically contain no artificial leavening. The mixture is piped through a pastry bag into short lines, giving the cookies their identifiable shape. The fine grain, light consistency, and subtle flavor of rice flour yields airy yet crispy ladyfingers. The recipe makes close to four dozen, so use what you need, pack the rest, and freeze for future use. They make delicious sandwich cookies glued together with chocolate ganache, Nutella, or raspberry jam (see page 94).

1. Place two oven racks in the middle positions and preheat the oven to 350°F. Line two baking sheets with parchment paper.

2. For the ladyfingers, sift the flours into a mixing bowl.

3. In a stand mixer fitted with the whisk attachment, beat the egg whites with the salt and cream of tartar until frothy. Slowly add the granulated sugar while the mixer is still running and continue to mix until the egg whites hold firm peaks. Add the vanilla and egg yolks and whip for another minute. Using a rubber spatula, gently fold in the sifted flours.

4. Transfer the ladyfinger batter to the pastry bag and pipe 2-inch strips, spaced 1 inch apart, onto the prepared baking sheets. Put the confectioners' sugar in a sieve and dust the piped ladyfingers.

5. Bake the ladyfingers for 10 minutes, then, rotate the baking sheets and switch their positions in the oven. Bake for another 6 to 8 minutes, until the edges turn golden. Rotating and switching the sheets halfway through the baking process will ensure that the ladyfingers bake evenly. Remove the sheets from the oven. Let the cookies cool completely before peeling them off the parchment paper.

6. To make the fool filling, start with the whipped cream. In a stand mixer fitted with the whisk attachment, whip the sour cream and heavy cream until soft peaks form. Transfer to a medium bowl and refrigerate. Wash the bowl; you will need it again shortly.

7. Combine the egg whites and sugar in a heat-resistant mixing bowl. Whisk over a pot of barely simmering water, making sure the bottom of the bowl isn't touching the water. Beat until all the sugar is dissolved and the mixture is slightly warm, 2 to 3 minutes. Pour the egg white mixture into the clean bowl of the stand mixer and, with the whisk attachment, beat at high speed until medium peaks form.

8. Using a rubber spatula, fold the strawberry jam and pistachios into the whipped egg whites with as few strokes as possible. Then fold in the whipped cream. The mixture should be uniformly pink.

9. To assemble the fool, cover the bottom of six dessert cups with ladyfingers. Spoon a generous dollop of fool cream in each cup. Build another layer of ladyfingers and fill the cups with the remaining fool mixture. Repeat until the cups are full. Finish with a final layer of fool cream and a light sprinkle of chopped pistachios. Alternatively, you can build a family-style fool in a large trifle dish, alternating layers of ladyfingers and fool cream. Refrigerate for at least 2 hours or overnight before serving.

RECIPE CONTINUES

Variation

Strawberry Icebox Cake

Bakers with busy schedules may opt to make a frozen version of this dessert in advance (up to 1 week), and serve it as an icebox cake at their convenience. Line a 9- to 10-inch springform pan with plastic wrap, assemble layers of ladyfingers followed by fool cream as if you were building a trifle. Start with a layer of cookies and finish with a layer of cream, taking care to spread evenly to avoid air pockets. Decorate the top with the chopped pistachios. Cover with plastic wrap and freeze. To unmold, run an offset spatula along the sides of the pan, loosen the springform lock, and slice as you would a regular cake.

Strawberry Jam

MAKES 1 CUP

¾ cup (150 g) sugar

½ cup (120 ml) water

½ vanilla bean

4 cups (480 g) strawberries, hulled and halved

Put the sugar in a medium saucepan. Add ½ cup of water to moisten the sugar, but do not stir. Split the vanilla bean lengthwise with a paring knife, scrape out the pulp with the back of the knife, and put both pulp and pod into the pot. Cook over high heat until the mixture comes to a boil. Lower the heat to medium and reduce the mixture to a thick syrup, 3 to 5 minutes. Add the strawberries and cook for 5 minutes while stirring constantly. Stirring is crucial because it breaks down the berries while preventing overcaramelization, which may cause the jam to stick to the bottom of the pot. To test the jam's readiness, chill a small plate in the freezer, spoon a bit of jam onto it, and run your finger through the jam. If your finger leaves a trace on the plate, the jam is ready. Transfer to a bowl and let cool completely. Remove the vanilla bean and discard. The jam can be stored in the refrigerator for up to 1 month.

Persian–Style Rice Fritters

MAKES 2 DOZEN FRITTERS

For the syrup

2 cups (400 g) sugar

Juice of ½ lemon

½ cup (120 ml) water

2 tablespoons honey

2 tablespoons rose water (see page 30)

For the batter

½ cup plus 2 tablespoons (90 g) rice flour

¾ cup (105 g) all-purpose flour

⅛ teaspoon baking soda

½ teaspoon baking powder

⅛ teaspoon kosher salt

¼ teaspoon ground cardamom

1 large egg

¼ cup (50 g) sugar, plus extra for coating

¼ cup plus 3 tablespoons (105 ml) buttermilk

2 teaspoons honey

1 tablespoons plus 1½ teaspoons rose water

Vegetable oil for frying (about 1 quart)

The first time I had these sweet fritters was at a Nowruz or Persian New Year celebration, hosted by my Iranian American friend and fellow chef Samir Mohajer. The table was covered in delectable Persian dishes, but a silver platter of shiny syrup-covered zalabia, as they're called in Farsi and Arabic, caught my eye. Zalabia is a popular dessert that can be found all over the Middle East. The ones sold at Persian dessert shops in L.A. look like elongated curvy fingers, while the ones sold as street food in Cairo are more like perfect doughnut holes, but when people make them at home, they tend to take more whimsical shapes.

My take on the dish deviates slightly from the original. Instead of saturating the fritters in syrup, I first toss them in granulated sugar, then finish with a light syrup drizzle. I've seen zalabia in pastry cases, looking delectable many hours after being fried; they keep well, so evidently the syrup helps. Still, I prefer eating them fresh and warm. Never omit the rose water in the syrup; it is what gives the fritters their defining Middle Eastern flavor.

The rice flour adds a satisfying chew and uniquely crunchy exterior. The batter is loose in order to yield a light fritter, so it must be spooned directly into the hot oil. I like to make the batter ahead of time and fry shortly before serving when I entertain. I always find a couple of curious volunteers wanting to help. Since they're basically finger food, I like to serve them for dessert on a platter at the center of the table and have guests pick them up with their hands. Zalabia always enliven a dinner party, sparking enlightening conversations about travel, food, and breaking bread with strangers in faraway lands.

RECIPE CONTINUES

1. For the syrup, combine the sugar, lemon juice, water, and honey in a small saucepan over medium heat and bring to a boil. Lower the heat to a simmer and stir briefly to help the sugar dissolve. Cook for 2 minutes or until slightly thickened, around 220°F on a digital thermometer. Remove from the heat and stir in the rose water. Set aside until completely cooled.

2. To make the batter, sift the flours, baking soda, baking powder, salt, and cardamom into a mixing bowl. Make a well in the center with your hands. Whisk the egg, sugar, buttermilk, honey, and rose water together in a separate bowl. Pour the liquid mixture into the well in the dry ingredients. Using a whisk, slowly mix from the center out, drawing the dry ingredients into the wet ingredients. Whisk well to work out any lumps. The batter should resemble a thick pancake batter.

3. Fill a large, heavy pot with frying oil (such as canola) about 3 inches deep and heat over medium heat until the oil reaches 360°F on a digital thermometer. Line a plate with paper towels and have a slotted spoon nearby.

4. Using a spoon, scoop the batter into 1-ounce (28 g) lumps and drop directly into the hot oil. You can use a second spoon to help you dislodge the lump from the other spoon with ease. Fry for 1 to 2 minutes on each side, using a slotted spoon to flip the fritters. To test for doneness, choose a sacrificial fritter and cut through the middle to gauge whether the others will need more or less frying time. When done, the fritters should have the texture of a doughnut cooked all the way through. Work in batches of four or five fritters at a time, taking care not to overcrowd your pot. Remove the golden fritters with a slotted spoon and put on the prepared plate. Let them rest.

5. When the fritters are cool enough to handle but still warmish, toss them in sugar. Drizzle with syrup and serve immediately.

Sweet and Spicy Rice Snack Mix

MAKES 1½ QUARTS

Equipment: 13-by-9 ceramic or glass baking dish

For the snack mix

½ cup (65 g) macadamia nuts, raw or unsalted dry-roasted

2¼ cups (42 g) puffed brown rice cereal

¾ cup (50 g) unsweetened shredded coconut

1 tablespoon black sesame seeds

For the spicy caramel

3 tablespoons unsalted butter

¼ cup plus 2 tablespoons packed (80 g) dark brown sugar

3 tablespoons light corn syrup

½ teaspoon kosher salt, plus extra for sprinkling

1 tablespoon hot sauce such as Tabasco, Cholula, or Sriracha

¼ teaspoon baking soda

Move aside, Chex Mix! Crunchy, salty, spicy, and sweet, this homemade snack mix is incredibly addictive and easy to make. Next time you host a cocktail party, skip the bar nuts and opt for this; your guests will be blown away. It requires nothing more than tossing dry ingredients in a fiery caramel, then baking at a low temperature until perfectly crunchy. Plus, the mix keeps for a very long time—if you can manage not to eat it within a day. Package in decorative bags for the ultimate holiday gift.

Rather than highly processed pretzels or wasabi peas, the base of this recipe is puffed rice. Puffed rice is made by heating rice kernels with steam in a pressurized environment—similar to the process of popping corn. But unlike corn, you can't puff rice at home. Fortunately, you can find minimally processed puffed brown rice at the grocery store. Read the label to rule out additives and sweeteners. Feel free to get creative and try different ingredients, like peanuts or soy nuts, in the mix. Just be sure to use no more than 4 cups of dry ingredients total. Also, refrain from adding anything that could moisten the mix, such as bacon or fresh chiles. They'll significantly shorten its shelf life.

1. Place an oven rack in the middle position and preheat the oven to 350°F.

2. Scatter the macadamia nuts on a baking sheet. Toast until just golden, 7 to 8 minutes. Remove from the oven and let cool. Using a chef's knife, roughly chop the nuts. Lower the oven temperature to 325°F.

3. Lightly coat the baking dish with nonstick spray. Put the chopped nuts, puffed rice cereal, coconut, and sesame seeds in it.

4. To make the spicy caramel, melt the butter in a medium saucepan. Add the brown sugar, corn syrup, salt, and hot sauce and bring to a boil while stirring constantly. Remove from the heat, add the baking soda, and stir vigorously. Wait 1 minute for the foam to dissipate. Pour your caramel over the rice mixture and stir with a rubber spatula until all the ingredients are evenly coated. Spread into an even layer.

5. Bake the snack mix for 15 minutes. Then stir the mix with a rubber spatula and bake for 15 to 20 minutes more. While the snack mix is baking, line a baking sheet with parchment paper.

As soon as the rice mixture comes out of the oven, turn it out onto the baking sheet, spreading gently to break the mix into smaller clumps. Sprinkle lightly with additional salt. The mixture will be hot. As tempting as it may be, resist touching it with your hands at this point. Let cool completely. Store at room temperature in an airtight container for up to 2 weeks—probably longer, but I always seem to eat it before it has a chance to expire.

Tres Leches

Equipment: 9-inch square cake pan

For the sponge cake

½ cup plus 2 tablespoons (90 g) brown rice flour

½ cup plus 2 tablespoons (90 g) all-purpose flour

¼ teaspoon kosher salt

1 tablespoon baking powder

4 large eggs, separated

1 cup (200 g) sugar

1 teaspoon vanilla extract

2 tablespoons water

For the Tres Leches bath

One 14-ounce can sweetened condensed milk

One 14-ounce can evaporated milk

1 cup (240 ml) heavy cream

For the meringue frosting

¾ cup (150 g) sugar

½ cup (120 ml) water

2 large egg whites

1 teaspoon vanilla extract

Tres Leches was a very trendy dessert when I was growing up in Costa Rica. I first made it with my mom, who learned the recipe in a cooking class taught by a friend. Imagine my amusement when a few decades later, here in the United States, Tres Leches cakes, doughnuts, ice creams, and cocktails began popping up everywhere. According to culinary folklore, Nestlé developed the recipe in the 1960s and printed it on the labels of condensed and evaporated milk cans, hoping to market their use in Latin America. The recipe was so successful that many countries adopted it as their own, incorporating variations here and there.

In its purest form, Tres Leches is a sponge cake drenched hot from the oven in a mixture of condensed milk, evaporated milk, and heavy cream. Once cooled, it's covered with meringue. The dessert is heavily soaked, so it must be baked in the dish in which it will be served. Some modernized versions consist of round cakes lightly brushed with the tres leches, rather than soaked in them. But in my book, those don't qualify as the Tres Leches I know and love.

Tres Leches has been in my family repertoire for thirty years, so I've long felt obliged to stick with the original. That is, until I developed this version, which incorporates brown rice flour to produce a light, chiffonlike crumb—a move that even my brother, Ignacio, the toughest Tres Leches judge I know, applauded.

1. Place an oven rack in the middle position and preheat the oven to 350°F. Lightly coat the cake pan with nonstick spray.

2. For the sponge cake, sift the flours, salt, and baking powder into a bowl.

3. In a stand mixer fitted with the whisk attachment, beat the egg whites on high speed until frothy. Slowly add the sugar while the mixer is still running and continue to mix until the egg whites hold medium peaks. Add the egg yolks one at a time and mix to combine. Combine the vanilla with the water in a cup. Using a large rubber spatula, carefully fold the flour mixture into the egg mixture, alternating with the vanilla water. Transfer the batter to the prepared cake pan and even out the surface with a spatula. Bake until the top is golden and a toothpick inserted in the center comes out clean, 30 minutes. To prevent the cake from sinking in the middle, avoid opening the oven early or moving the pan.

4. While the cake is baking, make the tres leches bath. Combine the condensed milk, evaporated milk, and heavy cream in a blender and blend on low speed for 45 seconds to 1 minute.

5. Remove the baked cake from the oven and carefully poke multiple holes in it with a skewer or toothpick. Pour the tres leches bath over the cake in three additions, waiting a few minutes after each addition to allow the cake to absorb as much as possible. You're drenching the cake directly in the pan so all the liquid is captured. Let the soaked cake cool completely and then refrigerate while you make the frosting.

6. To make the frosting, combine the sugar with the water in a small saucepan. Cook over medium-high heat until the sugar reaches the thread stage, about 230°F on a digital thermometer. In a stand mixer fitted with the whisk attachment, whip the egg whites on high speed while you slowly add the hot syrup in a thin, steady stream. Continue mixing until the frosting is fluffy and shiny. Add the vanilla and whisk just to combine.

7. Immediately spread the frosting evenly across the pan of Tres Leches. Refrigerate for at least 2 hours before serving. Always serve chilled, cut into squares, with some of the pooling liquid spooned onto the plate. Tres Leches will keep well, covered, in the refrigerator for a couple of days.

Almond Streusel Coffee Cake

MAKES ONE 9-INCH CAKE, SERVING 8 TO 10

Equipment: 9- or 10-inch springform pan

For the streusel

½ cup (45 g) sliced almonds

4 tablespoons (½ stick/55 g) cold unsalted butter, cut into ½-inch cubes

¼ cup (50 g) granulated sugar

1 tablespoon packed dark brown sugar

3 tablespoons all-purpose flour

3 tablespoons brown rice flour

⅛ teaspoon ground cinnamon

Pinch of kosher salt

For the cake batter

1 cup (140 g) all-purpose flour

1 cup (140 g) brown rice flour

1 teaspoon baking powder

½ teaspoon baking soda

½ teaspoon kosher salt

10 tablespoons (1¼ sticks/140 g) unsalted butter

1¼ cups (250 g) granulated sugar

2 large eggs

1 cup plus 1 tablespoon (240 g) sour cream

½ cup (160 g) raspberry or strawberry jam, homemade (page 94 or 188) or store-bought

Most bakers have a coffee cake recipe they swear by. What makes this version special is the decision to weave dollops of jam into the batter before topping with a generous layer of toasty, almond-filled streusel.

Streusel, an Old German word meaning "something strewn," is a versatile and delicious crumble used in coffee cakes, muffins, fruit crisps, cobblers, breakfast bars, and many other baked goods. While it's not particularly difficult to make, it requires close attention to ingredient temperatures and an understanding of when to stop mixing. Take it too far, and you'll end up with cookie dough. Nuts are common in streusel toppings, and for good reason. Besides adding flavor and texture, they pair well with common streusel building blocks like brown sugar and cinnamon. Both the streusel and the cake batter are made with a good helping of brown rice flour. It makes the cake incredibly tender and the streusel satisfyingly crispy.

The best baking vessel for this cake is a springform pan. Because springform pans don't require inverting the cake onto a plate, you won't lose even a fleck of streusel.

1. Place an oven rack in the middle position and preheat the oven to 350°F. Lightly coat the springform pan with nonstick spray.

2. For the streusel, scatter the almonds on a baking sheet. Toast in the oven for 5 to 7 minutes or until golden brown. Let cool completely.

3. Combine the cubed butter, sugars, flours, cinnamon, and salt in a mixing bowl. Quickly cut the cold butter cubes into the dry ingredients by pinching the butter with your fingertips until the mixture resembles a coarse meal with crumbs the size of hazelnuts. Toss in the toasted almonds and refrigerate until ready to use.

4. To make the cake batter, sift the flours, baking powder, baking soda, and salt into a bowl. In a stand mixer fitted with the paddle attachment, cream the butter and granulated sugar on medium speed until airy and lighter in color, about 3 minutes. Add the eggs one at a time, beating well after each addition. Add the sour cream and half of the flour mixture, mixing just to combine. Add the remaining flour mixture and mix until thoroughly combined.

5. Transfer the batter to the prepared pan. Smooth the top with an offset spatula. Using the back of a small spoon, make 8 indentations on the surface of the cake, at least 1 inch apart. Fill each indentation with a spoonful of the jam and scatter the streusel across the top of the cake, making sure the entire surface is covered.

6. Bake for 30 minutes. Then rotate the pan and bake for another 30 to 40 minutes, until a skewer inserted in the center comes out clean. Rotating the pan halfway through the baking process will ensure that the cake bakes evenly. Let cool completely. To unmold, run an offset spatula or paring knife along the side of the pan and loosen the springform lock. Transfer to a cake plate and slice into wedges with a serrated knife to serve. The cake will keep for up to 2 days in an airtight container at room temperature.

Gallo Pinto

For the beans

1 cup (200 g) dried black beans

½ yellow onion, quartered

1 chile de árbol

1 bay leaf

1 teaspoon kosher salt

For the rice

1 teaspoon cumin seeds

½ cup (120 ml) extra virgin olive oil

1 yellow onion, finely diced

1 red bell pepper, finely diced

1 cup chopped cilantro

2 garlic cloves, minced

2 teaspoons kosher salt

2 cups (400 g) medium-grain brown rice

6 cups (1.5 liters) water

In Costa Rica, where I grew up, this panfried rice and bean concoction is considered a national dish. Many Latin American countries have their own version, but I'm inclined to think gallo pinto is the best one. It's traditionally served for breakfast with eggs sunny-side up, fried fresh cheese, and corn tortillas. In most households, it's common to find beans simmering on the stove alongside a rice cooker filled to the brim. This way one can always make gallo pinto with just a moment's notice. Starting from scratch is a longer cooking project, about 1½ hours of total cooking time, but you can break it up in steps by making the beans a day or two ahead.

The recipe calls for white rice, but more health-conscious Costa Ricans use brown rice, as I do here. I purchase dried black beans from Latino markets, where they're restocked often and are therefore fresher. Refrain from using canned beans—one integral element of gallo pinto's deep flavor comes from adding the beans' cooking broth. Heirloom beans of excellent quality from Rancho Gordo (see Sourcing on page 336) are also available online. Take your time to prepare a well-seasoned sofrito. Just like mirepoix in classic French cooking, this blend of aromatic vegetables—onion, red bell pepper, cilantro, and garlic—is used as a flavorful base.

This recipe is ideal for entertaining and feeds 6 to 8 hungry guests. Not cooking for a crowd? Don't worry; the leftovers keep for up to 3 days in the refrigerator and reheat very well. Some even say gallo pinto tastes better the next day.

1. Rinse the black beans in a colander and place in a medium saucepan. Add the onion, chile, and bay leaf and pour in enough water to cover the beans by 3 inches. Bring to a boil, then simmer over medium heat until the beans are very tender, 50 to 60 minutes. Season with the salt. Drain, reserving the cooking liquid.

2. For the rice, toast the cumin seeds in a small sauté pan over medium heat until they start releasing their assertive aroma. Let the seeds cool for a few minutes before you crush them to a powder in a mortar and pestle or spice grinder.

3. Heat the olive oil in a large saucepan over medium-high heat. Add the onion, red pepper, cilantro, and garlic. Cook the vegetables until soft, stirring constantly with a wooden spoon, 5 to 6 minutes. Stir in the ground cumin and salt. Add the rice and stir to mix the grains thoroughly with the sofrito. Add the water, bring to a boil, lower the heat, and simmer until the rice is tender, about 40 minutes. Cover with a lid and rest for 10 minutes.

4. Fluff the rice with a fork to separate the grains. Stir in the black beans with 1 cup (240 ml) of their cooking liquid and cook over medium-high heat until the liquid reduces in volume almost completely, 3 to 4 minutes. Taste for salt and adjust the seasoning as necessary. Let sit for a few minutes before serving. Store leftovers in the refrigerator. To reheat, sauté in a pan until warm all the way through.

rye

SECALE CEREALE

Rejoice! Rye is back!

Rye is a newer grain, cultivated only within the last two to three thousand years. The grain originated in Anatolia (near modern-day Turkey) and entered Europe as a weed alongside more important crops, like wheat and barley. However, rye thrived in diverse conditions, so people began cultivating it intentionally. Farmed on soils too poor for other grains, rye became vital for feeding the masses. In fact, nobility in Western societies typically ate wheat bread, while peasants ate rye bread. Ironically, peasant bread made with the "poverty grain" proved more nutritious.

Rye's ability to thrive in cold, damp environments made it ubiquitous in Scandinavia, Eastern Europe, and Russia, where it has long been a staple crop. In Nordic countries, rye bread is considered a source of national identity. Its influence also stretches beyond these regions, inspiring diverse and long-lasting culinary traditions across the whole of Europe. In Denmark, for example, the Danish word for "bread" was actually "rye bread" until the 1800s. Danish rye is the base of smørrebrød, a beloved open-face sandwich topped with traditional Scandinavian ingredients like smoked salmon, shrimp, dill, sliced red onions, beets, and tart-sweet berries. In nearby Finland, rye bread is referenced in the *Kalevala* (the national Finnish epic), featured prominently in paintings, and included in proverbs. During long Icelandic winters, dark, sweet rye bread was baked

Opposite: Rye Focaccia (page 211)

underground by proximity to powerful hot springs. In the Balkans, leftover rye is used to make a refreshing fermented beverage called *kvass*. In Russia and other Baltic countries, such as Estonia, Latvia, Lithuania, Belarus and Ukraine, rye breads are deeply sour. These varieties differ from rye breads found in central and southern Europe, where rye is combined with a high proportion of other grains to yield breads resembling those made with wheat.

Rye became a widely cultivated crop in colonial America after coming to the New World with sixteenth- and seventeenth-century European colonists, but production dropped drastically when wheat drew farmers to the western territories. Rye's history often narrates a tale of neglect followed by rediscovery, where diverse varieties become hard to come by only to be found again years later. Take, for example, Finnish rye, otherwise known as "rediscovered rye." The variety originated in central Russia over a thousand years ago, before spreading across Finland and Norway. The popular grain became a reliable source of food, in turn spurring population growth. However, the variety fell out of favor and was eventually thought extinct around the start of World War I. Luckily, it was rediscovered in the 1970s when a few remaining kernels were found under the floorboards of an old Norwegian grain-drying sauna. With them, a new crop of Finnish rye flourished, yet it took over twenty years for concerned seed savers to build a significant seed stock. Rediscovered rye has since been added to the Svalbard Global Seed Bank, a visionary project funded by the Norwegian government consisting of a high-tech vault located in the Arctic Circle where seeds from species all over the globe are cataloged and stored in perpetuity.

Rye is a great source of antioxidants, vitamins, and minerals, like vitamin E, calcium, iron, and potassium. These nutrients are readily retained because rye is typically less refined than wheat. Like other whole grains, it also supports a healthy digestion. Rye is also good for the environment. It's tolerant of high soil acidity, grows well in cool climates, and is drought resistant due to a root system that uses 20 to 30 percent less water than wheat. It performs well at high altitudes and as far north as the Arctic. In addition to thriving in poor conditions, rye has the incredible ability to revitalize soil. It makes an excellent cover crop—reducing soil erosion, enhancing water retention, contributing green manure, and containing weed growth without the need for herbicides. With a deep, complex root system, rye is an effective nutrient catch crop that can absorb unused nitrogen in the soil.

It's tempting to equate wheat and rye, especially because they're both foundational bread ingredients. Plus, rye is a cereal grass, sharing genetic similarities with wheat and barley. But rye and wheat are quite different, especially in the kitchen. Rye has minimal gluten, so dough made with it doesn't develop structure or elasticity like wheat. This is what differentiates true rye bread from the lofty loaves we associate with Jewish delis. Deli breads are almost entirely wheat, flavored heavily with caraway seeds. The dense, dark bread found in Scandinavia, Russia, and Eastern Europe, on the other hand, is a different kind of rye, a true rye. This bread has a deep, robust flavor that's both sour and nutty—you can actively taste the fermentation required to transform gummy, coarse rye flour into bread. It's a bread that wholly engages the senses. Slicing into it reveals a dark mosaic of seeds and grains with a spongy, almost damp, texture, and an earthy scent reminiscent of nature.

Rye is most often utilized in one of three forms. The first and most common is milled as a dark, fragrant flour, incorporated in everything from bread to cookies. There are also rye flakes, which are similar to rolled oats and traditionally made into porridge. And finally, you can cook whole rye berries the same way you cook other whole grains and add them to pilafs, soups, or grain salads.

The importance of rye, a culturally significant grain that grows well, revitalizes the soil, and offers excellent nutrition, has been overlooked for far too long. In the foreseeable future, rye production and rye baking will surely increase; we're indeed on the verge of a rye renaissance. So, if rye is destined to remain a "distant aunt," second to the more appreciated wheat, maybe we've at least begun acknowledging that it's the cool aunt with fabulous hair who just might go save the world.

How to Purchase and Use

Rye Berries and Rye Chops

Rye berries are the prettiest berries I've ever seen. They're long and elegant, slimmer than wheat berries, with a greenish-blue hue. The flavor is more assertive than wheat, with an earthy, slightly acidic taste. Like many other grains, the berries can be cooked in salted boiling water until tender. Cooked rye berries have a pleasantly chewy texture and can be added to salads, pilafs, soups, or stews. They're often soaked in water and sprouted for use in Nordic and German-style rye bread. This simple process is easy to do at home and takes 2 to 3 days. Rye chops are cracked or coarsely cut rye berries, commonly added to bread. When I want to add the flavor and texture of rye kernels to a recipe, I find whole berries far more satisfying than chops. Rye berries and chops can be found in bulk bins at health food stores or packaged in good grocery stores. If your local mill has rye berries, definitely stock up. Chances are they're a single variety grown on a single farm.

Rye Flakes

Just like oats, rye berries can go through steel rollers to be flattened into flakes. The flakes are very versatile and can be made into a hot cereal, like oatmeal. They can be used in pretty much every way rolled oats are, from the Oatmeal Date Cookies on page 149 to my granola on page 151. Unlike oats, which are commonly steamed and then rolled, rye berries are roasted and then rolled. The resulting flake has a nutty flavor and crispy texture. My go-to brand is Eden Foods (see Sourcing on page 336), and the Rye Müesli on page 205 is my favorite rye flake recipe.

Whole-Grain Rye Flour or Dark Rye Flour

Shopping for rye flour can be confusing. Like wheat, rye is often sifted after milling to remove portions of bran and germ. I recommend avoiding flours labeled "white" rye, "medium" rye, or "deli" rye, which are all forms of refined rye flour. Most producers never use the label "whole-grain" rye, instead opting for names like dark rye or pumpernickel, which don't necessarily explain the product. Always read the label to ensure you're buying whole-grain flour. King Arthur Pumpernickel Flour and Bob's Red Mill Dark Rye Flour are good options. I strongly recommend purchasing whole-grain rye flour from an independent mill. The flour will be fresher and likely ground from a single variety grown on a single farm. To find an independent mill near you, see Sourcing on page 336. Store flour in a cool pantry and try to use it within 3 months of purchase. To keep track, I recommend labeling the bag with the date of purchase.

Rye Müesli

¼ cup (45 g) buckwheat groats

2½ cups (260 g) rye flakes

¼ cup (20 g) sliced almonds

¼ cup (35 g) shelled pistachios

2 tablespoons shelled sunflower seeds

1 tablespoon flaxseed

¼ cup (40 g) dried cherries

½ cup (65 g) dried apricots, small diced (about 8 apricot halves)

½ teaspoon ground cinnamon

¼ teaspoon ground cardamom

⅛ teaspoon ground cloves

⅛ teaspoon freshly grated nutmeg

¼ teaspoon kosher salt

This popular cold breakfast cereal was created by Swiss physician Maximilian Bircher-Benner in the early 1900s. He developed it as an appetizer, like bread or soup, for his sanatorium near the Swiss Alps. The original recipe called for blending rolled oats, nuts, and seeds with two raw apples—skin, seeds, and flesh included. Cream, honey, and lemon juice were added to moisten the heartier dry ingredients. Bircher's müesli was well received by his patients, who benefited from the nutrient- and fiber-rich staple. Soon enough müesli became the breakfast of choice of the Swiss elite. By 1950 it was made commercially and exported to other European countries. In the United States, müesli became popular in the 1960s, when the whole food movement gained momentum. Modern-day preparations include an array of ingredients, but it's generally recommended to maintain a ratio of 80 percent grain to 20 percent dried fruits, nuts, and seeds. Like granola, müesli can be adapted to fit the cook's preference. In many European countries and Australia, it's still served as a simple cereal with raw apples, milk, or yogurt.

My version of müesli calls for rye flakes instead of traditional rolled oats. Rye flakes are thicker and toothier, and give the müesli a pleasant chew. It's a simple blend of ingredients tossed together in a bowl, and requires no cooking. Once made, it can be kept in an airtight container for up to 6 months. My ideal bowl of müesli contains ¼ to ½ cup of cereal with an equal amount of milk, a drizzle of honey, and fresh fruit, like berries, sliced bananas, or apple chunks. You can also prepare your müesli overnight oats style (see Leah's Overnight Oats on page 168) by soaking for at least 4 hours. Because it travels well and has a long shelf life, müesli packed in decorative mason jars with a handwritten label makes a great housewarming gift or a delicious addition to a care package for your kids in college or at sleepaway camp.

For higher nutritional value, use unsweetened dried fruits and raw nuts and seeds, avoiding any labeled "roasted," "toasted," or "salted."

Stir all the ingredients together in a large bowl until well combined. Store in an airtight container at room temperature. To serve, combine ½ cup of müesli in a cereal bowl with ½ cup of yogurt or your milk of choice and top with sliced bananas, berries, or a diced apple. Müesli will keep for up to 6 months in a cool, dark pantry.

Chocolate Dynamite Cookies

½ cup plus 2 tablespoons (80 g) dark rye flour

2 tablespoons Dutch-processed cocoa powder

¼ teaspoon baking powder

½ teaspoon kosher salt

6 tablespoons (¾ stick/85 g) unsalted butter, cut into 1-inch cubes

2 cups (350 g) bittersweet chocolate chips

1 cup (200 g) sugar

2 large eggs

½ teaspoon vanilla extract

Are you ready to be invited to every potluck, picnic, and dinner party? If yes, mark this page. Take a batch of these to your next social gathering and you're guaranteed to make a splash, becoming everyone's new best friend. As the name suggests, these cookies elicit explosive reactions in all who try them. Rich and gooey, with a tender interior and crispy edges, these wheat-free, entirely whole-grain cookies are reminiscent of a fudgy brownie loaded with chocolate chips.

The dough is simple, but you can't rush the process. It begins with melted butter and chocolate, which makes the mixture quite sticky. To make the dough malleable you must chill it for at least 1 hour. Although it may be tempting, never skip this step. I enjoy melty, freshly baked cookies, so I bake shortly before serving—a euphoric experience indeed. The baked cookies will sit well at room temperature and are just as enjoyable once cooled.

1. Sift the rye flour, cocoa powder, baking powder, and salt into a bowl.

2. Place the butter and half of the chocolate chips in a large heat-resistant bowl. Place the bowl over a pot of barely simmering water, making sure the bottom of the bowl doesn't touch the water. Stir with a heat-resistant rubber spatula to encourage the chocolate and butter to melt. Remove from the heat when the chocolate and butter are melted.

RECIPE CONTINUES

3. In the bowl of a stand mixer fitted with the paddle attachment, combine the melted chocolate mixture with the sugar on low speed. Add the eggs one at a time, mixing briefly after each addition. Add the vanilla and the sifted ingredients, continuing to mix on low speed until a uniform dough forms. Stir in the remaining chocolate chips and mix just to combine. The dough will be very sticky, almost like a cake batter.

4. Transfer the dough to a separate container, cover with plastic wrap, and refrigerate for at least 1 hour or overnight.

5. Place two oven racks in the middle positions and preheat the oven to 350°F. Line two baking sheets with parchment paper.

6. Remove the cookie dough from the refrigerator. Divide the dough into 16 equal portions, about 1½ ounces (42 g) each. Working quickly, roll each into a ball. Place the cookies on the prepared sheets, spaced at least 2 inches apart. They will expand and grow significantly as they bake.

7. Bake for 8 minutes. Then rotate the sheets, switch their positions in the oven, and bake for another 7 to 8 minutes, until the tops of the cookies are no longer shiny (except for a few visible melty chocolate chips). Rotating and switching the sheets halfway through the baking process will ensure that the cookies bake evenly. The ideal cookie will be set around the edges with a softer, almost underdone center. Remove the cookies and let cool completely or enjoy while still slightly warm.

Chocolate Cherry Scones

½ cup plus 1 tablespoon (135 ml) heavy cream

¼ cup (30 g) Dutch-processed cocoa powder

½ teaspoon almond extract

½ cup plus 2 tablespoons (90 g) all-purpose flour, plus extra for dusting

½ cup plus 2 tablespoons (80 g) dark rye flour

¼ cup plus 1 tablespoon (65 g) granulated sugar

2 teaspoons baking powder

4 tablespoons (½ stick/55 g) cold unsalted butter, cut into ½-inch cubes

½ cup (90 g) bittersweet chocolate chips

¼ cup (40 g) unsweetened dried sour cherries

For finishing

2 tablespoons heavy cream

2 tablespoons decorative crystal sugar or granulated sugar

Robust, chocolaty, and punctuated by bright bursts of tart cherry, this scone is an ideal in-between-meals snack or accompaniment to tea or coffee. Rye's earthy hues pair beautifully with chocolate's bold intensity, and because of its low protein content, rye flour yields an exceptionally tender scone. The quality of chocolate in this recipe is crucial. Make sure to use bittersweet chocolate chips and Dutch-processed cocoa powder. I recommend unsweetened dried sour cherries, although sweetened varieties will work too. I cut the scones on the smaller side—they're rich and decadent, so a smaller portion does the trick.

1. Place an oven rack in the middle position and preheat the oven to 350°F. Line a baking sheet with parchment paper.

2. Put the ½ cup plus 1 tablespoon (135 ml) heavy cream in a small nonreactive saucepan and bring to a boil over medium heat. Remove from the stove and use a whisk to quickly mix in the cocoa powder, making sure there are no lumps. Stir in the almond extract. Transfer to a nonreactive container and let cool completely.

RECIPE CONTINUES

3. Combine the flours, sugar, and baking powder in a mixing bowl. Toss the cold butter cubes in the dry ingredients. Quickly cut the cold butter cubes into the dry ingredients by pinching the butter with your fingertips until the mixture resembles a coarse meal with crumbs the size of hazelnuts. Mix in the chocolate chips and dried cherries. Make a well in the center and pour the cooled cocoa and cream mixture into the well. Mix with both hands until the mixture forms a ragged dough. The dough shouldn't be uniform, and you should be able to see bits of butter laced throughout the dough.

4. Transfer the dough to a lightly floured surface. Pat the dough down until it forms a disk about 5 inches in diameter and 1 inch thick. Using a large knife, slice the disk in half and each half into thirds to get six equal wedges. Transfer each individual scone to the prepared baking sheet, placing them at least 2 inches apart. Brush each scone with the additional heavy cream and sprinkle with the decorative or granulated sugar.

5. Bake for 15 minutes. Then rotate the baking sheet and bake the scones for 10 to 15 minutes more, until the tops crack and the edges start to brown. Rotating the sheet halfway through the baking time will ensure that the scones bake evenly. Let cool for at least 30 minutes before serving.

Rye Focaccia

For the poolish

1 cup plus 1 tablespoon (255 ml) cold (65° to 70°F) water

⅓ cup (40 g) bread flour

⅓ cup (40 g) dark rye flour

¼ teaspoon instant yeast

For the dough

1 cup (130 g) dark rye flour

1 cup (155 g) whole wheat flour

5 cups (675 g) bread flour

3½ cups (815 ml) cold (65° to 70°F) water

1½ teaspoons instant yeast

¼ cup (60 ml) lukewarm (95° to 108°F) water

2 tablespoons fine sea salt

¼ cup (60 ml) extra virgin olive oil, plus extra as necessary

Coarse sea salt such as Maldon or fleur de sel

Cracked black pepper

Whole-grain rye flour adds a nice rusticity to this focaccia bread, which is light, fluffy, and chewy. To truly appreciate its flavor, I garnish simply with olive oil, sea salt, and cracked black pepper. If I happen to have a special ingredient on hand, like marash pepper or fresh summer savory, I may sprinkle some on top. But for the most part, it's all about the dough.

Like most bread recipes in this book, focaccia is prepared over 2 days. Most of the work is done on day one, leaving just the baking step for day two. The dough is made with poolish, a loose pre-fermented dough that adds complexity of flavor and improved texture. Whole grains absorb more water than refined flour, so resist adding extra flour even if the hydration seems high and your dough feels sticky. This focaccia is all about the grains, but there's a good amount of sifted bread flour to break up the whole grains' density and ensure the airy crumb focaccia is known for.

While many of the breads in this book keep for up to a week, this rye focaccia must be enjoyed the day that it's baked. Leftovers can be turned into croutons or bread crumbs.

The focaccia should rest in the refrigerator overnight. This cold period slows down the fermentation while deepening the flavor. Follow the Prep and Baking Schedule to make the recipe just in time to have fresh focaccia for a weekend luncheon.

RECIPE CONTINUES

Prep and Baking Schedule

Prep Day (day prior to baking):

1. Make the poolish and ferment for 2 hours.

2. Hydrate or autolyse the flours 1 hour after making the poolish.

3. Mix the poolish, hydrated flours, and remaining ingredients into a dough. Ferment for 1½ to 2 hours.

4. Shape on a baking sheet. Refrigerate overnight.

Baking Day:

1. Remove the dough from the refrigerator 1 hour before baking.

2. Preheat the oven.

3. Bake. Cool. Enjoy later that day.

Prep Day

1. For the poolish, combine the cold water with the bread flour, rye flour, and yeast. The water temperature is important to ensure that the poolish rises at a slower rate; warmer water can cause the poolish to ferment too quickly, impacting the flavor of the focaccia. Cover with a kitchen towel or plastic wrap and ferment at room temperature for 2 hours or until bubbles form on the surface.

2. One hour after you make the poolish, hydrate or autolyse the flours: Combine all of the flours for the dough with the cold water and mix by hand until a mass forms. Cover with plastic wrap or a clean kitchen towel and let rest for 1 hour. This resting phase, in which the flour is allowed to hydrate, is known as the autolyse. Autolysing the flour promotes elasticity as well as enzymatic activity, contributing to gluten development and the focaccia's open structure.

3. When the poolish is ready, you can mix the dough. In a small cup, sprinkle the yeast over the lukewarm water. Be sure to use the correct temperature water; any hotter and the yeast can deteriorate. Stir with a spoon and let sit for 5 minutes to activate. Transfer the flour and water mixture to the bowl of the stand mixer. Add the poolish and dissolved yeast.

4. Fit the mixer with the dough hook attachment, mix for 5 minutes on low speed, then increase the speed to medium-high and mix for 2 minutes. Finally, sprinkle in the fine sea salt and mix on low speed until thoroughly combined, about 2 minutes. Transfer the dough to a large bowl lightly coated with olive oil. Cover with plastic wrap or a clean kitchen towel and allow it to rise at warm room temperature. After 30 minutes, moisten your hands with water and dig under the front end of the dough, stretch it out, and fold it back on top of the dough. Repeat from the back end and then from each side. Finally, turn the dough over and tuck it into a ball. This process is known as stretching and folding and helps strengthen the dough. After each series of stretching and folding, the dough should feel significantly firmer.

5. Cover the dough and let it rest for 30 minutes. Then stretch and fold a second time, just as you did before. Let it rest for another 30 minutes and stretch and fold one last time for a total of three times. Let the dough ferment for 30 minutes more for a total time of 2 hours before shaping.

Opposite: Use your fingertips to dimple the dough and coax it into a rectangular shape.

RECIPE CONTINUES

6. Coat an 18-by-13-inch rimmed baking sheet generously with ¼ cup olive oil. Transfer the dough to the sheet and coat your hands with additional oil. Use your fingertips to dimple the dough and coax it into a rectangular shape. Try to keep the thickness as even as possible. Once you start stretching the dough, it will begin springing back. Let the dough rest for 10 minutes and then stretch and dimple again, trying to extend the dough as much as possible. Don't worry if the dough doesn't fill the entire baking sheet, especially the corners. As the dough rests overnight it will expand. Wrap the sheet with plastic and refrigerate overnight.

Baking Day

1. Remove the focaccia from the refrigerator, take off the plastic, and let sit at room temperature for 1 hour.

2. Place an oven rack in the middle position and preheat the oven to 450°F.

3. Dimple the focaccia with your fingertips one more time, drizzle with additional olive oil, and sprinkle with coarse sea salt and cracked pepper or any other desired toppings. Bake for 15 minutes, then rotate the baking sheet and bake for another 15 minutes, until golden and crusty. Rotating the sheet halfway through the baking process will ensure that the focaccia bakes evenly. Let cool completely before cutting into squares, triangles, or strips.

Everything Rye Bagels

For the rye sponge

½ cup (65 g) dark rye flour

¼ teaspoon fine sea salt

⅛ teaspoon instant yeast

⅓ cup (80 ml) cold (65° to 70°F) water

For the dough

⅔ cup (180 ml) lukewarm (98° to 105°F) water

1 teaspoon instant yeast

2 cups (270 g) bread flour, plus extra for dusting

¾ cup (115 g) whole wheat flour

3 tablespoons whole milk

1 tablespoon plus 1½ teaspoons sugar

1½ teaspoons fine sea salt

1 teaspoon barley malt syrup

For the topping

1½ teaspoons caraway seeds

1½ teaspoons nigella seeds

1½ teaspoons poppy seeds

1 tablespoon plus 1½ teaspoons sesame seeds

3 tablespoons onion flakes

¼ cup barley malt syrup

What makes a good bagel is the subject of a perennial debate. New Yorkers claim their tap water is the reason you can find a real bagel only in their city, but it takes only a basic understanding of bread making to know that a decent bagel can be made anywhere. These chewy round rolls with a shiny exterior and a hole in the center usually achieve their characteristic chewiness with bread flour, which is high in gluten. Kneading the dough sufficiently also builds a strong structure, capable of remaining tight after proofing, poaching, and baking. As for the shiny crust, you must simmer the bagels in malted water for a few seconds on both sides before baking.

If good bagels require high-gluten flour, why even consider using rye? Rye flour is infamously low in gluten and high in starch. Breads made entirely from rye flour are prone to collapsing because they lack sufficient strength to hold their shape. But when paired with the right amount of high-gluten flour, rye makes a gorgeous bagel with a rustic exterior and a desirably dense crumb that remains chewy and flavorful.

If you've made bread before, you're ready for bagels. If you haven't, read the directions carefully, so you can anticipate the dough's various stages. Always opt for dark rye flour, which is whole grain and contains the most bran. To prepare the dough, you'll have to make a rye sponge a few hours in advance. Nutritious rye yields a very active sponge and shouldn't be allowed to ferment for more than the indicated time. The final dough should be firm. Rather than rolling ropes and connecting them to form a loop, I use an unorthodox yet fun shaping method: roll each dough portion into a tight ball, then poke a hole

RECIPE CONTINUES

in the center with your index finger and stretch from the inside out. The bagels are shaped the night before and allowed to rest overnight in the refrigerator. As tempting as it is, don't try to make this a one-day process; let the bagels have their sleep! This slow, cold rise is key to both texture and flavor. You can follow the suggested Prep and Baking Schedule to make the recipe just in time to have bagels ready for breakfast in the morning.

These days you can buy artisan everything toppings in specialty shops, but I recommend making your own. You can use it to garnish other breads like the Rye Focaccia on page 211 or the Potato Rolls on page 62 or sprinkle over avocado toast or deviled eggs. To really highlight the oniony flavor that everything topping is known for, the recipe calls for more onion flakes than the other ingredients. But you can play with the amounts in favor of your favorite component.

Bagels are best eaten the day they're baked, but leftovers keep for another day stored in a paper bag at room temperature. I always suggest toasting the day-old bagels, though. Rye bagels are delicious schmeared with the timeless duo of cream cheese and lox. If you're looking for alternative serving ideas, try homemade jam and ricotta or labneh, sumac, and avocado. There's really no wrong topping for a bagel.

Prep and Baking Schedule

Prep Day (day prior to baking):

1. Make the sponge. Ferment for 4 hours.
2. Make the bagel dough when the sponge is ready. Rest for 20 minutes.
3. Shape the bagels and refrigerate overnight.

Baking Day:

1. Remove the bagels from the refrigerator 30 minutes before baking.
2. Preheat the oven.
3. Poach, bake, and cool. Enjoy shortly afterward.

Prep Day

1. To make the sponge, stir the flour, salt, yeast, and cold water together in a small bowl and mix with a wooden spoon or rubber spatula until well combined. The water temperature is important to ensure that the sponge rises at a slower rate; warmer water can cause the sponge to ferment too quickly, impacting the flavor of the bagels. Cover tightly with plastic wrap or a kitchen towel and ferment at room temperature for 4 hours.

2. When the sponge is ready, you can make the dough. Pour the lukewarm water into a bowl and sprinkle the yeast over it. Stir and set aside to activate for 5 minutes. Be sure to use the correct temperature water; any hotter and the yeast can deteriorate. In a stand mixer fitted with the dough hook attachment, combine the dissolved yeast mixture, rye sponge, flours, milk, sugar, salt, and barley malt syrup. Mix on low speed for 2 minutes just to combine. Increase the speed to medium and mix until the dough feels firm and bouncy, about 2 minutes.

RECIPE CONTINUES

Place the dough on a lightly floured surface and knead briefly to shape into a smooth ball. Place the dough in a bowl lightly coated with nonstick spray, cover tightly with plastic wrap, and let rest at room temperature for 20 minutes so the gluten can relax.

3. Coat a baking sheet with nonstick spray. Cut the dough into six equal pieces, about 4 ounces (115 g) each. Shape each piece into a tight ball. With your index finger, poke a hole in the middle of the ball to create a hollow center. Stretch the hole until it measures 1 to 1½ inches in diameter. Transfer the shaped bagels to the prepared sheet, making sure they're spaced at least 2 inches apart. Cover with plastic wrap and refrigerate overnight. The bagels will be ready to poach the next day.

Carefully poach the bagels.

Baking Day

1. Remove the bagels from the refrigerator and let them sit, uncovered, at room temperature for 1 hour.

2. Place an oven rack in the middle position and preheat the oven to 400°F. Coat a baking sheet with nonstick spray.

3. Make the everything topping by combining the caraway seeds, nigella seeds, poppy seeds, sesame seeds, and onion flakes in a small bowl.

4. To poach the bagels, bring a medium saucepan of water to a boil. Lower the heat until the water is at a simmer and stir in the barley malt syrup. The barley malt will help the exterior of the bagels brown while giving them an attractive sheen. Working in batches of 2 or 3 bagels at a time, carefully poach for 30 seconds, flip with a slotted spoon, and poach for 30 more seconds. Use the slotted spoon to transfer the poached bagels to the prepared baking sheet, spaced 2 inches apart. You will notice the bagels have a prettier side, usually the side that went into the poaching water first. Make sure the prettier side is up. Sprinkle each bagel generously with everything topping, about 1 tablespoon per bagel.

5. Bake the bagels for 15 minutes. Then rotate the baking sheet and bake for another 15 minutes, until the bagels are golden brown. Rotating the sheet halfway through the baking process will ensure that the bagels color evenly. Cool on a wire rack for 1 hour before serving.

Black Olive Boule

Equipment: 8-inch round banneton, 4½-quart Dutch oven with lid, lame, digital thermometer

To feed the starter

2 tablespoons bread flour

2 tablespoons whole wheat flour

1 teaspoon sourdough starter (see page 102)

3 tablespoons cold (65° to 70°F) water

For the dough

2 cups (270 g) bread flour, plus extra for dusting

1⅓ cups (170 g) dark rye flour

1⅓ to 1½ cups (320 to 360 ml) warm (90° to 95°F) water

2 teaspoons barley malt syrup

2 teaspoons fine sea salt

1 cup (135 g) pitted kalamata olives

2 to 3 tablespoons rice flour for dusting the banneton (optional)

When I first fell for rye it was with feverish enthusiasm. The relationship didn't start in a professional kitchen, which is where I do most of my work, but rather with a rogue group of local hobbyist bakers, known as LABB (Los Angeles Bread Bakers). These couple thousand bakers communicate online and occasionally meet for classes, community wood-oven bakes, and bakery and brewery tours in the Los Angeles area. The first time I baked with them, I made real pumpernickel with nothing but rye flour alongside founder Erik Knutsen, his wife, Kelly, and a dozen other bakers. I was instantly hooked on the compact, brick-like density of Old World rye breads and continued experimenting with 100 percent rye breads long after the class.

I wanted to feature these creations at Friends & Family but felt the local clientele wasn't ready for such a dense, robust style of rye bread. To better introduce them to the grain, I decided to develop an irresistible rye and black olive loaf and feature it in a popular dish: our Olive Oil Fried Eggs. Farm-fresh eggs are fried in olive oil until perfectly crisp on the edges, then served with fiery harissa, thick yogurt, fried chickpeas, herbs, and a chunk of grilled rye olive boule. My guerrilla marketing strategy proved effective, and many customers would take a black olive boule home after trying the dish.

This black olive boule is made with bread and whole-grain rye flours. It requires an active sourdough starter and takes 2 days to make. You can follow the suggested Prep and Baking Schedule. Most of the work happens on day one, with just baking left for day two. You'll need a few bread baking tools for this loaf: a proofing

RECIPE CONTINUES

basket, a bread lame, and a Dutch oven with a lid. I highly recommend using rice flour to prevent the shaped boule from sticking to the proofing basket, but you may use bread flour instead. Like most sourdough breads, the boule will keep for up to a week stored in a paper bag at room temperature.

My favorite way to enjoy the black olive boule at home is as a quick, easy, open-face, vegan sandwich: toast a slice of black olive bread, rub with a peeled garlic clove, top with two thick slices of ripe tomato and a few rings of thinly sliced red onion, and finish with olive oil and coarse sea salt. Two of these are my go-to dinner on many summer nights. For the Olive Oil Fried Eggs recipe that made this bread popular at Friends & Family, see page 224.

Prep and Baking Schedule

Prep Day (day prior to baking):

In the morning:
1. Feed the starter anytime between 6:00 and 10:00 a.m. The starter will be ready to use in 8 to 10 hours.

2. Weigh the flours.

In the late afternoon (8 to 10 hours after feeding the starter):
1. Hydrate or autolyse the flours.

2. Mix the starter, hydrated flours, and remaining ingredients into a dough. Ferment for 3½ to 4 hours.

3. Shape the bread and put it in a banneton proofing basket. Refrigerate overnight.

Baking Day:

In the morning:
1. Remove the bread from the refrigerator 1 hour before baking.

2. Preheat the oven and Dutch oven 30 minutes before baking.

3. Bake. Cool. Enjoy later that day.

Prep Day

1. The day before you'd like to bake the bread, feed the starter by combining the flours and sourdough starter with the cold water. Cover and let it ferment at room temperature for 8 to 10 hours, until it has increased in volume and formed bubbles on the surface.

2. About 8 hours after the starter was fed, hydrate or "autolyse" the flours: In a medium bowl, combine the flours for the dough with at least 1⅓ cups of the warm water, adding more as needed to attain a wet, sticky dough. Cover and let rest for 1 hour. This resting phase, in which the flour is allowed to hydrate, is known as the autolyse. Autolysing the flour promotes elasticity as well as enzymatic activity and contributes to gluten development in the dough.

3. In a stand mixer fitted with the dough hook attachment, mix the autolysed flours with the fed sourdough starter on medium speed for 2 minutes. Stop the mixer occasionally, scraping the sides of the bowl with a rubber spatula to promote even mixing. Add the barley malt along with 1 tablespoon of water and mix for another 2 minutes at medium speed. Add the salt along with 1 additional tablespoon of water and mix for another 2 minutes at medium speed. Decrease the speed to low, add the olives, and mix for 3 to 4 minutes or until well incorporated.

4. Transfer the dough to a medium bowl and cover with a clean kitchen towel or plastic wrap. Let sit at room temperature for 30 minutes. After 30 minutes, moisten your hands with water and dig under the front end of the dough, stretch it out, and fold it back on top of the dough. Repeat from the back end and then from each side. Finally, turn the dough over and tuck it into a ball. This process is known as stretching and folding and helps strengthen the dough. After each series of stretching and folding, the dough should feel significantly firmer.

5. Cover the dough and let it rest for 30 minutes. Then stretch and fold a second time, just as you did before. Let it rest for another 30 minutes and stretch and fold one last time for a total of three times. Let the dough ferment for 1½ hours more for a total time of 4 hours before shaping.

6. To shape into a boule, transfer the dough to a floured surface. Gently flatten the dough into a rough rectangle and bring all four corners to the center. Pinch the corners together with your fingertips. Invert the boule on the work surface and, using your hands, gently rotate against the surface to tighten the boule further and seal the bottom where the corners connected. Flour an 8-inch banneton generously (my preferred flour for this task is rice flour) and place the boule inside with the seam side up. Refrigerate uncovered overnight.

RECIPE CONTINUES

Baking Day

1. Remove the dough from the refrigerator 1 hour prior to baking and let it sit at room temperature.

2. Place an oven rack in the lower position and place a lidded Dutch oven on it. Preheat the oven to 450°F for 30 minutes.

3. Cut a piece of parchment paper a few inches wider than the boule. Invert the banneton on the parchment paper to release the bread. Using a lame or a sharp paring knife, cut a crosshatch (#) about ½ inch deep on the surface of the boule. These cuts will serve as steam release vents when the bread expands in the oven.

4. Using oven mitts, carefully put the hot Dutch oven on a heat-resistant surface and remove the lid. Lift the parchment paper from the sides to transfer the bread and parchment to the Dutch oven. Put the lid back on and place the Dutch oven back in the oven. Bake for 30 minutes—the lid helps retain enough steam inside the pot, allowing the surface of the bread to remain supple and expand. Remove the lid and bake for another 15 to 20 minutes—removing the lid will help the bread's exterior caramelize and bake into a chewy crust. The bread is ready when the crust is a dark mahogany brown and a digital thermometer inserted in the center reads 200° to 208°F. Using oven mitts, carefully remove the Dutch oven from the oven. Gently invert it over a cooling rack to release the bread. Let cool completely before slicing.

Opposite: Dan's Olive Oil Fried Eggs (page 224) and Black Olive Boule (page 219)

Dan's Olive Oil Fried Eggs

SERVES 1

1 slice Black Olive Boule (page 219)

½ cup (118 ml) extra virgin olive oil, plus extra for brushing

2 large eggs

Kosher salt

2 tablespoons well-drained canned chickpeas

¼ cup parsley leaves

2 tablespoons Greek yogurt

2 teaspoon harissa

6 pitted kalamata olives, cut in half

This dish of fried eggs, harissa, and yogurt, served with a slice of black olive bread, is a best-seller at Friends & Family. My husband, Dan, put it together many years ago while working the brunch shift at Campanile. Loosely inspired by the cuisine of North Africa, this inventive combination of flavors and textures can be enjoyed for breakfast, lunch, or dinner. It's a multisensory experience in which every bite on the plate is different. Every component plays a role: deeply spiced harissa enlivens the dish; cool, tangy yogurt makes it creamy and balanced; crispy chickpeas and parsley amp up the texture; briny olives bring their salty punch; while runny yolk adds dreamy richness. The olive bread is there to mop up every bit, ensuring nothing is left on the plate. You might feel tempted to reduce the amount of oil, but to get the crispy lacy edges when you fry the eggs, you really do need that much. You can reserve the leftover oil to cook more eggs later in the week.

1. Place an oven rack in the middle position and preheat the oven to 350°F.

2. Brush the bread with olive oil, put on a baking sheet, and toast for 5 minutes, until golden but not crisped all the way.

3. Line a plate with paper towels.

4. Heat up the olive oil in a 6-inch nonstick pan over medium-high heat until it starts to smoke. Crack the eggs into a small bowl and season with salt. To test whether the oil is hot enough, drop a 1-inch piece of bread into the oil. If the bread causes the oil to bubble rapidly, it's ready to fry the eggs. Carefully drop the eggs into the hot oil. They will start to sizzle and bubble right away. Cook until the edges are golden, the whites are firm, and the yolk is still runny, about 2 minutes. Use a slotted spoon to remove from the oil and transfer to the paper towels. In the same oil, fry the chickpeas and parsley leaves for 30 seconds or until the parsley is crispy. Remove with the slotted spoon and transfer to the paper towels with the eggs. Season with salt. To serve, spoon the yogurt onto a plate, spread harissa over it with the back of a spoon, put the fried eggs on top of the yogurt and harissa, and garnish with the olives, fried chickpeas, and parsley. Enjoy immediately with the toasted black olive bread on the side.

Eliisa's Ring Bread

MAKES TWO 8-INCH RING BREADS

For the sprouted rye berries

⅓ cup (50 g) rye berries

For the rye leaven

1 tablespoon sourdough starter (see page 102)

1 cup (125 g) dark rye flour

¾ cup (180 ml) cold (65° to 70°F) water

For the bread dough

2½ cups (315 g) dark rye flour, plus extra for kneading and dusting

1½ teaspoons fine sea salt

¾ cup (180 ml) cold (65° to 70°F) water

This is a perfect place to start if you've never made 100 percent rye bread. The dough is easy to handle and shape and doesn't require any hard-to-come-by ingredients or sophisticated equipment.

The recipe was given to me by my friend Eliisa Kuusela, a Finnish baker and cookbook author based in Tampere. We first met in an online sourdough forum. While traveling in Oslo a few months later, I took a detour to meet Eliisa in person. She picked me up in her red VW bus, opened the door, and handed me a beautiful blue and white linen tea towel. I was about to thank her effusively for the thoughtful present when I realized the token wasn't the towel but what it held inside. I unveiled a round flat bread with a profound sour aroma. Eliisa explained that it was called "ring bread," because a circle of dough is punched out of the center, making it look like a ring. The same dough is used to make "vagabond rye," a more traditionally shaped bread that keeps for a long time. In olden times, vagabonds could toss the bread in their sack while traveling.

While showing me around Helsinki, Eliisa pointed out various ring breads at bakeries and market stalls. After a day of adventures, including my first sauna experience and a dive into the near-freezing Baltic Sea, I finally tried Eliisa's bread. I knew immediately that the intriguing Finnish bread would be my new obsession. Luckily, Eliisa was happy to share her recipe. By the end of the week I was recipe testing in my Los Angeles kitchen.

The bread is not difficult to make, but you'll have to time the process with precision. Leaven,

RECIPE CONTINUES

a sourdough preferment, is prepared the day before the mixing, shaping, and baking take place. The shaped bread must proof for about 6 hours before baking, so I like to start the process early in the morning and bake the bread midday. Like most rye breads, this one must cool completely and rest for a few hours before serving. If you play your cards right (see the Prep and Baking Schedule), you can build your leaven on Friday morning, make and bake the bread on Saturday, and have delicious Finnish ring bread for a Sunday morning smoked fish, cured meat, and hard cheese feast. It's also delicious split in half and filled with mashed avocado, hummus, or even egg salad. But my all-time favorite way to eat it is with good butter and berry jam—and when I say berry jam, you bet I'm talking about that lingonberry jam I got at IKEA.

I find the ring bread doesn't keep as long as other rye breads—probably because it doesn't have a dense middle to retain moisture. I recommend you enjoy it within 2 days.

Prep and Baking Schedule

2 to 3 days prior to baking:
1. Sprout the rye berries. This process will require that you rinse and drain the berries daily, 2 to 3 days in a row.

Prep Day (day prior to baking):
In the morning:
1. Mix the rye leaven.
2. Ferment for 24 hours.

Baking Day:
In the morning:
1. Mix the dough and shape it into ring breads.
2. Ferment for 6 hours.

In the early afternoon:
1. Bake. Cool. Enjoy the next day.

Prep Day

1. Start the process of sprouting the rye berries 2 to 3 days before making the bread. Soak the rye berries in cold water for 5 minutes. Drain and put in a glass container with a lid. Let sit overnight on the kitchen counter. Repeat the same process for two consecutive days. When you see that the berries are starting to germinate—they'll have an incipient stem protruding from within— you can refrigerate them until ready to use.

2. One day before baking the bread, make the rye leaven. In a medium bowl, stir together the starter and rye flour with the cold water. Cover and let ferment on the kitchen counter for about 24 hours.

RECIPE CONTINUES

1. Divide the dough into two equal pieces, about 1 pound (450 g) each. Knead each into a ball.

2. Using a rolling pin, flatten each dough ball into a disk about 8 inches in diameter, dusting with rye flour as necessary to prevent sticking.

3. Use a 2-inch round biscuit cutter or the rim of a glass to punch a hole in the center.

4. Use a skewer to poke decoratively across the surface of the bread.

Baking Day

1. Line two baking sheets with parchment paper. In a large bowl, combine the fermented rye leaven with the rye flour, salt, sprouted rye berries, and cold water, mixing with your hands until a dough forms. Knead the dough on a surface floured with rye flour until it comes together in a smooth ball. Divide into two equal pieces, about 1 pound (450 g) each. Knead each into a ball. Using a rolling pin, flatten each dough into a disk about 8 inches in diameter, dusting with rye flour as necessary to prevent sticking. Use a 2-inch round biscuit cutter or the rim of a glass to punch a hole in the center. Using the back of a chef's knife, score each disk into six equal sections (as if you were cutting a cake into six wedges). Use a skewer to poke decoratively across the surface of the bread. Transfer the ring breads and their holes to the prepared baking sheets. Cover your breads and holes with a clean kitchen towel and let rise at room temperature for 6 hours.

2. Place two oven racks in the middle positions and preheat the oven to 450°F.

3. Bake the breads for 12 to 15 minutes or until a thermometer inserted into the middle of the bread reads 200°F or slightly higher. Remove the breads from the oven and immediately wrap each in a clean kitchen towel. Let rest for at least 12 hours before slicing. Save the holes for yourself—I usually enjoy them later that evening as a midnight snack, split in half with a little butter. To serve, cut sections or wedges along the scored lines, split each in half, and fill with your favorite spread.

Danish Rye Bread

MAKES 1 LOAF

Equipment: 8½-by-4½-inch loaf pan

For the sprouted rye berries

½ cup (95 g) rye berries

To feed the starter

⅔ cup (80 g) bread flour

2 teaspoons sourdough starter (see page 102)

⅓ cup (80 ml) cold (65° to 70°F) water

For the rye leaven

2 cups (250 g) dark rye flour

1¼ cups (300 ml) cold (65° to 70°F) water

For the seed mixture

½ cup (80 g) pumpkin seeds (pepitas)

⅓ cup (50 g) sunflower seeds

2 tablespoons flaxseed

For the dough

2¼ cups (305 g) dark rye flour, plus more for finishing

2 teaspoons fine sea salt

1 cup (240 ml) boiling water

Opposite (clockwise from bottom left): slices of Danish Rye Bread, Black Olive Boule (page 219), Eliisa's Ring Bread (page 225)

Did you know Denmark ranks among the happiest countries in the world? As far as I'm concerned, their rye bread is a contributing factor. A few trips to Copenhagen were enough to get me hooked on rugbrød. This traditional Danish rye is dense in both flavor and texture and is the base of the iconic open-face sandwiches known as smørrebrød.

After months of experimenting with my own Danish rye, Toronto-based baker and cooking instructor Matthew Duffy suggested prefermenting the majority of the flour and mixing the final dough with boiling water. The preferment facilitates acidity development, and the hot water gelatinizes the flour, encouraging a stable rise in the oven. Matt's version was most similar to the loaves I had in Denmark; I knew I was getting close. I tweaked his recipe one last time, under the tutelage of resident Friends & Family Dane and baker, Maja Almskou. "It needs more give," Maja said, so I continued experimenting until I found the perfect ratios of seeds, rye berries, and whole-grain rye flour.

Keep in mind that this bread requires planning ahead, since you'll have to sprout the rye berries, a process that takes 2 to 3 days. You will also need active sourdough starter to make the rye leaven, a sourdough preferment that is prepared the day before the mixing, shaping, and baking take place. The bread takes 2 days to make. You can follow the suggested Prep and Baking Schedule.

This bread is made with 100 percent rye flour, plus a small amount of residual wheat from the sourdough starter. Minimal wheat flour means there isn't much gluten to sustain the bread's

RECIPE CONTINUES

structure, so you'll have to pay close attention to the proof. Rye doughs are particularly active and must be baked before their lack of strength causes collapse. This happens much faster than in wheat-based breads. Once baked, the bread must sit for a day before being sliced; otherwise the interior will be gummy. This last step is very important, so be patient. When it's ready to eat, slice thinly, enjoy as is, or toast at a low setting. This bread is definitely meant for smoked fish, creamy cheese, and rye lovers. The loaf will keep for a week wrapped tightly with plastic and stored at room temperature.

Prep and Baking Schedule

2 to 3 days prior to baking:

1. Sprout the rye berries. This process will require that you rinse and drain the berries daily, 2 to 3 days in a row.

Prep Day (day prior to baking):

In the morning:

1. Feed the starter anytime between 6:00 and 10:00 a.m. The starter will be ready to use in 8 to 10 hours.

Later that day (8 to 10 hours after feeding the starter):

1. Mix the rye leaven. Ferment overnight at room temperature.

Baking Day:

1. Soak the seed mixture.

2. Mix the bread dough and transfer to a loaf pan. Ferment for 1 to 1 ½ hours.

3. Bake. Cool. Enjoy the next day.

Prep Day

1. Start the process of sprouting the rye berries 2 to 3 days before making the bread. Soak the rye berries in cold water for 5 minutes. Drain and put in a glass container with a lid. Let sit overnight on the kitchen counter. Repeat the same process for two consecutive days. When the berries start to germinate—they'll have an incipient stem protruding from within—you can refrigerate until ready to use.

2. The day prior to baking the bread, feed the starter by combining the bread flour and sourdough starter with the cold water. Cover and let it ferment at room temperature for 8 to 10 hours, until it has increased in volume and formed bubbles on the surface.

3. To prepare the rye leaven, stir the fed sourdough starter and rye flour with the cold water in a medium bowl. The water temperature is important to ensure that the leaven rises at a slower rate; warmer water can cause it to ferment too quickly, impacting the flavor and structure of the bread. Cover with plastic wrap and let ferment on the kitchen counter for 12 to 18 hours.

Baking Day

1. Soak the pumpkin seeds, sunflower seeds, and flaxseed in cold water for 5 minutes. Drain and set aside.

2. Coat the loaf pan with nonstick spray.

3. To mix the dough, transfer the fermented rye leaven to a large bowl. Add the flour and salt followed by the boiling water and mix quickly and vigorously with a rubber spatula. Mix in the sprouted rye berries and seeds until thoroughly combined. This will be a very strange dough, sticky, dark, and claylike, possibly unlike any other dough you've made. You won't be able to knead it, but mixing with a rubber spatula will suffice. Transfer immediately to the prepared loaf pan. Use a wet spatula to prevent the dough from sticking to it and spread the top as evenly as possible. The dough should come almost all the way to the top of the pan. Sprinkle generously with additional rye flour. Proof at warm room temperature for 1 to 1½ hours, until it has risen above the edge of the pan and the top has pronounced cracks.

4. Place an oven rack in the middle position and preheat the oven to 450°F.

5. Carefully cover the bread loosely with aluminum foil; be mindful not to punch the risen top. Bake the bread for 30 minutes, then remove the foil and bake for another 30 to 40 minutes or until a digital thermometer inserted in the middle reads 208°F. Let the bread cool in the pan on a cooling rack for 30 minutes. Then remove from the pan, put back on the cooling rack, and let rest uncovered overnight. The bread will be ready to eat the next day. Slice thinly and enjoy with a schmear of butter or your favorite spread. I like mine with almond butter and honey or avocado and coarse salt. Later in the week, when the bread starts to stale, toast it briefly to bring it back to life.

Chocolate Babka with Rye Streusel

Equipment: 8½-by-4½-inch loaf pan

For the dough

1 teaspoon instant yeast

½ cup (120 ml) cold (65° to 70°F) water

¾ cup (100 g) bread flour

½ cup plus 2 tablespoons (90 g) all-purpose flour, plus extra for dusting

½ cup plus 2 tablespoons (80 g) dark rye flour

2 tablespoons granulated sugar

2 teaspoons kosher salt

1 large egg

3 tablespoons unsalted butter, at room temperature

For the chocolate filling

¾ cup (135 g) bittersweet chocolate chips

2 tablespoons unsalted butter, at room temperature

¼ cup packed (55 g) dark brown sugar

1 tablespoon Dutch-processed cocoa powder

Pinch of kosher salt

For the rye streusel

¼ cup (30 g) dark rye flour

¼ cup (35 g) all-purpose flour

2 tablespoons granulated sugar

⅛ teaspoon ground cinnamon

Pinch of kosher salt

8 tablespoons (1 stick/115 g) cold unsalted butter, cut into ½-inch cubes

1 egg, beaten, for brushing

Babka can be considered both coffee cake and sweet bread. It came to America with Jewish bakers of Eastern European descent during the World War II era. In recent years it has experienced a rise in popularity, perhaps due to the contagious babka enthusiasm of many talented young bakers with strong social media platforms.

Babka is typically built as a jellyroll filled with cinnamon, dried fruits, or chocolate. The roll is then cut in half and braided to expose the filling. It can be baked in a loaf pan or as a free-form bread. I've noticed that many modern versions lack the traditional streusel topping, a choice I find sacrilegious. Why deny yourself a toasty bite of crumble topping on your babka, especially when said topping is made of aromatic rye flour?

The dough is enriched with eggs and butter. I've included rye flour in the dough because it pairs nicely with the chocolate filling, but also because rye and babka hail from the same region of the world. Why not bring the two together in a festive fashion?

To make the recipe less labor intensive, I recommend making the dough the day before and assembling and baking it the next day.

I know this might be asking a lot, but please let the baked babka cool completely before digging in. Letting the filling set completely ensures that your slices will show the arty twists and turns babka is known for. If the chocolate still seems gooey and you try cutting it, you'll be left with a chocolaty mess. Babka is best the day it is made, so I usually enjoy it in the afternoon with coffee. It will still be good the next day, but after that it will start to dry out.

1. Make the dough the day before baking the babka. Sprinkle the yeast over the cold water, stir with a spoon, and let it sit for 5 minutes.

2. Sift the flours, granulated sugar, and salt into the bowl of a stand mixer. Add the egg and dissolved yeast to the sifted flours. Fit the stand mixer with the dough hook attachment. Mix on low speed until a dough forms, about 2 minutes. Add the butter, increase the speed to medium, and continue mixing just to incorporate, about 2 more minutes. Transfer the dough to a lightly floured surface and knead into a ball. Place in a bowl lightly coated with nonstick spray and cover tightly with plastic wrap. Let rest in the refrigerator overnight.

3. The next day, for the filling, put the chocolate chips in a heat-resistant bowl and melt over a pot of barely simmering water, making sure the bottom of the bowl doesn't touch the water. Remove the bowl from the heat when all the chocolate pieces are melted. Add the butter and stir with a rubber spatula until completely melted. Add the brown sugar, cocoa powder, and salt and stir until well combined. Set aside at room temperature until ready to use.

4. Coat the loaf pan with nonstick spray.

5. Remove the dough from the refrigerator and place it on a floured work surface. Using a rolling pin, flatten the dough into a 10-inch square, about ¼ inch thick, using flour as needed to prevent sticking. With an offset spatula, spread the chocolate mixture over the dough as evenly as possible, leaving a ½-inch border at the top.

Roll up the dough like a jelly roll and pinch the seam together. Roll it back and forth to form a tight cylinder and place seam side down on the work surface; by now your log should be about 14 inches long. Using a chef's knife, slice the cylinder in half lengthwise. Carefully braid the two strands by twisting them around each other, pinching their ends together so they won't uncoil. Gently compress the braid to coerce it into the prepared loaf pan, making sure to tuck the ends downward so they're not exposed. Cover the pan loosely with plastic wrap and let the babka rise at room temperature for 1½ to 2 hours, until the strands of braided dough look puffy and soft to the touch or they no longer bounce back when you press gently with a moistened index finger.

6. While the dough is rising, make the rye streusel. In the bowl of a food processor fitted with the steel blade, combine the flours, granulated sugar, cinnamon, and salt, and pulse just to combine. Add the cold butter pieces and pulse until a coarse meal begins to form. It's important to stop before the streusel begins clumping together, which will happen quickly. The resulting streusel will be somewhat uneven with tiny and not-so-tiny pebbles. Refrigerate until ready to use.

7. Place an oven rack in the middle position and preheat the oven to 350°F.

8. Once the babka is proofed, brush with the beaten egg and sprinkle generously with all of the rye streusel. It might look like a lot of streusel topping, but it's so delicious you wouldn't

RECIPE CONTINUES

1. With an offset spatula, spread the chocolate mixture over the dough as evenly as possible.

2. Leave a ½-inch border at the top.

3. Roll up the dough like a jelly roll.

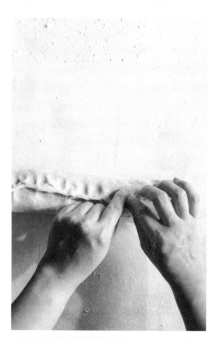

4. Pinch the seam together. Roll it back and forth to form a tight cylinder about 14 inches long.

5. Using a chef's knife, slice the cylinder in half lengthwise.

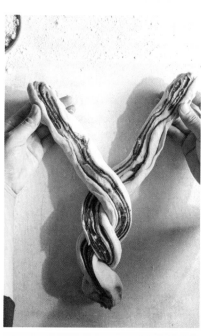

6. Carefully braid the two strands by twisting them around each other.

want to miss any of it. Bake for 20 minutes, then rotate the pan and bake for another 15 to 25 minutes, until the streusel is a rich golden brown. Rotating the pan halfway through the baking process will ensure that the babka bakes evenly. To test for doneness you can also insert a digital thermometer in the center and check the internal temperature; the babka will be properly baked at 185°F. Cool completely before removing from the pan, about 1 hour. Slice with a serrated knife for the cleanest cuts.

sorghum

SORGHUM BICOLOR

Get to know sorghum, the grain of the future.

If you travel through rural pockets of the South in late September, particularly the Appalachia regions that thread through North Carolina, Tennessee, Kentucky, and West Virginia, you might find yourself lucky enough to come across a sorghum harvest. Once a common annual occurrence throughout the region, the sorghum harvest is the process of turning sorghum stalks—tall, thin plants similar to corn stalks—into sorghum syrup. Lasting from early mornings well into the cool nights, the harvest traditionally uses horses pulling a wheel to mill sorghum stalks into juice. Then, like maple syrup, the juice is boiled down, yielding a dark, viscous syrup reminiscent of molasses, but with more varied notes of bitterness, sourness, and even smoke that many liken to savory caramel.

The sorghum harvest was a linchpin in Southern Appalachia communities, bringing neighbors together each year in the joint production of a common good, and sorghum was once the primary sweetener of the region. As such, sorghum is deeply embedded in the culinary culture of Appalachia. Dishes like hot biscuits drizzled with sorghum syrup are a regional delicacy, while sorghum pie is a smoky-sweet celebration.

Sorghum is grown for three different purposes: sorghum syrup, livestock feed, and human consumption. The variety used for livestock feed is known as *forage sorghum*, and it constitutes the majority of sorghum produced worldwide. A niche variety known

Opposite: Trouble Cookies (page 257)

as *sweet sorghum* is used to make syrup, while grain sorghum is grown exclusively for culinary use. Grain sorghum is available as whole-grain kernels or ground into flour, and the range of recipes that can be prepared with it encompasses savory porridges, grain salads, quick breads, cookies, cakes, and even beer.

Although it's not a common modern-day kitchen ingredient, sorghum has been a key food source for millennia, with origins tracing back eight thousand years ago to southern Egypt. It was domesticated in Ethiopia and Sudan, and from there it spread to the rest of Africa. During the Arab Agricultural Revolution, a period that extended from the eighth to the thirteenth century, sorghum was planted extensively in parts of the Middle East, North Africa, and Southern Europe. The grain was also known in India and traded elsewhere along the Silk Road. In fact, the name *sorghum* is descriptive of the grain's migration through the region. It comes from the Italian *sorgo*, which in turn is derived from the Latin *Syricum granum,* meaning "grain of Syria."

Sorghum was most likely brought to the Americas from West Africa during the slave trade era. Benjamin Franklin is responsible for one of the first recorded mentions of sorghum in the country when he wrote about sorghum being used to make brooms in 1757. This description isn't surprising—far more than just a food source, sorghum's long stalks have also been used for thatch, fencing, baskets, brushes, and brooms.

A nutrient-dense food, sorghum is a primary food source for many of the world's most food-insecure populations, particularly in Africa, where it thrives in both the tropics and the deserts and is mostly consumed as a hearty and nutritious savory porridge. In Ethiopia the staple flatbread injera is sometimes made with sorghum instead of teff—an ancient grain domesticated three thousand years ago, known for its small size, cocoa color, and sweet-mild flavor. In the Middle East, sorghum kernels are often cooked like couscous, while in various regions of India, like the Maharashtra state and northern Karnataka state, sorghum is used to make a version of roti. In neighboring Bangladesh, it's added to the traditional lentil stew known as *khichuri*, while in China it's a popular base for making distilled beverages. There's even a Chinese film named after it: *Red Sorghum* (1988), about a young woman's life working at a distillery for sorghum liquor.

From a sustainability standpoint, sorghum presents clear advantages. Perhaps most importantly, it's easy to grow. Unlike the much more well-known quinoa, which can be cultivated only at high altitudes and is relatively expensive to grow, sorghum flourishes in a variety of conditions and requires less water than other grains, such as corn. Because stalks can grow close to each other, sorghum requires less acreage, preventing the overdevelopment of agricultural land. As climate change–induced drought continues to affect agricultural land around the world, the ability to grow food in hot, dry conditions will become increasingly more vital. Sorghum is among the most efficient crops in conversion of solar energy and use of water—two resources growing ever more important. And on top of everything, it's markedly cheap to produce (hence its extensive use as livestock feed). Not only is it inexpensive and prolific, but sorghum's nutrient density and versatility mean that this grain can serve as a rock-solid dietary foundation. It can even be popped like corn!

I often refer to sorghum as "the grain of the future," with an enthusiasm that is seldom shared by many. But if we consider the challenges agriculture has yet to experience in the era of climate change, we would start looking at sorghum in a whole new light. In today's unstable environmental and agricultural landscape, we would do well to look to the practices of farmers in Ethiopia, India, and the American South for inspiration to grow and consume sorghum. Unlike diet and ingredient fads that drift in and out of public consciousness, sorghum isn't just a cool ingredient with a strange name. Sorghum is high in antioxidants and naturally gluten-free. In recent years, it has become an important source of fiber for those with celiac disease or gluten intolerance. I can't wait to see more chefs, bakers, brewers, and confectioners get creative with sorghum in the coming decades.

How to Purchase and Use

Sorghum Kernels

Sorghum kernels and flour are sometimes called *jowar* or *milo*, as they're known in other parts of the world. The kernels can be cooked like rice or barley and used in porridges, grain salads, and pilafs. They have a heartiness similar to steel-cut oats and a nutty, mildly sweet flavor. Sorghum kernels are also sold as "popping sorghum"—their hulls trap moisture and explode when heated, just like popped corn. Sorghum kernels can be cooked in water until soft, about 50 minutes. Throw cooked kernels into a salad with a punchy vinaigrette like the Sorghum and Albacore Tuna Salad on page 272, or substitute sorghum for couscous to make a modernized tabbouleh. I toss it into soups and panfry it with vegetables just like fried rice. Sorghum kernels are sold as whole-grain sorghum by Bob's Red Mill and Shiloh Farms and can be ordered online. The whole grain keeps well, so there's no harm in ordering a larger amount and storing it for up to year.

Sorghum Flour

Sorghum flour is smooth, sweet, and velvety. It's great for soft batters and crisp cookies, because it rarely clumps. When purchasing, look for whole-grain unbleached organic sorghum flour. Refined sorghum flours are readily available, but the tender husks in the whole-grain counterpart add volume and complexity of flavor. When ground, mild sorghum flour can complement or replace wheat flour. As such, you can substitute sorghum in most existing recipes that call for all-purpose flour. It may take some experimentation, but there's great potential for success. Sorghum doesn't contain gluten—the protein that allows wheat to bind and stretch—so I combine it with all-purpose flour when I need more structure. My preferred ratio is one part whole-grain sorghum to one part all-purpose flour. Sorghum can leave a starchy feel in your mouth, but this problem is solved by blending with all-purpose flour. Generally speaking, sweet sorghum flour, white sorghum flour, and jowar (a popular name in health food stores and macrobiotic markets) are the same thing. Farmer Larry Kandarian offers limited amounts he mills himself at my local farmers' market, but when that's not an option, my preferred brand is Bob's Red Mill. Store flour in a cool pantry and try to use it within 3 months of purchase. To keep track, I recommend labeling the bag with the date of purchase.

Sorghum Syrup or Molasses

Sorghum syrup, or sorghum molasses, is a prominent ingredient in the American South. Sorghum syrup's taste varies depending on where it was grown, when it was harvested, and how it was processed, meaning that each batch has a specific terroir indicative of the land it came from, very much like wine. Interestingly, more sorghum is grown in the United States for syrup than for flour. This natural sweetener is made by processing juice from the stalks of specific sorghum varieties. The juice is cooked into a concentrated syrup, similarly to how sugarcane juice is reduced to molasses. Thanks to their comparable viscosity and flavor, sorghum syrup can be substituted for molasses. I sometimes use it as I would honey, but its flavor is more pronounced. Over time, sorghum syrup has permeated my holiday baking, replacing molasses in classics like gingerbread and molasses cookies. I like blending softened butter with sorghum syrup as an accompaniment to buttermilk biscuits, pancakes, or corn bread. And after sweetening homemade whipped cream with a touch of sorghum, you'll never want to use anything else.

If your local health food store doesn't carry it, a quick online search will point you in the right direction. Much sorghum syrup is still produced by small family farms almost exclusively in the South, each one claiming that theirs is best. Recent purchases include Uncle John's Sorghum Molasses, Golden Barrel Sorghum Syrup, Muddy Pond Sorghum, and Oberholtzer's Kentucky Sorghum. I tend to like dark sorghum syrups, but it's possible to find more golden syrups with a milder flavor, such as Loveless Cafe Old-Fashioned Sorghum molasses (see Sourcing on page 336).

Fried Apple Cider Dumplings

MAKES ABOUT 20 DUMPLINGS

For the batter

1 cup plus 2 tablespoons (160 g) all-purpose flour

1 cup plus 2 tablespoons (145 g) sorghum flour

1 teaspoon baking powder

1 teaspoon kosher salt

½ teaspoon ground cinnamon

¼ teaspoon freshly grated nutmeg

⅓ cup (80 ml) buttermilk

⅓ cup (80 ml) sparkling apple cider

4 tablespoons (½ stick/55 g) unsalted butter, at room temperature

⅔ cup (130 g) granulated sugar

1 large egg

1 large egg yolk

1 teaspoon vanilla extract

Vegetable oil for frying (about 1 quart)

For the cinnamon sugar

½ cup (100 g) granulated sugar

½ teaspoon ground cinnamon

¼ teaspoon kosher salt

Confectioners' sugar for dusting

As a longtime resident of Southern California, I often fantasize about autumnal experiences that never fully realized in my neck of the woods—think apple picking, falling leaves, and chunky scarves. When Friends & Family baker Ari Smolin, who had spent the last few years in New York, came to work at the bakery, we quickly discovered our shared love of all things fall. Her stories of wandering among apple trees, freshly pressed cider in one hand and a bag of cinnamon-sugar-coated doughnuts in the other, made me want to drop everything and book it to the East Coast. After months of having her work with me on this book, doing everything from proofreading to recipe testing, I realized that we couldn't forgo an homage to the apple cider doughnuts she longed for every fall. And so we put our heads together to make some pretty stellar fried sorghum and cider dumplings.

The cider dumplings are a breeze to make. It's almost hard to believe something so delicious can be whipped up so effortlessly. The batter comes together in just a few minutes and requires no rising or resting time before frying. A hefty proportion of sorghum flour yields a delicate batter with compelling texture, while buttermilk and sparkling cider ensure light, tender dumplings.

They're really fun to make on a lazy Sunday in early fall. Kids could help roll the dumplings in cinnamon sugar. Like most fritters, the dumplings should be eaten within 4 hours of frying. Ari recommends gobbling them up with a glass of cider on a chilly autumn afternoon.

RECIPE CONTINUES

1. For the batter, sift the flours, baking powder, salt, cinnamon, and nutmeg into a bowl. Combine the buttermilk and cider in another bowl.

2. In a stand mixer fitted with the paddle attachment, cream the butter and granulated sugar for 2 minutes or until a paste forms. Add the egg on low speed, followed by the egg yolk, mixing to combine after each addition. Add the sifted flour mixture, alternating with the buttermilk and cider, in three additions. Scrape the sides of the bowl with a rubber spatula, add the vanilla, and mix just to combine.

3. Fill a large heavy pot with frying oil (such as canola) about 3 inches deep, place over medium heat, and heat until the oil reaches 360°F on a digital thermometer. Line a plate with paper towels and have a slotted spoon nearby.

4. Using a spoon, scoop the batter into 1-ounce (28 g) lumps and drop directly into the hot oil. You can use a second spoon to help you dislodge the lump from the other spoon with ease. Fry for 1 minute on each side, using a slotted spoon to flip the dumplings. To test for doneness, choose a sacrificial dumpling and cut through the middle to gauge whether the others will need more or less frying time; they should be cooked all the way through like doughnuts. Work in batches of four or five dumplings at a time, taking care not to overcrowd your pot. Don't be alarmed if your dumplings split or crack while frying; these crispy nooks and crannies add a delicious crunch. Remove the golden dumplings with a slotted spoon and put on the prepared plate. Let them rest until cool enough to handle.

5. Make the cinnamon sugar by combining the granulated sugar, cinnamon, and salt in a bowl. Toss the dumplings in the cinnamon sugar. If you, like me, think everything is more irresistible with confectioners' sugar, go forth and dust your dumplings!

Ginger Scones

Equipment: 2¾-inch plain biscuit cutter

1 cup (130 g) sorghum flour

2 cups (260 g) Sonora wheat flour (see page 102 for more on heirloom wheats) or all-purpose flour

½ cup (100 g) sugar, plus extra for sprinkling

1 tablespoon plus 1 teaspoon baking powder

1 cup (2 sticks/225 g) cold unsalted butter, cut into ½-inch cubes

1 cup (150 g) chopped crystallized ginger

1 cup (240 ml) heavy cream, plus extra for brushing

The original version of these scones traces back to the groundbreaking La Brea Bakery, founded by my mentor, Nancy Silverton, in 1989. From the very start, La Brea Bakery grew at an exponential pace. At the height of its popularity, it supplied bread for its sister restaurant, Campanile, and some of the best chefs in Los Angeles. Not long after opening, their freshly baked baguettes could be found in fine grocery stores, and bread-loving customers would line up outside the small space on La Brea Avenue every morning. While the bread department quickly evolved into a wholesale bakery with distribution across the country, the pastries continued to be baked in house exclusively for the store. The entire pastry production took place in a tiny kitchen located on the second floor of the retail space. Four bakers would show up at midnight to prepare all the items that were to stock the shelves the next morning, including my favorite, the ginger scone. Over the next decade the bakery continued to expand and in time outgrew its production space.

When we opened Friends & Family, I wanted to make a ginger scone that honored the delicious La Brea Bakery version. In this grain-forward incarnation, the refined flour is replaced with whole-grain Sonora wheat and sorghum flours to enrich the scones with more fiber and the melt-in-your-mouth effect that sorghum adds to many recipes. I'm proud to say we make these ginger scones by hand every day at Friends & Family. When I shape a batch of them, I always think about that tiny La Brea Bakery kitchen and the many delicious pastries generations of bakers made there.

RECIPE CONTINUES

1. Line a baking sheet with parchment paper.

2. Combine the flours, sugar, and baking powder in a large bowl. Toss the cold butter cubes into the dry ingredients. Quickly cut the cold butter cubes into the dry ingredients by pinching the butter with your fingertips until the mixture resembles a coarse meal with crumbs the size of hazelnuts. Mix in the crystallized ginger and make a well in the center. Pour the cream into the well of dry ingredients. Toss gently with both hands (the way you would toss a salad) until the mixture forms a crumbly dough that barely comes together.

3. To shape the scones, transfer the dough to a lightly floured surface. Pat down into a disk about 1 inch thick. Using the biscuit cutter, cut as many scones as possible. Gather up the scraps, pat down again, and cut a few extra scones. Place the scones on the prepared baking sheet at least 2 inches apart. Chill in the freezer, uncovered, for 30 minutes.

4. Place an oven rack in the middle position and preheat the oven to 375°F.

5. Remove the scones from the freezer. Brush each one with cream and sprinkle generously with sugar. Bake for 12 minutes. Then rotate the baking sheet and bake for another 12 minutes or until the scones are a rich golden color on top. Rotating the sheet halfway through the baking process will ensure that the scones bake evenly. Let cool for at least 15 minutes before serving. Scones should be eaten fresh, but if you have leftovers, store in an airtight container and reheat in a toaster oven.

Quintessential Peanut Butter Cookies

6 tablespoons (¾ stick/85 g) unsalted butter, at room temperature

½ cup (135 g) smooth peanut butter

¼ cup plus 3 tablespoons (90 g) granulated sugar, plus extra for rolling

¼ cup packed (55 g) dark brown sugar

¼ teaspoon kosher salt

¾ teaspoon baking soda

¼ teaspoon baking powder

1 large egg

½ teaspoon vanilla extract

½ cup (65 g) sorghum flour

½ cup (70 g) all-purpose flour

Old-school peanut butter cookies always hit the spot. There's nothing wrong with the classic, but when your kitchen is full of flour samples from around the country it's easy to get curious. I decided to try sorghum in this simple recipe after a successful week spent adding it to many of my cookies.

Peanut butter cookies are relatively simple to make, but they can be a bit tricky. They contain a large amount of fat in the form of butter and peanut butter, which can cause them to be overly soft. The oily peanut butter can also make them crumbly and reluctant to come together. I tested a version made solely with sorghum flour, but, just as I suspected, the cookies had a hard time keeping their shape. A second test with a safe ratio of one part whole-grain sorghum flour to one part all-purpose flour worked really well. The peanut butter you choose will also make a difference. I suggest a uniform, smooth peanut butter. Rolled in sugar and baked to perfection, these are exactly what peanut butter cookies should be: crispy edges surrounding tender centers, full of nutty, nostalgia-evoking goodness.

1. In a stand mixer fitted with the paddle attachment, cream the butter, peanut butter, and sugars on medium-high speed for 2 to 3 minutes. Add the salt, baking soda, and baking powder and mix for another minute. Add the egg and vanilla and mix to combine. Add the flours and mix on low speed until a uniform dough forms. The dough will be very soft at this point. Transfer the dough to a sheet of parchment paper or plastic wrap. Flatten into a disk with your

RECIPE CONTINUES

hands, then wrap tightly and refrigerate for at least 30 minutes (and up to 2 days)—chilled dough will be much easier to handle.

2. Place two oven racks in the middle positions and preheat the oven to 375°F. Line two baking sheets with parchment paper.

3. Divide the chilled dough into sixteen equal portions, about 1½ ounces (45 g) each. Working quickly so that the dough doesn't warm up, round each portion with your hands. You can freeze the cookie dough balls for up to 2 weeks in a freezer bag to be baked from frozen at a later time. Keep in mind that frozen cookies may take longer baking time. Roll the cookies in granulated sugar and place on the prepared baking sheets, at least 3 inches apart to prevent the cookies from touching as they spread when they bake. Press the cookies in a cross-hatch pattern with a fork, flattening to ½-inch thickness. Bake for 8 minutes. Then rotate the sheets, switch positions in the oven, and bake for another 7 to 8 minutes, until the cookie edges are golden. Rotating and switching the sheets halfway through the baking process will ensure that the cookies bake evenly. Let the cookies cool completely on the baking sheets. The cookies will keep in an airtight container at room temperature for up to 2 days.

Chocolate Chip Cookies

MAKES 16 COOKIES

8 tablespoons (1 stick/115 g) unsalted butter, at room temperature

½ cup (100 g) granulated sugar

½ cup packed (112 g) dark brown sugar

½ teaspoon baking soda

¼ teaspoon kosher salt

1 large egg

1 teaspoon vanilla extract

¾ cup (100 g) sorghum flour

¾ cup (105 g) all-purpose flour

1 cup (175 g) bittersweet chocolate chips

Coarse sea salt such as Maldon or fleur de sel (optional)

Whenever someone new to ancient grains asks where to start, I recommend making a familiar staple, like chocolate chip cookies. I've made these using every grain in the book, including all heirloom wheat varieties I came across while developing these recipes. I know these cookies so well, I use them as my measuring stick. Each flour may behave a bit differently, but I can confidently say that, with the exception of corn, the cookies work beautifully with all mother grains. Every version taught me something new and distinctive about its featured flour: what the flour tastes like, how it responds to fat, if it browns quickly or slowly, and if it creates a chewy or crispy texture. It was pretty hard to decide which chapter these cookies belong in, but I finally settled on placing them here, in the sorghum chapter, to underline how an unusual flour can be used in traditional recipes. I've also included on page 253 a list of seven variations showing how to make them with other grains.

Because it's gluten-free and therefore less structured, I blend sorghum flour with all-purpose flour in a one-to-one ratio. The same ratio applies if trying the recipe with other gluten-free grains, such as buckwheat or rice. These cookies are sublime with rye, and their texture is remarkable with spelt. But when made with sorghum flour, this recipe yields beautiful golden rounds, with crispy edges and tender centers. Sorghum's complex, sweet notes will have you making this cookie time and time again.

RECIPE CONTINUES

1. In a stand mixer fitted with the paddle attachment, cream the butter and sugars on medium-high speed for 2 to 3 minutes. Add the baking soda and kosher salt and mix for another minute. Add the egg and vanilla and mix to combine. Add the flours and mix on low speed until a uniform dough forms. Add the chocolate chips and mix until well distributed in the dough. The dough will be very soft at this point. Transfer the dough to a sheet of parchment paper or plastic wrap. Flatten it into a disk, wrap tightly, and refrigerate for at least 30 minutes (and up to 2 days)—chilled dough will be much easier to work with.

2. Place two oven racks in the middle positions and preheat the oven to 350°F. Line two baking sheets with parchment paper.

3. Divide the chilled dough into sixteen equal portions, about 1½ ounces (45 g) each. Working quickly so that the dough doesn't warm up, round each portion with your hands. You can freeze the cookie dough balls for up to 2 weeks in a freezer bag to be baked from frozen at a later time. Keep in mind that frozen cookies may take longer baking time. Place the cookies on the prepared baking sheets, at least 3 inches apart to prevent the cookies from touching as they spread when they bake. If desired, top each cookie with a few flakes of coarse sea salt. Exercise restraint—it's still salt. Bake for 8 minutes. Then rotate the sheets, switch their positions in the oven, and bake for another 8 minutes, until the cookie edges are brown but the centers are still a little gooey. Rotating and switching the sheets halfway through the baking process will ensure that the cookies bake evenly. Let the cookies cool completely on the baking sheets or enjoy while still warm. The cookies will keep in an airtight container at room temperature for up to 2 days.

Bittersweet Chocolate

Use your preferred brand of bittersweet chocolate chips in this recipe; just make sure the label indicates it contains 60 to 70 percent of cacao solids. A great grocery store brand is Guittard. Specialty stores offer a vast variety of high-quality chocolate brands too, top among them Valrhona, El Rey, and Callebaut, but they don't always offer chips. If that's the case, you can chop larger bars into smaller pieces with a chef's knife. To further highlight the chocolate flavor, garnish the cookies with a few flakes of crunchy salt such as Maldon salt or fleur de sel (see page 32).

Variations

Barley Chocolate Chip Cookies

Soft-textured cookies that look very appealing. Hints of vanilla come through. Very kid friendly. Replace the sorghum and all-purpose flours with:

½ cup plus 2 tablespoons (80 g) barley flour

½ cup plus 2 tablespoons (90 g) all-purpose flour

Buckwheat Chocolate Chip Cookies

Sober version of this cookie. Really highlights the affinity between chocolate and buckwheat. The earthy flavor of buckwheat comes through. For the more adventurous baker. Replace the sorghum and all-purpose flours with:

½ cup plus 2 tablespoons (95 g) buckwheat flour

½ cup plus 2 tablespoons (90 g) all-purpose flour

Oatmeal Chocolate Chip Cookies

Lacy texture with a toasted-grain flavor. Tastes great with milk and makes delicious ice cream sandwiches. Replace the sorghum and all-purpose flours with:

½ cup (105 g) old-fashioned rolled oats

½ cup (70 g) oat flour

½ cup (70 g) all-purpose flour

Rice Chocolate Chip Cookies

Slightly sweeter than other versions with a nice, almost snappy crunch. Texture-rich with a pleasant grit from the finely ground rice. Replace the sorghum and all-purpose flours with:

½ cup plus 2 tablespoons (90 g) brown rice flour

½ cup plus 2 tablespoons (90 g) all-purpose flour

Rye Chocolate Chip Cookies

Elegant, more adult version of this cookie with a slightly sour-bitter flavor from the rye. This is the version we offer at Friends & Family. Replace the sorghum and all-purpose flours with 1¼ cups (160 g) dark rye flour.

Sonora Wheat Chocolate Chip Cookies

Pretty and tasty cookie with crispy edges and chewy center. Very close to the classic version of this American staple with a hint of toasted wheat bran flavor. Replace the sorghum and all-purpose flours with 1¼ cups (160 g) Sonora wheat flour.

Spelt Chocolate Chip Cookies

A great cookie for grain novices to make and eat. Uniform in flavor and texture with a delicious crunch. Replace the sorghum and all-purpose flours with 1¼ cups (165 g) spelt flour.

barley

sor

buckwheat

sonora

rice

spelt

oat

Trouble Cookies

¼ cup plus 2 tablespoons (60 g) whole raw cashews

8 tablespoons (1 stick/115 g) unsalted butter, at room temperature

¾ cup plus 2 tablespoons packed (200 g) dark brown sugar

1 large egg

1 teaspoon vanilla extract

½ cup plus 2 tablespoons (80 g) sorghum flour

½ cup plus 2 tablespoons (90 g) all-purpose flour

½ teaspoon baking powder

1 teaspoon baking soda

¼ teaspoon kosher salt

¾ cup (70 g) unsweetened shredded coconut, plus extra for decorating

½ cup (90 g) English toffee chips, such as Heath Toffee Bits

When I noticed how guests would often choose chocolate chip cookies over other treats, I decided to create a cookie so irresistible no one would even consider the chocolate-studded competition. I kept the classic brown sugar–based dough intact but combined it with other delicious morsels. It took a few tries, but the result surpassed all my expectations. My assistant and I ate so many we made ourselves sick, and everyone from our dishwasher to our office manager had the same issue. Once you eat one, you just can't stop. They remained nameless until we finally dubbed them Trouble Cookies. Naturally sweet sorghum flour becomes caramely when enriched with butter and brown sugar. You'll indeed be in trouble when you try these irresistible cookies, loaded with coconut, toasted cashews, and toffee bits. Even the most disciplined will have a hard time eating only one.

Opposite: Chocolate Dynamite Cookies (page 207), Sorghum Molasses Cookies (page 259), Oatmeal Date Cookies (page 149), Trouble Cookies, Quintessential Peanut Butter Cookies (page 247)

RECIPE CONTINUES

1. Place an oven rack in the middle position and preheat the oven to 350°F.

2. Scatter the cashews on a baking sheet. Toast until golden, 8 to 10 minutes. Let cool before chopping into pieces the size of a pea.

3. In a stand mixer fitted with the paddle attachment, cream the butter and brown sugar. Add the egg and vanilla and mix for 1 minute. Add the flours, baking powder, baking soda, and salt and mix until incorporated, 2 minutes. Mix in the toasted cashews, coconut, and toffee until just combined.

4. The dough will be very soft at this point. Transfer the dough to a sheet of parchment paper or plastic wrap. Flatten into a disk with your hands, then wrap tightly and refrigerate for at least 30 minutes (and up to 2 days)—chilled dough will be much easier to handle.

5. Place two oven racks in the middle positions and preheat the oven to 375°F. Line two baking sheets with parchment paper.

6. Divide the chilled dough into sixteen equal portions, about 1½ ounces (45 g) each. Working quickly so that the dough doesn't warm up, round each portion with your hands. You can freeze the cookie dough balls for up to 2 weeks in a freezer bag to be baked from frozen at a later time. Keep in mind that frozen cookies may take longer baking time. Place the cookies on the prepared baking sheets, at least 3 inches apart to prevent the cookies from touching as they spread when they bake. Press gently with the palm of your hand to flatten and decorate with a sprinkle of shredded coconut. Bake for 7 minutes. Then rotate the sheets, switch their positions in the oven, and bake for another 7 minutes, until the cookie edges are brown but the centers are still a little gooey. Rotating and switching the sheets halfway through the baking process will ensure that the cookies bake evenly. Let the cookies cool completely on the baking sheets. The cookies will keep in an airtight container at room temperature for up to 2 days.

Sorghum Molasses Cookies

MAKES 14 COOKIES

8 tablespoons (1 stick/115 g) unsalted butter

1¼ cups packed (265 g) dark brown sugar

1 large egg

2 tablespoons vegetable oil

¼ cup (60 ml) sorghum syrup

1 teaspoon kosher salt

1½ teaspoons baking soda

¾ teaspoon cream of tartar

2 cups (260 g) Sonora wheat flour or any other heirloom wheat flour (for more on heirloom wheats, see page 279)

½ teaspoon ground cloves

½ teaspoon ground ginger

1 teaspoon ground cinnamon

Granulated sugar for rolling

A perfect molasses cookie should be chewy yet soft, spiced but not spicy, and homey as well as interesting. Sorghum syrup is exemplary at achieving these standards. Since sorghum syrup is made almost identically to molasses (in fact, it's sometimes called sorghum "molasses" instead of "syrup"), I use it in very similar ways. I find the flavor of sorghum syrup more complex, hitting notes that can elevate a simple recipe to a new level. For this recipe, I recommend punchy, smoky, and dark sorghum syrup that you can buy online from reputable artisan sources (see Sourcing on page 336). It may take planning ahead, but finding a good sorghum syrup is worth going the extra mile. You may notice that my spice usage here is somewhat conservative. This lets the sorghum syrup shine; the spices just round out its flavor.

Portion these on the bigger side, so they can develop proper, chewy edges and soft centers. Don't skip the step of rolling them in granulated sugar before baking; it lends an irresistible sparkling exterior.

RECIPE CONTINUES

1. In a stand mixer fitted with the paddle attachment, cream the butter and brown sugar at medium speed for 2 to 3 minutes. Add the egg and mix for 1 minute. Add the oil and sorghum syrup and mix on low speed for 1 minute before adding the salt, baking soda, cream of tartar, flour, and spices. Mix until a uniform dough forms. The dough will be very soft at this point. Transfer the dough to a sheet of parchment paper or plastic wrap. Flatten into a disk with your hands, then wrap tightly and refrigerate for at least 30 minutes (and up to 2 days)—chilled dough will be much easier to handle.

2. Place two oven racks in the middle positions and preheat the oven to 350°F. Line two baking sheets with parchment paper.

3. Divide the dough into 14 equal portions, about 2 ounces (55 g) each. Working quickly so the dough doesn't warm up, shape each portion into a ball with your hands. You can freeze the cookie dough balls for up to 2 weeks in a freezer bag to be baked from frozen at a later time. Keep in mind that frozen cookies may take longer baking time. Roll the balls in sugar and place on the prepared baking sheets, at least 3 inches apart to prevent the cookies from touching as they spread when they bake. Bake for 7 minutes. Then rotate the sheets and switch their positions in the oven. Bake for another 7 minutes, until the edges are just set and the centers have cracked. Rotating and switching the sheets halfway through the baking process will ensure that the cookies bake evenly. Let the cookies cool completely on the baking sheets. The baked cookies keep well in an airtight container at room temperature for up to 2 days.

Sorghum Pecan Pie

Equipment: 9-inch glass pie pan

2 cups (335 g) raw pecan halves

1 baked pie shell made from Sonora Wheat Pie Dough (page 288)

⅓ cup packed (70 g) dark brown sugar

¼ teaspoon kosher salt

3 large eggs

1 cup (240 ml) light sorghum syrup or ½ cup dark sorghum syrup plus ½ cup light corn syrup or Lyle's Golden Syrup

1 tablespoon bourbon (optional)

8 tablespoons (1 stick/115 g) unsalted butter, melted and cooled slightly

Every Thanksgiving we make about a hundred pecan pies to sell alongside our pumpkin, apple, and chocolate varieties. Pecan may not be the most popular pie, but those who prefer it do so with devotion. Many declare our pecan pie their all-time favorite because it isn't too sweet. The secret? Sorghum syrup. Ironically, something that sounds (and is) viscous, sticky, and sugary offsets the sweetness in this dessert. Many pecan pie recipes call for corn syrup, but we stir this unique, southern ingredient into our custard, honoring the dessert's all-American origin. Add a touch of bourbon—another esteemed southern staple—and you're on your way to an unforgettable pie. The quality of your pecans is paramount. I recommend purchasing raw pecan halves. They take only a few minutes to roast and chop at home, yielding a result far superior to prechopped pecan pieces.

For this recipe, use a light sorghum syrup for a more balanced pie. I recommend Old-Fashioned Sorghum from The Loveless Cafe (see Sourcing on page 336). If working with darker sorghum syrup, use instead ½ cup sorghum syrup plus ½ cup light corn syrup or Lyle's Golden Syrup.

Serve at room temperature with a dollop of Sorghum Whip (page 264).

RECIPE CONTINUES

1. Place an oven rack in the middle position and preheat the oven to 350°F.

2. Scatter the pecans on a baking sheet and toast in the oven for 8 to 10 minutes, until a pecan cut in half is golden throughout. Let the toasted pecans cool completely. Chop 1 cup into chickpea-size pieces and save the other cup whole for decorating the top of the pie. Put the chopped pecans in the blind-baked pie shell.

3. Lower the oven temperature to 300°F.

4. To make the custard filling, in a bowl, whisk together sugar, salt, eggs, sorghum syrup, and bourbon (if using). Whisk in the melted butter. Let the custard rest on the kitchen counter for 20 minutes so the bubbles you created while whisking can dissipate.

5. Reserve ½ cup of custard filling and pour the rest over the chopped pecans in the shell. Toss the reserved pecan halves in the reserved custard until they're well coated. Arrange decoratively on top of the pie filling. Coating the pecans in custard prevents them from browning excessively in the oven while making them glossy. Put the pie pan on a baking sheet and bake for 1 hour, until the filling is set but slightly jiggly in the center. Remove from the oven and let cool completely. The pie will keep in an airtight container at room temperature for 2 days.

Sorghum Gingerbread
with Sorghum Whip

Equipment: 9-inch square or round cake pan

For the gingerbread

1½ teaspoons baking soda

1½ cups (360 ml) boiling water

1¼ cups (150 g) sorghum flour

1¼ cups (175 g) all-purpose flour

2 teaspoons ground cinnamon

2 teaspoons ground ginger

¼ teaspoon ground cloves

2 teaspoons baking powder

8 tablespoons (1 stick/115 g) unsalted butter, at room temperature

1 cup (200 g) sugar

2 large eggs

1 cup (240 ml) sorghum syrup, plus 2 tablespoons for brushing

For the sorghum whip

¾ cup (180 ml) heavy cream

2 tablespoons sour cream

1 to 2 tablespoons sorghum syrup

I first made this recipe after Glen Roberts, founder of South Carolina's Anson Mills, sent me a pint of sorghum syrup. It arrived shortly after a long sorghum conversation, involving many how-to videos of syrup boiling in gigantic pots. After opening the jar, I could see why people call it "sorghum molasses"—the two are almost identical in appearance. I decided to try it in gingerbread, where molasses always makes sense. The sorghum syrup added layers of flavor and a pleasant intensity. To keep things in the family, I substituted sorghum flour for half of the flour, yielding a soft, silky crumb. Just like that, sugarcane-based molasses was pushed to the back of the cupboard and my jar of sorghum syrup took its place.

Brushing lightly with sorghum syrup right after pulling the cake from the oven enhances the sorghum flavor and adds shininess. Serve a slice with sorghum whip for dessert and embrace the opportunity to introduce friends to the flavor and history of this incredible grain.

1. Place an oven rack in the middle position and preheat the oven to 350°F.

2. Cut a 9-inch square (or circle if using a round cake pan) of parchment paper. Lightly coat the bottom of the pan with nonstick spray and line it with the parchment.

3. Dissolve the baking soda in the boiling water and let cool completely. Dissolving the soda in water ahead of time helps disperse it more

thoroughly throughout the other ingredients, exposing it more evenly to the acid present in the recipe.

4. Sift the flours, spices, and baking powder into a bowl and stir to combine.

5. In a stand mixer fitted with the paddle attachment, cream the butter and sugar at medium speed for 2 to 3 minutes. Add the eggs, one at a time, mixing well after each addition. Add the sorghum syrup and mix for another minute. Using a rubber spatula, scrape the sides and bottom of the bowl. Add the sifted flour mixture, alternating with the baking soda water, in three batches.

6. Transfer the batter to the prepared pan and bake for 30 minutes. Rotate the pan and bake for 20 minutes more, until a toothpick inserted in the center of the cake comes out clean. Rotating the pan halfway through the baking process will ensure that the cake bakes evenly. If desired, brush the top of the cake with the additional sorghum syrup while still warm. Let the cake cool completely before cutting into slices and serving each slice with a dollop of sorghum whip. The cake will keep in an airtight container at room temperature for another day.

7. To make the sorghum whip, whip the heavy cream and sour cream at high speed until soft peaks form. Add sorghum syrup to taste. Whip just to incorporate. Transfer to a separate bowl and refrigerate until ready to serve. You will have enough whip to serve with 8 to 10 slices of cake.

Carrot Snack Cake with Cream Cheese Frosting

Equipment: 9-inch square or round cake pan

For the cake

½ cup (50 g) walnut halves

¾ pound (336 g) carrots, peeled

1½ cups (200 g) sorghum flour

2 teaspoons ground cinnamon

1½ teaspoons baking powder

½ teaspoon baking soda

1 teaspoon kosher salt

1 cup (240 ml) vegetable oil

1 cup (200 g) granulated sugar

½ cup packed (105 g) dark brown sugar

2 teaspoons vanilla extract

3 large eggs

⅓ cup (50 g) golden raisins

⅓ cup (25 g) unsweetened shredded coconut

One 8-ounce can crushed pineapple, drained

For the cream cheese frosting

1 cup (one 8-ounce package/225 g) cream cheese, at room temperature

¾ cup (150 g) granulated sugar

Pinch of kosher salt

1½ cups (360 ml) heavy cream

Because of its mild flavor, sorghum flour is ideal for creating gluten-free versions of many classic desserts, such as this carrot cake, for customers with dietary restrictions. But the absence of gluten in sorghum necessitates some recipe adjustments to make sure the resulting product holds together.

After some trials, I realized that to make a successful sorghum-based carrot cake, it's best to bake it as a single layer snack cake rather than a multilayer cake. To finish it, I like to leave the sides uncovered and just frost the top with a lightened cream cheese frosting. This presentation produces a silky, velvety cake that won't fall apart. It is also less time consuming than a layered cake and travels so well that it has become my favorite dessert to take to a potluck or picnic.

Carrots, plump golden raisins, and grated pineapple add moisture to the cake, while the cream cheese frosting protects it from drying out. That said, the cake keeps for 2 to 3 days in the refrigerator. You could also bake the cake a day ahead and frost shortly before serving.

Keep in mind that cakes made exclusively with sorghum flour can leave a starchy mouthfeel. Most people don't mind it, but if the presence of gluten is not a health risk for you and you'd like to reduce this effect, reduce the amount of sorghum flour to ¾ cup (100 g) sorghum flour and add ¾ cup (105 g) all-purpose flour.

1. Place an oven rack in the middle position and preheat the oven to 350°F.

2. Cut a 9-inch circle of parchment paper (or a square if working with a square pan). Lightly coat the bottom of the cake pan with nonstick spray and line it with the parchment.

3. Scatter the walnuts on a baking sheet and toast in the oven for 8 to 10 minutes, until a nut cut in half is golden in the center. Remove from the oven, let cool, and then chop roughly.

4. Shred the carrots with a grater. You should end up with 2 cups (270 g) of grated carrots.

5. Sift the flour, cinnamon, baking powder, baking soda, and salt into a large bowl. Make a well in the center with your hands.

6. Whisk the oil, sugars, vanilla, and eggs together in a separate bowl. Pour the oil mixture into the well in the dry ingredients and whisk from the center out, drawing the dry ingredients into the liquids gradually until a uniform batter forms. Stir in the grated carrots, walnuts, raisins, coconut, and pineapple. Transfer the batter to the prepared pan and bake for 30 minutes. Then rotate the pan and bake for 30 minutes or until a toothpick inserted in the center of the cake comes out clean. Rotating the pan halfway through the baking process ensures that the cake bakes evenly. Let the cake cool completely before removing it from the pan.

7. While the cake is baking, make the frosting. In a stand mixer fitted with the paddle attachment, beat the cream cheese, sugar, and salt on medium speed until light and fluffy, 3 minutes. In a separate bowl, whisk the heavy cream by hand until medium peaks form. Switch to the whisk attachment, add the whipped cream to the cream cheese mixture, and whip to incorporate. Invert the cooled cake onto a serving plate. Cover the top with the frosting, swirling it decoratively with a spatula or the back of a spoon. Refrigerate until ready to serve.

Hazelnut Brown Butter Cake

Equipment: 9-inch springform pan

For caramel crème anglaise

½ cup (100 g) granulated sugar

½ vanilla bean

¼ cup (60 ml) water

1 cup (240 ml) heavy cream

1 cup (240 ml) whole milk

½ teaspoon kosher salt

5 large egg yolks (save egg whites for the cake)

Coarse sea salt such as Maldon or fleur de sel

For the cake

2 scant cups (225 g) raw hazelnuts

1 cup (2 sticks/225 g) unsalted butter

½ vanilla bean

1½ cups (225 g) confectioners' sugar, plus extra for dusting

¾ cup (100 g) sorghum flour

5 large egg whites

⅓ cup (65 g) granulated sugar

Early in my career I was offered the pastry chef role at a small, soon-to-open restaurant. I wasn't sure what the chef's menu would be like and was a little lost as to what I should serve for dessert. After a brief meeting, the chef handed me a small paper with five ingredients written on it: hazelnuts, brown butter, powdered sugar, flour, and egg whites. No quantities or instructions. After playing around with proportions and methods, this cake was born. I listed it on the dessert menu to be served with caramel crème anglaise and a sprinkle of fleur de sel. The cake was well received by both my boss and our customers and always outsold the other sweets.

When we opened Friends & Family, I needed a delicious, decadent gluten-free cake for our catering menu. I decided to convert this trusty standby with sorghum flour. The sorghum was so delicate that it filled in beautifully, leaving the cake's flavor unaltered. I'm still touched by the reactions this cake elicits from first-time tasters.

Keep in mind that cakes made exclusively with sorghum flour can leave a starchy mouthfeel. Most people don't mind it, but if you'd like to reduce this effect, change the amount of sorghum flour to ¼ cup plus 2 tablespoons (50 g) and add ¼ cup plus 2 tablespoons (55 g) all-purpose flour. You could also make it entirely with ¾ cup (90 g) barley flour, which is very compatible with brown butter. Be advised that both of these variations contain gluten.

1. For the crème anglaise, put the sugar in a small saucepan. Cut the vanilla bean in half lengthwise with a paring knife, scrape out the sticky pulp with the back of the knife, and add both pulp and pod to the saucepan. Add the water and cook over medium heat until the sugar caramelizes and turns a deep mahogany brown. Remove from the heat and quickly stir in the cream and milk. Don't worry if the cold liquids harden the caramel. Add the kosher salt, return the saucepan to the stove, and cook over medium heat until the caramel dissolves again and comes to a boil. Whisk the yolks thoroughly in a mixing bowl. Slowly add the hot liquid mixture to the yolks in a thin, steady stream while whisking vigorously. Strain through a fine-mesh sieve into a heat-resistant container and refrigerate until ready to serve.

2. Place an oven rack in the middle position and preheat the oven to 350°F.

3. Lightly coat the bottom and sides of the springform pan with nonstick spray.

4. For the cake, scatter the hazelnuts on a baking sheet and toast for 8 to 10 minutes, until a nut cut in half is golden in the center. Let cool completely.

5. To make the brown butter, put the butter in a medium saucepan. Cut the vanilla bean in half lengthwise with a paring knife, scrape out the sticky pulp with the back of the knife, and add both pulp and pod to the pot. Cook over medium-low heat until the butter is golden brown, 7 to 8 minutes. Keep a watchful eye; butter can burn easily if left unattended. Remove the pod with a slotted spoon and let the brown butter cool slightly.

6. In a food processor, grind the toasted hazelnuts and confectioners' sugar to a fine meal. Add the sorghum flour and pulse just to combine.

7. In a stand mixer fitted with the whisk attachment, beat the egg whites at high speed until frothy. Slowly add the granulated sugar while the mixer is still running and continue to mix until the egg whites hold firm peaks. Fold the ground hazelnut mixture into the beaten egg whites with a rubber spatula. Add the brown butter and continue to fold until fully incorporated. Transfer the cake batter to the prepared pan and bake for 20 minutes. Then rotate the pan and bake for 20 minutes more. Rotating the pan halfway through the baking process will ensure that the cake bakes evenly. The cake will look done after 30 minutes, but continue baking to develop a crunchy exterior. Let the cake cool in the pan for 10 minutes. To unmold, run an offset spatula or paring knife along the side of the pan and loosen the springform lock. Transfer to a cake plate. Put confectioners' sugar in a sifter and dust the surface generously. Slice and serve while warm with the chilled caramel crème anglaise and a sprinkle of coarse sea salt. Leftovers keep in an airtight container at room temperature for 2 to 3 days. The cake will reheat well for a few minutes in a toaster oven.

Salted Sorghum Ice Cream

MAKES 1 QUART

1¼ cups (300 ml) whole milk

1¼ cups (300 ml) heavy cream

½ cup (120 ml) sorghum syrup

¾ cup (150 g) sugar

½ teaspoon kosher salt

½ vanilla bean

6 large egg yolks

I'm of the opinion that sorghum's sci-fi-sounding name deters potential admirers from giving it a shot. When I first served this ice cream, I intentionally avoided naming it Sorghum Syrup Ice Cream, opting instead for "Milo," as it's known in other regions of the world. But food giant Nestlé manufactures an instant chocolate drink powder under the same name, and I grew afraid that it could further confuse the public on the already puzzling matter of sorghum. So let's call it salted sorghum ice cream, shall we?

The ice cream base is sweetened with artisan sorghum syrup from Kentucky and served with a syrup drizzle on top. I steep the base with a vanilla bean, which complements the syrup beautifully, but you can omit the vanilla if desired. Most available sorghum syrup is high quality—it's still a rare ingredient that requires expert labor to produce. Depending on the maker, its color will range from amber to almost black. The darker the color, the stronger its flavor. I prefer a darker syrup for this recipe. Sorghum ice cream is delicious solo or as an accompaniment to many desserts in this chapter, from Sorghum Pecan Pie (page 261) to Fried Apple Cider Dumplings (page 243).

1. Combine the milk, cream, sorghum syrup, sugar, and salt in a nonreactive pot. Cut the vanilla bean in half lengthwise with a paring knife, scrape out the sticky pulp with the back of the knife, and add both pulp and pod to the pot. Heat over medium heat until it comes to a boil, stirring occasionally, then remove from the heat.

2. Whisk the egg yolks in a large bowl to break them up. Temper the egg yolks by slowly adding a ladleful of the hot milk mixture while whisking the yolks vigorously. Continue adding the hot milk to the yolks until you've added all of it. Strain through a fine-mesh sieve into a separate container. Cover and place in the refrigerator to chill until completely cold, at least 4 hours and up to 2 days.

3. Churn in an ice cream machine, following the manufacturer's instructions. Pack the churned ice cream into an airtight container and place in the freezer to firm up completely, at least 4 hours, but preferably overnight.

Sorghum and Albacore Tuna Salad

SERVES 4

1 cup (200 g) sorghum kernels

¼ cup (60 ml) fresh lemon juice

¼ cup (60 ml) extra virgin olive oil

½ teaspoon kosher salt, plus extra if necessary

One 5-ounce can albacore tuna packed in water, drained

1 teaspoon minced drained capers

2 tablespoons finely diced celery

1 tablespoon finely diced red onion

1 tablespoon minced chives

1 tablespoon minced dill

1 tablespoon minced parsley

6 pitted green olives, roughly chopped

1 tablespoon finely diced preserved lemon

1 avocado, peeled, pitted, and sliced

Whole-grain sorghum is a great base for other savory ingredients. In this dish the mildly flavored sorghum becomes a nutritious meal when combined with albacore tuna and a lemony vinaigrette. The salad can be prepared ahead of time and will keep well in the refrigerator for up to 2 days. Sliced avocado adds a creamy morsel to this multitextured dish.

Sorghum's exterior is very starchy, and soaking the grains overnight before cooking is highly recommended. It is also very feisty (taking up to 50 minutes to soften), but once cooked, this meal comes together fairly quickly. Use canned albacore tuna packed in water for this recipe, favoring brands labeled "wild" or "pole and line caught." Preserved lemon or lemon pickle is a popular North African condiment made by pickling the fruits in abundant salt and lemon juice. Buy it in Middle Eastern markets and specialty stores or online.

1. Put the sorghum in a nonreactive container. Add enough cold water to cover by 3 inches. Cover with a lid and let it soak overnight on the kitchen counter.

2. The next day, drain the sorghum through a strainer and rinse under running water until the water runs clear. Put in a medium pot with approximately 2 quarts water and bring to a boil over high heat. Reduce to a simmer and cook for 40 to 50 minutes, until tender.

3. Drain in a colander, then spread the grains on a baking sheet to prevent them from clumping as they cool.

4. Put the lemon juice in a bowl. Add the olive oil in a steady, slow stream while whisking vigorously. Season with the salt. Add the cooled sorghum to the bowl and toss. Flake the tuna with a fork, add to the grains, and toss just to combine. Add the capers, celery, red onion, chives, dill, parsley, olives, and preserved lemon and toss gently until thoroughly combined. Check the seasoning and add salt if necessary. Transfer to a serving platter and garnish with the avocado. The salad keeps well in the refrigerator for up to 2 days, but skip the avocado and garnish right before serving.

wheat

TRICUM

Wheat, the mother grain.

In a book about eight grains nutritionally, historically, economically, and culturally relevant enough to be considered mother grains, wheat is *the* mother grain. It's a true juggernaut, with so many applications it's hard to imagine human life without it. The world of wheat is filled with a diversity of flavors, textures, and colors. It encompasses a broad spectrum stretching far beyond the narrow representation in our modern diet. We've learned to see wheat as an inert substance, a stable bag on the shelf. But wheat is alive and as seasonal as tomatoes or peaches, with flavor profiles running the gamut from nutty einkorn to assertive red fife to corn-like durum.

We call wheat and other grasses "cereals" because in ancient Rome, where wheat fueled an empire, the goddess Ceres was worshipped as the guardian of grain. Einkorn, a wild grass grown in the Middle East for millennia, is the oldest wheat species we know of. It originated in the Fertile Crescent, near modern-day Iraq, over twelve thousand years ago. Early civilizations realized they could pulverize wheat into a rudimentary flour by crushing it with stones. This unlocked its vital nutrients and made it more digestible, leading to more extensive cultivation of the grain. Wheat domestication was a crucial step in early human evolution; it enabled nomads to settle down and fostered the beginnings of farming. Over the next few thousand years, wheat expanded north, west, and east. Spreading as far as Scandinavia, India, and China prompted wheat to

Opposite: Brioche Pecan Sticky Buns (page 305)

adapt to new environments and microclimates. As a result, thousands of varieties with distinct characteristics were born in regions across the globe.

It was most likely the Egyptians who first used wheat to bake bread, around three to five thousand years ago. This process, needless to say, was revolutionary; it made wheat's nutrition and calories portable and accessible. Bread quickly became integral to daily life, making wheat essential to the health and growth of civilizations. Wheat eventually expanded beyond bread, laying the foundation for more specialized baking and pastry traditions.

In early America, wheat production was centered in the Middle Colonies of New York, Pennsylvania, New Jersey, and Delaware. Otherwise known as the "Bread Colonies," these territories were home to German, British, and Spanish migrants who brought wheat seeds from the Old World and built food-secured settlements around them. With the mid-nineteenth-century immigration boom came more varieties from Eastern European countries, like Poland and Ukraine. Wheat eventually became so prolific that over twenty thousand stone mills were in use nationwide, everywhere from New England to the Deep South. During this period wheat and the bread it produced were linked to regional agriculture. Farmers, millers, and bakers lived and worked in close proximity, propelling the growth of small, localized economies.

The Transcontinental Railroad made it possible to ship large quantities of grain across the country, while new processes like roller milling increased flour production exponentially. Industrial farmers soon began engineering wheat to better suit commercial flour production. They bred high-starch wheat yielding vast quantities of white flour. They also developed plants with short stalks and limited roots, diverting the plants' energy into producing large kernels easily harvested by machine. These changes meant fields could maintain more plants within less acreage, maximizing yields and profit.

Today this type of wheat makes up approximately 75 percent of American grain production and two-thirds of American grain consumption. It's grown commercially in forty-two states, with Kansas and North Dakota being the largest producers. The rest of wheat production is centered in the so-called Wheat Belt, a stretch of Middle America running from Canada to Texas.

Until the Industrial Revolution, farmers grew certain wheats for hardiness and flavor, breeding new versions to suit their needs as necessary. These heritage wheats are known as *landrace*. You'd be hard pressed to find many of them now, despite widespread pervasiveness in their heyday. Almost all the wheat we eat today is monolithic—a modern invention made by engineering rather than evolution. Industrialized flour is similar in taste, texture, and baking behavior, no matter when or where it was produced. This uniformity is helpful in the kitchen, ensuring that baked goods turn out the same every time. Function is the primary concern, rather than taste or health. The bran and germ, where key nutrients are stored, are removed, rendering commercial flour nutrient deficient. Furthermore, commercial wheat crops, which no longer resembled the tall, proud stalks grown by our ancestors, require more water, fertilizer, pesticides, herbicides, and fungicides.

Luckily, heritage grains haven't completely disappeared. Growers are rediscovering ancient varieties like einkorn, spelt, and emmer, while others experiment with newer heirloom breeds suited to their environments. On the receiving end, bakers and chefs are capitalizing on the diversity of taste and texture that heirloom wheat offers. Unearthing early varieties and working to make newer ones viable has drastically expanded the world of wheat. Over ten thousand varieties have been identified, a number likely to increase as breeding programs around the world work to develop new seeds.

American growers categorize wheat as belonging in larger groups encompassing many species: hard red winter, soft red winter, hard white, soft white, hard red spring, and durum. *Red* and *white* refer to naturally occurring pigments in the kernel. Red wheat's color ranges from yellowish orange to dark brown, while white wheat can be bone pale, cream-colored, or gray as clay. *Hard* and *soft* refer to the kernel's physical characteristics. It's believed that harder wheats are higher in gluten and protein, but this isn't always true. Winter and spring denote the season in which the variety is commonly planted.

This chapter covers the ancient wheats einkorn, spelt, emmer, Khorasan, and durum, as well as some red and white heirloom varieties I often work with such as Sonora and Öland. Vibrant and aromatic, these freshly ground grains are far more compelling than the usual refined all-purpose flour. Play with them to tap into their tremendous culinary potential, benefit from their higher nutritional value, and encourage farmers and millers to continue to work with them. See the Sourcing section on page 336 for suggestions on where to buy any of the varieties used in this chapter.

How to Purchase and Use

Einkorn

Native to Georgia, Armenia, and Turkey, einkorn is the oldest wheat variety we know. In fact, almost every wheat variety has descended from it. A highly nutritious grain, einkorn is high in protein, iron, thiamine, dietary fiber, B vitamins, and the antioxidant lutein. Einkorn can be purchased as whole wheat berries to be milled at home or as whole-grain flour. I often buy it milled from Grist & Toll (see Sourcing on page 336), located here in California. Store flour in a cool pantry and try to use it within 3 months of purchase. To keep track, I recommend labeling the bag with the date of purchase.

Spelt

Spelt is perhaps the best-known "ancient" wheat. I consider it a gateway for bakers starting to explore ancient grains. It behaves similarly to most wheat flour and performs well in many applications, from sourdough and enriched breads to cakes, cookies, and laminated pastries. Spelt is a good source of fiber, iron, and manganese. I almost always buy spelt flour from my local miller, Grist & Toll, but Bob's Red Mill, Arrowhead Mills, and other companies offer flour and berries that can be purchased in grocery stores or online. Store flour in a cool pantry and try to use it within 3 months of purchase. To keep track, I recommend labeling the bag with the date of purchase. The berries are similar to other wheat berries and can be cooked in similar ways. Their flavor isn't as pronounced as farro, but they have a subtle nutty taste.

Emmer or Farro

Emmer, more popularly known as farro, is an ancient wheat closely related to durum. It originated in the Central Mediterranean, where it's still grown and consumed. It can be found as whole berries or milled into flour. I almost always use whole berries, which I cook and incorporate in salads. It's my favorite grain to use in savory cooking—don't tell rice. With its wholesome flavor and delicious texture, cooked emmer is the ideal base for grain bowls, pilafs, and even risotto. Emmer flour is excellent in egg noodles and makes a hearty, flavorful loaf of bread. Emmer or farro berries can be found in good grocery stores, but their flour is harder to come by. Look for domestically grown emmer; many berries sold in the United States are imported from Italy. Arizona-based Hayden Flour Mills offers both berries and flour on its website.

Khorasan Wheat

Often sold under the brand name Kamut, this variety originated in the ancient province of Khorasan, located in northern Iran and portions of Afghanistan. Despite arriving in the 1950s, Khorasan didn't catch on in the United States until the late seventies, when father-son farming duo Mack and Bob Quinn began growing it in Montana. In 1990, they trademarked it as Kamut. As a condition of this trademark, Kamut can only be grown organically, and farmers can't alter the seed in any way. While the trademark holders surely acted in the grain's best interest, I take issue with the ownership of a common good that results from registering it under a brand name. This has stopped me from in-depth experimentation with Kamut. Regardless, my apprehension shouldn't deter you from favoring this nutritious ancient wheat. The Khorasan kernel is visually striking—large and slender with an amber hue. Khorasan berries are popular among clean-eating advocates and can be used similarly to emmer. They're particularly popular in Italy, a country responsible for about half of its production worldwide. Khorasan flour's high protein content makes it a favorite of many bread bakers. Bob's Red Mill offers both Kho-rasan berries and flour for purchase in grocery stores and on its website. Store flour in a cool pantry and try to use it within 3 months of purchase. To keep track, I recommend labeling the bag with the date of purchase.

Durum

As its Latin name implies, durum is one of the hardest wheats. Its stubborn kernel resists milling, so grinding it into flour is a complex, multi-step process. It's popular among pasta and bread makers for its high protein content. Naturally drought resistant, durum is cultivated in the southwestern United States. The most common durum product is semolina, made by grinding endosperm into a meal, texturally similar to fine cornmeal. In fact, I swap semolina for cornmeal every now and again. They absorb liquid similarly and produce the same results, with durum imparting a more wheaty flavor. Semolina flour is widely available, although whole-grain durum is harder to find. Bob's Red Mill offers semolina flour at most well-stocked grocery stores, and Arizona-based Hayden Flour Mills offers it online. Store flour in a cool pantry and try to use it within 3 months of purchase. To keep track, I recommend labeling the bag with the date of purchase.

Heirloom Red and White Wheats

When it comes to heirloom wheat varieties, it's important to work with whatever your local grain hub has to offer. Part of the challenge, and indeed the reward, is constantly discovering new wheats to bake with. When I travel throughout the United States, and even abroad, I'm often fascinated by wheats I've never even heard of. On my last visit to Chicago, I made bread with stoic Turkey Red, a variety widely grown in the Midwest but uncommon on the West Coast. In Norway, I had my hands full with Dala and Öland wheat. How lucky are we to live in a world where recipes can take on different personalities depending on the local flour? Exploring heirloom wheat is a personal journey, and no two bakers have the same experience.

Although online availability is slowly growing, heirloom wheats are produced by small operations and typically require sourcing at a local level. Certain independent mills commonly omit the name of the specific variety, packing flour under broader labels like "hard red wheat" or "hard white." The flour may come from a single variety or be a blend of several wheats.

Many of us run into heirloom wheats while shopping at the local farmers' market, visiting a mill, or venturing into homesteader shops—all of which are accessible if you live in a large city like Los Angeles. For others, it's imperative to network and find your own sources. A great word of advice from Ellen King, a friend and fellow baker who owns and operates Hewn Bakery in Evanston, Illinois: Don't obsess and fall for a specific wheat. Chances are the supply will run out when the season ends. Keep an open mind and embrace new wheats. Using the same recipes and techniques, you can achieve similar baked goods with slightly different characteristics.

Einkorn Shortbreads

Equipment: 2½-inch round cookie cutter

¼ cup (30 g) confectioners' sugar

¼ cup packed (55 g) dark brown sugar

8 tablespoons (1 stick/115 g) unsalted butter, cut into ½-inch cubes, at room temperature

¾ cup (85 g) einkorn flour

½ cup (70 g) all-purpose flour

1 teaspoon kosher salt

My grandma, Yenita, made butter cookies to package and sell to neighbors nearly every day. For years after her passing, no one in the family attempted to make her cookies, not even me. Perhaps we were afraid they wouldn't be as scrumptious as hers. As an adult, I finally overcame my hesitation and tested every butter cookie recipe I could find, longing to re-create Yenita's cookies. From the classic Danish variety sold in blue tins in supermarkets to sophisticated shortbread made with high-end butter, I'm eternally comparing cookies to those of my childhood. These einkorn shortbreads aren't exactly like Yenita's, but they do come close. Conceptually, both recipes branch from the same family tree, although this one is perhaps a more modern take on my grandma's recipe. They both have the lingering flavor of butter and the melt-in-your-mouth effect that quintessential shortbread is known for. Einkorn is an enticing ancient wheat variety that can transform simple shortbread into complex cookies packed with bold, diverse flavors. It shines when combined with good butter and a pinch of salt. A long bake at a low temperature gives the shortbread a toasty, wheaty flavor. To appreciate einkorn in all its glory, make sure to use whole-grain flour.

1. Place an oven rack in the middle position and preheat the oven to 300°F. Line a baking sheet with parchment paper.

2. In a food processor, pulse the confectioners' sugar and brown sugar for 1 minute. Add the butter and pulse to combine. Add the flours and salt and pulse until the dough just comes together. Turn the dough out onto the work surface and knead into a disk about 6 inches in diameter. Put the disk between two 16-by-12-inch pieces of parchment paper, and with a rolling pin roll the dough from the center out until it is ½ inch thick. Peel off the top sheet of parchment. Using a 2½-inch round cookie cutter, stamp out cookies and transfer them to the prepared baking sheet, spaced 1 inch apart. Using a small heart, star, or clover cookie cutter, stamp out a design in the center of each cookie. Gather the scraps and reroll as you did before to cut a few more cookies.

3. Bake the cookies for 15 minutes. Then rotate the baking sheets and switch their positions in the oven. Bake for another 10 to 15 minutes, until light golden. Rotating and switching the sheets halfway through the baking process will ensure that the cookies bake evenly. Remove from the oven and let cool completely on the baking sheets. Enjoy with a soothing cup of tea. The cookies can be stored in an airtight container at room temperature for up to 3 days.

Semolina Cookies with Fennel Pollen

Equipment: 3½-inch fluted or plain round cookie cutter

8 tablespoons (1 stick/115 g) cold unsalted butter, cut into ½-inch cubes

¾ cup (95 g) confectioners' sugar

1 cup (165 g) fine semolina flour

1 cup (140 g) all-purpose flour

¼ teaspoon kosher salt

3 large egg yolks

½ teaspoon vanilla extract

2 tablespoons granulated sugar

1 teaspoon fennel pollen

Semolina, a granular flour ground from the endosperm of durum wheat, is a common cookie ingredient throughout the Mediterranean, from Italy to the Levant. Whenever I make these cookies, I reminisce about my days as a young pastry cook at Campanile, where my mentor, Nancy Silverton, introduced us to myriad hyper-regional Italian treats.

Semolina gives these simple and understated cookies a pleasantly gritty texture, while fragrant fennel pollen sprinkled on just before baking lends a delicate aniselike flavor. These tiny golden beads are collected by hand from fennel flowers, mostly in Italy and California. You can find fennel pollen in the spice section of well-stocked grocery stores or in specialty spice shops.

The wafer-thin, subtly sweet cookies are a perfect accompaniment to afternoon espresso. Add one to a few scoops of gelato for an Italian-esque dessert or, in the summer, serve alongside a bowl of berries with a dollop of whipped cream. The semolina makes these cookies crisp, so they'll keep for a week in an airtight container at room temperature.

RECIPE CONTINUES

1. In a stand mixer fitted with the paddle attachment, combine the butter, confectioners' sugar, semolina, all-purpose flour, and salt. Mix on low speed until the butter mixture resembles a coarse meal with butter pieces no larger than a pea, about 3 minutes. Add the egg yolks and vanilla and continue mixing until the dough comes together. Transfer the dough to a lightly floured surface and shape into a disk. Wrap in plastic and refrigerate for 30 minutes.

2. Place two oven racks in the middle positions and preheat the oven to 300°F. Line two baking sheets with parchment paper.

3. Place the dough between two 16-by-12-inch sheets of parchment paper. Use a rolling pin to roll the dough from the center out until it is ⅛ inch thick. Peel off the top sheet of parchment. Using a 3½-inch round cookie cutter, stamp out cookies and transfer them to the prepared baking sheets, spaced 1 inch apart. Gather the scraps, reroll just as you did before, and cut out more cookies. Combine the granulated sugar and fennel pollen in a bowl. Brush each cookie lightly with water so the sugar sticks to the cookies and sprinkle the tops of the cookies generously.

4. Bake for 20 minutes. Then rotate the sheets, switch their positions in the oven, and bake for another 10 to 15 minutes, until golden around the edges. Remove from the oven and let the cookies cool completely on the baking sheets. The cookies can be stored in an airtight container at room temperature for up to 1 week.

Spelt Blueberry Muffins

Equipment: Muffin tin

For the spelt streusel

3 tablespoons spelt flour

2 tablespoons granulated sugar

2 teaspoons packed dark brown sugar

Pinch of ground cinnamon

2 tablespoons cold unsalted butter, cut into ½-inch cubes

For the muffin batter

1½ cups (195 g) spelt flour

½ teaspoon baking soda

1 teaspoon baking powder

¼ teaspoon ground cinnamon

¼ teaspoon kosher salt

⅔ cup packed (150 g) dark brown sugar

⅓ cup (80 ml) vegetable oil

1 large egg

⅓ cup (80 ml) buttermilk

Finely grated zest of 1 lemon

½ cup (85 g) frozen blueberries (see headnote)

It's time to give the classic blueberry muffin a makeover, swapping out all the refined white flour for whole-grain spelt. If you haven't baked with spelt before, you're in for a pleasant surprise. It performs similarly to wheat flour and can be used as a one-to-one substitute in most recipes, making it easy to improvise and update your tried-and-true favorites. Spelt will introduce sweet and nutty notes to your recipes along with an impressive list of health benefits including greater circulation, stronger bones, improved immune system, lower bad-cholesterol levels, and better digestive functions.

We've baked a few dozen of these streusel-topped blueberry muffins every morning since the bakery opened. The recipe calls for frozen blueberries, which prevents the fruit from getting smashed while mixing the batter, but you can certainly use fresh berries—just be sure to fold in the fruit gently. Don't omit the spelt streusel topping. It adds delicious crunch to your muffins and helps keep them moist longer.

RECIPE CONTINUES

1. Place an oven rack in the middle position and preheat the oven to 350°F.

2. For the streusel, combine the spelt flour, sugars, and cinnamon in a medium bowl. Toss the cold butter cubes in the dry ingredients. Quickly cut the butter into the dry ingredients by pinching the butter cubes with your fingertips until the mixture resembles a coarse meal with pieces the size of a pea. Refrigerate the streusel until ready to use.

3. For the muffins, sift the spelt flour, baking soda, baking powder, cinnamon, and salt into a small bowl. Make a well in the center with your hands. Whisk the brown sugar, oil, egg, buttermilk, and lemon zest together in a separate bowl. Pour the liquid mixture into the well in the dry ingredients. Whisk to combine. Using a rubber spatula, gently fold in the blueberries.

4. Evenly distribute the muffin batter into 8 muffin cups, filling each cup with about ¼ cup (60 ml) of batter. Top each muffin with approximately 1 tablespoon of streusel. Bake for 12 minutes. Then rotate the tin and bake for 12 minutes more, until the muffins turn a rich golden brown and a toothpick inserted in the center of a muffin comes out clean. Rotating the tin halfway through the baking process will ensure that the muffins bake evenly. Let the muffins cool in the tin for at least 20 minutes before transferring them to a wire rack to cool completely. The muffins will keep in an airtight container at room temperature for 2 days.

Sonora Wheat Pie Dough

MAKES ENOUGH DOUGH FOR TWO 9-INCH PIE CRUSTS,
1 DOUBLE-CRUST PIE, OR 8 EMPANADAS

Equipment: 9-inch glass pie pan; dried beans or pie weights if you're making piecrusts

1¾ cups (245 g) Sonora wheat flour, plus extra for rolling

1 tablespoon granulated sugar

½ teaspoon kosher salt

12 tablespoons (1½ sticks/170 g) cold unsalted butter, cut into ½-inch cubes

¾ cup (170 g) cold cream cheese, cut into ½-inch cubes

¼ cup (60 ml) ice water

One fall morning, when I was the pastry chef at a small restaurant called Cooks County, I entered the pastry kitchen determined to develop a pie-crust I could get behind. Pie season was quickly approaching, and I had grown tired of the pie dough I had used for years. It was flaky and functional but not particularly interesting. As a starting point, I decided to use the cream cheese dough I had relied on many times before for tarts, quiches, and hand pies. When Nan Kohler, miller at Grist & Toll, gave me a bag of finely milled Sonora flour, I knew I'd feature it in the dough. After a few tweaks, this recipe came about.

Sonora is a soft heirloom wheat with a gorgeous creamy color and low gluten percentage, making it perfect for tender, flaky crusts. This delicious piecrust is easy to put together, serving me well every Thanksgiving when we sell hundreds of autumnal pies, including the Sorghum Pecan Pie on page 261. But in late summer, when I'm just starting to get in the mood for fall, I love making the Grapple Pie on page 291. It's also my favorite dough to make hand pies or empanadas such as the Sweet Corn Empanadas on page 293.

1. Combine the flour, sugar, and salt in a medium bowl. Toss the cold butter cubes and cream cheese cubes in the flour. Quickly cut the butter and cream cheese cubes into the dry ingredients by pinching the cubes with your fingertips until the mixture resembles a coarse meal with crumbs the size of hazelnuts. Make a well in the center and pour in the ice water. Mix gently with your hands until a raggedy dough forms;

don't worry if bits of butter or cream cheese are still visible. Transfer to a lightly floured surface and knead briefly into a ball. Divide the dough ball in half, shape each half into a disk, and wrap tightly with plastic. Refrigerate for at least 30 minutes and up to 2 days. If you plan to make a single piecrust with the dough, wrap the remaining disk tightly in plastic and store in the freezer for up to 1 month.

2. To shape a single piecrust, follow the instructions below. To shape the double-crust Grapple Pie, skip to page 292, step 4. To make the Sweet Corn Empanadas, skip to page 294, step 4.

3. Remove one disk from the refrigerator and roll out the dough on a lightly floured surface, forming a round about 11 inches in diameter. Pick up the dough by rolling it onto the rolling pin and lay it into the pie pan. Gently press the dough into the bottom of the pan, leaving a lip on the edge. Trim any excess dough with kitchen scissors, leaving 1 inch of dough hanging from the edge of the pie pan. Gather the dough to form a border along the edge of the pan. Crimp the border by pinching the dough with your fingertips, forming small triangles along the edge. Refrigerate the shaped piecrust for 20 minutes—chilling prevents the dough from shrinking.

4. Place an oven rack in the middle position and preheat the oven to 350°F. Cut a 12-inch parchment paper circle.

5. Place the pie pan on a baking sheet. Coat the pie pan lightly with nonstick spray and line it with the parchment. Fill it three-quarters of the way with dried beans or pie weights. Bake for 20 minutes. Then rotate the baking sheet and bake for 20 to 25 minutes more. Rotating the baking sheet halfway through the baking process will ensure that the pie shell bakes evenly. To check whether the shell is ready, carefully lift a section of the parchment and see if the bottom is golden. Let cool for at least 1 hour before removing the parchment paper and pie weights. Baking your piecrust before the filling goes in is known as "blind baking," and it's a crucial step in making a successful single-crust pie. The piecrust in now ready to use in your favorite pie recipe.

Crimp the border by pinching the dough with your fingertips, forming small consecutive triangles.

RECIPE CONTINUES

Grapple Pie

Equipment: 9-inch glass pie pan

2 pounds (910 g) firm apples (such as Spitzenburg, Fuji, Honeycrisp, or Braeburn), peeled, cored, and cut into ¼-inch wedges

3 cups (580 g) whole seedless purple grapes (such as Thomcord, Red Flame, or Autumn Royal), stemmed

⅓ cup (65 g) granulated sugar, plus extra for sprinkling

⅓ cup packed (70 g) dark brown sugar

6 tablespoons (¾ stick/85 g) unsalted butter, melted

¼ teaspoon kosher salt

1 tablespoon cornstarch

¼ cup (60 ml) water

1 recipe Sonora Wheat Pie Dough (page 288)

All-purpose flour for dusting

1 large egg, beaten

Before we get started, let's have a word about apples. Is there a more mythical fruit? From tales about their ruby-red seductiveness to belief in their palliative properties, from Johnny Appleseed's orchards to their purported role in bringing us an understanding of gravity, apples hold an important place in our psyche.

I found the apple of my dreams at an apple festival while living in Portland, Oregon. In the midst of a dizzying assortment of apples, I fell hard for Spitzenburgs, a firm, medium-size, delicious-to-eat and delicious-to-cook variety. They were discovered in the late 1700s near Esopus, New York. Lucky for me, they also grow in California, and it's still the variety I seek for the Thanksgiving pies we bake at Friends & Family every year. But there are many other heirloom varieties I favor, among them Pink Lady, Ashmead's Kernel, Arkansas Black, Braeburn, Honey Crisp, Cox, Winesap, and Fuji. You could use any of these to make my Grapple Pie or rely on your regional favorite.

When it comes to choosing the right grape, make sure to buy seedless purple grapes, which are more acidic than their green counterparts. My favorite variety for this pie is Thomcord, a hybrid of Concord and Thompson grapes. Autumn Royal (a long, slender, and meaty variety) and Red Flame (a sweet and juicy relative of Thompson grapes) are also great for baking.

You could make this pie as soon as the temperatures start to drop. Or, if you don't mind breaking with tradition, bake it for Thanksgiving dinner.

RECIPE CONTINUES

1. Place an oven rack in the middle position and preheat the oven to 350°F.

2. Combine the apples, grapes, sugars, melted butter, and salt in a large bowl. In a small bowl, stir the cornstarch with the water until there are no lumps. Add the cornstarch slurry to the fruit mixture and mix well. Transfer to a large roasting pan. Roast for 15 minutes, stir the filling with a wooden spoon, and roast for another 15 minutes. Let cool completely to room temperature. Cooking the fruits partially prior to building the pie will diminish the chances of having a soupy filling and a soggy bottom, while preventing the top crust from sinking in the middle.

3. Place an oven rack in the middle position and preheat the oven to 350°F.

4. Working with one disk at a time, roll out the dough on a lightly floured surface, forming a round about 11 inches in diameter. Pick up one of the rounds by rolling it onto the rolling pin and lay it in the pie pan. Gently press the dough into the bottom of the pan, leaving a lip on the edge. Carefully fill the pie pan with grapple filling, trying to form a mound in the center. Pick up the other dough round and lay it on top of the filling. Trim any excess dough with kitchen scissors, leaving 1 inch of dough hanging from the edge of the pie pan. Gather the dough to form a border along the edge of the pan. Crimp the top and bottom crusts together around the edge by pinching the dough with your fingertips, forming triangles along the edge, or gently pressing with a fork. With a paring knife, cut three 2-inch slits in the top crust to let steam escape while baking. Brush the top crust with the beaten egg and sprinkle generously with granulated sugar. Place the pie pan on a rimmed baking sheet to catch any drips and bake for 90 minutes, until the top crust is a rich golden brown and the filling starts to bubble through the slits. Let cool for at least 1 hour before serving. The pie will keep in an airtight container at room temperature for 2 days.

Sweet Corn Empanadas

MAKES 8 EMPANADAS

1 teaspoon cumin seeds

½ cup (120 ml) extra virgin olive oil

½ cup chopped red onion

½ cup diced red bell pepper

½ cup chopped cilantro

1 teaspoon ground turmeric

2 cups fresh corn kernels (from about 3 ears)

1½ teaspoons kosher salt

¼ teaspoon cayenne pepper

1 recipe Sonora Wheat Pie Dough (page 288)

All-purpose flour for dusting

1 egg, beaten

Empanadas or hand pies are a broad category that includes different kinds of sweet and savory fillings from all over Latin America and the Caribbean, where every country has its own take. In Puerto Rico, empanadas stuffed with picadillo (minced meat sautéed with vegetables and raisins) are large in size and are eaten for lunch or dinner. In Guatemala, black bean empanadas are made with fresh masa and fried until crispy. In Argentina, fried and baked empanadas are almost a religion and are filled with an array of ingredients including ham and cheese, stewed chicken, and creamed spinach. In Costa Rica, a buttery pastry crust is used to make sweet baked empanadas filled with pineapple or guava jam to be served with afternoon coffee, and around Easter, empanadas de chiverre or candied squash are enjoyed all week long. I first made these empanadas to add a savory pastry to our selection at Friends & Family. People love to eat them at room temperature on the go, with their hands. But I think they're even more delicious while they're still warm. We prepare them with corn in summer, but in the winter and fall, we use russet potatoes that have been peeled and cut into ½-inch cubes. You could try either version depending on the season.

1. Toast the cumin seeds in a skillet over medium-low heat until they begin releasing their aroma; this will be quick, about 1 minute. Make sure to swirl the pan nonstop, which will prevent them from burning. Let the seeds cool before pounding them with a mortar and pestle or spice grinder.

RECIPE CONTINUES

2. Heat the olive oil in a large sauté pan over medium-high heat. Sauté the onion, bell pepper, and cilantro, stirring occasionally, until the vegetables are translucent, 3 to 4 minutes. Stir in the turmeric and toasted cumin and then the corn kernels. Sauté for 2 more minutes, until the corn has softened. Season with salt and cayenne and transfer to a plate. Let the corn filling cool completely.

3. Place an oven rack in the middle position and preheat the oven to 375°F. Line a baking sheet with parchment paper.

4. Roll out the dough on a lightly floured surface into a 24-by-12-inch rectangle about ¼ inch thick. Use a 6-inch plate as a guide to trace and cut out six circles with a paring knife. Gather the scraps, roll them out, and cut two more circles, dusting the surface with more flour as needed. Brush the edges of the circles lightly with water. Put 3 to 4 tablespoons of filling in the center of each dough circle and fold in half to form a half-moon, pressing gently with a fork around the edges to seal. Transfer the shaped empanadas to the prepared baking sheet, spaced at least 2 inches apart. Using a paring knife, cut three ½-inch slits on top of each empanada. The slits are decorative, but also act as vents to release steam and prevent the empanadas from opening in the oven. Brush with the beaten egg and bake for 20 minutes. Rotate the baking sheet and bake for 20 minutes more, until the empanadas are golden. Rotating the sheet halfway through the baking process will ensure that the empanadas bake evenly. Remove from the oven. Serve warm or at room temperature. The empanadas will keep in an airtight container in the refrigerator for up to 2 days. Reheat in a preheated 350°F oven for 5 minutes or until warm all the way through.

Spretzels

Equipment: nonstick silicone baking mat

1 teaspoon instant yeast

¾ cup (180 ml) lukewarm (98° to 105°F) water

1 cup (130 g) spelt flour

1 cup (140 g) all-purpose flour, plus extra for dusting

2 tablespoons granulated sugar

1½ teaspoons kosher salt

One 12-ounce (350 ml) bottle pilsner or blond ale (optional)

¼ cup (70 g) baking soda

Coarse sea salt such as Maldon or fleur de sel

Pretzels are one of my favorite snacks. When I started to make my own, I settled on a combination of spelt and wheat flour that benefited from the soft texture and elegant flavor of spelt and relied on the strength of wheat. And with that, the spelt pretzel, or spretzel, was born.

Spelt is a perfect choice for several reasons: It's high in protein and fiber, easy to grow organically sans pesticides, and tastes great. Besides adding earthy and nutty undertones, spelt imparts the rich mahogany hue we've come to expect in a pretzel, without requiring lye, the substance that gives commercially produced pretzels their traditional dark brown color (but is also corrosive and dangerous if it comes in contact with the skin and eyes). I poach my spretzels in an alternative alkaline solution made with baking soda. Many recipes suggest you simply brush pretzels with alkaline solution, but for me, a pretzel is not a pretzel—nor a spretzel a spretzel—without poaching, which gives them their chewy, smooth exterior. For additional oomph and an authentic German kick, add beer to your poaching liquid. I recommend baking the spretzels on a baking sheet lined with a nonstick silicone mat. Alternatively, you can brush a baking sheet generously with vegetable oil. Don't line the sheet with parchment paper—because the spretzels will be damp after poaching and get stuck on the paper.

Try making spretzels for a movie night at home. From start to finish, they take 3 hours to make, so begin the process early enough to have them come out of the oven right before the opening credits. Have ready some cold beer and a side of mustard.

RECIPE CONTINUES

1. Sprinkle the yeast over the lukewarm water in a small bowl. Stir with a spoon to dissolve and let activate for 5 minutes.

2. Combine the flours, sugar, and salt in a bowl. Add the dissolved yeast mixture and mix by hand until a soft dough forms. Transfer the dough to a floured surface and knead into a tight ball. Place the dough in a bowl lightly coated with nonstick spray—the bowl should be large enough for the dough to double in size. Cover with a clean kitchen towel or plastic wrap and let rise in a warm place for 1 to 1½ hours, until the dough has doubled in size.

3. Line a baking sheet with a nonstick silicone baking mat coated lightly with nonstick spray. Alternatively, you can brush a baking sheet generously with vegetable oil.

4. Transfer the risen dough to a lightly floured work surface and divide into six pieces, about 2¾ ounces (80 g) each. Roll each piece into a ball, dusting with extra flour if necessary, and let them rest on the kitchen counter for 20 minutes. This waiting period allows the gluten to relax, which in turn makes shaping the pretzels much easier.

5. Roll each ball into a snake 20 inches long. Working with one snake at a time, shape a pretzel: form a loop, twist the two ends together once, and fold the twisted ends back toward the middle of the loop to form a classic pretzel shape. Put the shaped pretzels on the prepared baking sheet and proof uncovered for 30 minutes, or until they start looking puffy and soft to the touch.

6. Place an oven rack in the middle position and preheat the oven to 400°F.

7. Prepare the alkaline solution: Bring 2 quarts (2 liters) of water (or 1¾ quarts/liters of water plus one bottle of beer) to a simmer in a large nonreactive pot. Very slowly and carefully, add the baking soda—it will cause the liquid to bubble furiously, so add it gradually and make sure you're using a very large pot to prevent spills. Working in batches, use both hands to pick the proofed spretzels one by one off the sheet and drop them in the pot face side down. Poach the spretzels for 30 seconds on each side (use a slotted spoon to flip them gently in the simmering water) and return one by one to the baking sheet. One side of the spretzels will be prettier than the other—normally the side with the twist—so make sure the prettier side is looking up. Before baking, garnish each spretzel with coarse salt somewhat generously . . . be careful, though; salt is salt after all. You could also garnish with the everything topping on page 215.

8. Bake for 10 minutes, then rotate the sheet and bake for 5 to 10 minutes more, until the spretzels are a rich golden brown. Rotating the sheet halfway through the baking process will ensure that the spretzels bake evenly. Let cool for 10 minutes on the baking sheet. Use an offset spatula to remove them from the sheet. Enjoy while still warm or at room temperature.

Hot Cross Buns with Marzipan Crosses

For the dough

½ cup (70 g) dried black currants

1 cup plus 2 tablespoons (270 ml) whole milk

1¼ teaspoons instant yeast

2 cups (280 g) all-purpose flour

1½ cups (195 g) Sonora wheat flour or similar soft white wheat

¼ cup (50 g) sugar

1½ teaspoons kosher salt

¾ teaspoon ground cinnamon

¼ teaspoon ground allspice

1 teaspoon aniseed

1 large egg, plus 1 egg, beaten, for brushing

1 large egg yolk

6 tablespoons (¾ stick/85 g) unsalted butter, at room temperature

1 tablespoon chopped Candied Kumquats (page 47) or other citrus zest

For the crosses

4 ounces (110 g) marzipan or almond paste

For the syrup

½ cup (100 g) sugar

½ cup (120 ml) water

2 tablespoons dark rum such as Myers's

2 tablespoons unsalted butter

Hot cross buns hail from England, where similar versions have been made since the Middle Ages. As their name indicates, they were meant to be eaten warm, although that practice was abandoned long ago. The buns are made from a lightly spiced, enriched, and yeasted dough, speckled with raisins or currants. They're baked close to one another, so they touch while rising, and have tops marked with an icing cross, symbolizing the crucifixion. At one point, selling them off season was banned by royal decree. They're wildly popular in the United Kingdom, Canada, Australia, and New Zealand. In recent years, they've gained popularity in the United States, where we eat them on Easter Sunday rather than Good Friday, as is done elsewhere.

Purists take note: I've broken from tradition and made a few alterations. I still add spices and currants to the dough, but also mix in some candied citrus (preferably kumquats, which are in season around Easter). As it's traditionally done, I brush the baked buns with a syrup perfumed with a splash of dark rum—this makes them shiny and accentuates the spice flavor. The most radical departure concerns the crosses. Instead of piping them with icing, I roll ropes of marzipan and use them to create a cross on top. The marzipan caramelizes in the oven and adds a festive flavor to my unorthodox hot cross buns. You can always skip the adornment and just make the tasty buns. I usually bake lots of these for Easter brunch. Luckily, the recipe is broken down over 2 days: make the dough on day one and leave shaping and baking for day two. That way you won't have to wake up at an unreasonable hour on Easter morning.

RECIPE CONTINUES

1. The buns stick together as they rise.

2. Brush the tops of the buns with the beaten egg.

3. Place a marzipan cross on top of each bun, pressing gently so it sticks to the bun.

4. Gently brush the baked buns with the warm syrup, making sure to coat both buns and crosses.

1. Soak the black currants in cold water for 10 minutes. Drain and set aside.

2. Warm the milk in a small saucepan until lukewarm (between 98° and 105°F), transfer to the bowl of a stand mixer, and sprinkle the yeast on top. Stir with a spoon to dissolve and let activate for 5 minutes.

3. Fit the stand mixer with the dough hook attachment and combine the dissolved yeast mixture with the flours, sugar, salt, spices, egg, egg yolk, and butter on low speed for about 2 minutes, until the ingredients come together, stopping to scrape the sides of the bowl with a rubber spatula if necessary. Increase the speed to medium and mix for 2 minutes to develop the dough. Switch to the paddle attachment, add the candied kumquats and the drained currants, and mix for 1 more minute on medium speed, until the dough looks smooth and uniform. Transfer the dough to a floured surface and knead briefly into a ball. Lightly coat a medium bowl with nonstick spray and place the dough in it. Cover with a clean kitchen towel or plastic wrap and let the dough rise at room temperature for 1½ to 2 hours, until doubled in size. Punch the risen dough ball in the middle to degas it. Cover with plastic wrap and refrigerate overnight.

4. The next morning, remove the dough from the refrigerator and let it sit at room temperature for 30 minutes.

5. Line a baking sheet with parchment paper.

6. Transfer the dough to a lightly floured surface. Divide the dough into twelve equal portions (about 75 g each) and roll each one into a ball. Arrange the buns on the prepared sheet in three rows of four buns each, spaced ¾ inch apart. They will stick to one another as they rise. Cover the buns with a clean kitchen towel and let them rise again at room temperature for 1½ to 2 hours, until puffy and soft to the touch or until they no longer bounce back when you gently press with a moistened index finger.

7. While the buns are rising, make the marzipan crosses. Divide the almond paste into six portions and roll each portion into a thin 12-inch-long rope. Cut each rope into four 3-inch-long pieces. Form 12 crosses by placing one 3-inch piece across another. Place the crosses on a baking sheet and cover with a clean kitchen towel to prevent them from drying out.

8. Place an oven rack in the middle position and preheat the oven to 350°F.

9. Brush the tops of the buns with the beaten egg and place a marzipan cross on top of each bun, pressing gently so it sticks to the bun. Bake for 10 minutes. Then rotate the baking sheet and bake for another 12 to 15 minutes, until the buns are golden. Rotating the pan halfway through the baking process will ensure that the buns bake evenly. Remove the buns from the oven and let them cool.

10. To make the syrup, combine the sugar and water in a small saucepan and bring to a boil over medium-high heat. Reduce the heat and simmer for 1 minute. Remove from the heat, add the rum and butter, and whisk to emulsify. Gently brush the baked buns with the warm syrup, making sure to coat both buns and crosses. Serve once the buns are completely cool.

Cardamom Buns

For the dough

1 teaspoon instant yeast

¾ cup (180 ml) lukewarm (98° to 105°F) water

2 cups (280 g) all-purpose flour, plus extra for dusting

1½ cups (195 g) Öland wheat or spelt flour

1 teaspoon kosher salt

¼ cup (50 g) sugar

½ teaspoon cardamom seeds, crushed, or 1 teaspoon ground cardamom

½ cup (120 ml) whole milk

2 tablespoons honey

6 tablespoons (¾ stick/85 g) unsalted butter, at room temperature

For the cardamom filling

8 tablespoons (1 stick/115 g) unsalted butter, at room temperature

½ cup packed (105 g) dark brown sugar

1 teaspoon cardamom seeds, crushed, or 2 teaspoons ground cardamom

1½ teaspoons ground cinnamon

½ teaspoon kosher salt

For decorating

¼ cup (50 g) sugar

½ teaspoon cardamom seeds, crushed, or 1 teaspoon ground cardamom

1 large egg, beaten

Swedish pearl sugar (optional; see page 160)

A few years ago I took a short midwinter trip to Copenhagen, eager to try every Danish rye bread I could get my hands on. When it was time to leave, a friend offered me a ride to the airport and insisted we stop by his new favorite bakery, Juno. Afraid of missing my early-morning flight, I hurriedly bought yet another loaf of rye and a knot-looking bundle, topped with a sprinkle of sugar and what appeared to be cardamom seeds. After rushing through airport security and finding my seat on the plane, I unearthed my purchase.

If there was ever a moment when time stood still, skies cleared, and seas parted, this was it. Rather than devour the pastry in a few bites, I carefully undid the strips of tender dough, seasoned generously with aromatic cardamom. The edges were toasty and chewy, the center was soft and yielding, and the smell was heady and intoxicating. I returned to the United States ready to re-create this precious concoction.

I soon learned that the buns, known as *karde-mummabullar*, are more Swedish than Danish. They've become somewhat of a trendy item in bakeries all over Scandinavia. After many trials not quite hitting Juno's high mark, I networked with Erica Landin-Löfving, a Swedish American food writer and baker in her own right, who kindly developed a kardemummabullar recipe for this book.

To acknowledge their Nordic roots, I like making these buns with Öland flour. Öland (spelled *Øland* in Danish and Norwegian) is an ancient wheat named after its Swedish island of origin. It nearly disappeared in the 1960s, but enthusiastic seed savers reintroduced it, and it's now one of the most popular heirloom wheats in Nordic cuisine. Naturally high in protein, Öland wheat is ideal for making everything from lean sourdoughs to enriched brioche-style doughs, like the one used to make kardemummabullar. It can be purchased online through Maine Grains (see Sourcing on page 336), but you can use another hard white or hard red wheat varietal that's accessible in your area. On occasion I've made this recipe with spelt flour and achieved great results. Erica suggests using cardamom seeds from green cardamom pods, extracted by hand and crushed with a mortar and pestle. Removing the seeds from the pods can be laborious, but I promise it's well worth it. If you must skip this step, ground cardamom substitution quantities are conveniently included in the recipe. You could seek desiccated cardamom—cardamom seeds already removed from the pods—which is sometimes available in the spice section of well-stocked grocery stores or online.

After the Sonora Wheat Croissants on page 313 and the Pain d'Amande on page 309, this project is one of this book's most ambitious. Read the recipe carefully and don't rush. The dough should rest in the fridge overnight, so you'll need at least 2 days. Believe me when I say you won't regret a single minute invested in these buns.

1. For the dough, sprinkle the yeast over the lukewarm water in a small bowl. Stir with a spoon to dissolve and let activate for 5 minutes.

2. Sift the flours into a bowl.

3. In a stand mixer fitted with the dough hook attachment, combine half of the sifted flours with the salt, sugar, and cardamom. Add the dissolved yeast, milk, and honey, and mix on low speed until a batter forms, about 2 minutes, stopping to scrape the sides of the bowl with a rubber spatula if necessary. Gradually add the remaining flour and continue mixing until a dough forms, about 2 minutes. Add the butter, increase the speed to medium, and continue mixing just to incorporate, about 2 more minutes. Transfer the dough to a lightly floured surface and knead into a ball. Lightly coat a medium bowl with nonstick spray and place the dough in it. Cover with a clean kitchen towel or plastic wrap and let rest in the refrigerator overnight, where it will rise at a slower rate, thus developing a more complex fermented flavor.

4. The next day, remove the dough from the refrigerator and let it rest for 1 hour at room temperature.

5. In the meantime, make the cardamom filling. In a stand mixer with the paddle attachment, cream the butter and brown sugar until a paste forms. Add the cardamom, cinnamon, and salt and mix until well combined.

RECIPE CONTINUES

1. Spread the filling evenly on top of the dough with an offset spatula.

2. Fold the dough in thirds, as you would a letter.

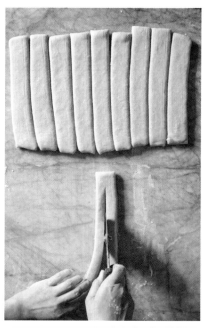

3. Using a knife or pastry cutter, cut ten strips 1½ inches wide. Then cut each strip in half lengthwise, leaving the top end uncut by about 1 inch.

4. Spread the strip apart. Coil the strip around itself into a tight wheel.

5. Drape the loose end over the middle of the bun.

6. Tuck the end underneath the center of the coil.

6. Line two rimmed baking sheets with parchment paper and coat each lightly with nonstick spray.

7. Transfer the dough to a lightly floured surface. Using a rolling pin, roll the dough into an 18-by-12-inch rectangle. Spread the filling evenly on top of the dough with an offset spatula. Fold the dough in thirds, as you would a letter. You should end up with a 12-by-6-inch rectangle. Dust your work surface with additional flour if needed and roll the folded dough into a 10-by-15-inch rectangle. Using a knife or pastry cutter, cut ten strips 1½ inches wide. Then cut each strip in half lengthwise, leaving the top end uncut by about 1 inch. Each strip should resemble a pair of pants with two separate legs that are connected at the top. Put the strips on a baking sheet, cover with plastic wrap, and refrigerate for 30 minutes—the chilled strips will be much easier to shape. Working with one strip at a time, spread the legs apart—now you have a long strip, about 20 inches in length. Coil the strip around itself into a tight wheel, drape the loose end over the middle of the bun, and tuck the end underneath the center of the coil. Place the ten formed buns on the prepared baking sheets at least 3 inches apart. Let them rise, covered with plastic wrap or a clean towel, for 1½ to 2 hours, until puffy and soft to the touch or until they no longer bounce back when you press gently with a moistened index finger.

8. Place an oven rack in the middle position and preheat the oven to 375°F.

9. Prepare the decorating sugar by mixing the granulated sugar with the cardamom. Brush the buns with the beaten egg and sprinkle them generously with the cardamom-sugar mix. Finish with Swedish pearl sugar, if using. Bake one sheet at a time for 15 minutes. Then rotate the tray and bake for another 5 minutes or until golden on the outside. Baking one sheet at a time will help the buns bake more evenly and retain their shape better. Resist the temptation to leave them in the oven longer or they could dry out. These could be served a few hours after baking, but my personal preference is to attack them minutes after they come out of the oven. Cardamom buns should always be eaten the day they're baked, but if you have leftovers, store them in an airtight container and reheat in a toaster oven the next day—they won't be as soft, but the rich cardamom flavor will still shine through.

Brioche Pecan Sticky Buns

Equipment: 9-inch square cake pan

For the brioche dough

1 teaspoon instant yeast

1 cup (120 ml) lukewarm (98° to 105°F) water

3 cups (475 g) hard white wheat flour

2 tablespoons granulated sugar

1 tablespoon kosher salt

3 large eggs

1 cup (2 sticks/225 g) unsalted butter, at room temperature

All-purpose flour for dusting

For the sticky caramel

½ cup (1 stick/115 g) unsalted butter

½ vanilla bean

1 cup packed (215 g) dark brown sugar

½ cup (120 ml) heavy cream

For the cinnamon filling

1 cup (110 g) pecan halves

8 tablespoons (1 stick/115 g) unsalted butter

½ cup packed (112 g) dark brown sugar

1½ teaspoons ground cinnamon

⅛ teaspoon freshly grated nutmeg

¼ teaspoon kosher salt

This French-style butter-enriched dough is sometimes considered the measuring stick by which a baker is ranked. It's traditionally prepared with high-gluten bread flour, but whole-grain flours can also yield excellent results. With their naturally high fiber content, whole grains actually perform quite well in buttery doughs such as this one, creating a fine-crumb bread with a strong structure. For aesthetic reasons I prefer making brioche with hard white varietals like Prairie Gold or Starr, but the recipe will work just as well with hard red wheat flours and even einkorn or spelt.

Technique-wise, there are a few important factors to consider. First, always use room-temperature butter—not softened to the point of becoming oily, but soft enough that you can easily leave an indentation with your finger. Second, always cool your dough before shaping. Most brioche recipes require overnight refrigeration, and for good reason. High fat content makes the dough difficult to handle at room temperature. Plan on giving your dough at least 2 hours in the refrigerator, or even better, chill it overnight.

Brioche is baked in many traditional shapes. Perhaps the most well known is *brioche à tête*, a bun with a smaller bun, or head, on top, baked in round fluted molds. In the United States, brioche is used for anything from doughnuts to all-American burger buns. My all-around favorite pastry to make with brioche is pecan sticky buns. They're utterly delicious, fun to assemble, and always well received. If you aren't a caramel fiend like me, just let them be cinnamon rolls and skip the sticky caramel (see the variation). But in my opinion, the sticky kind are best.

RECIPE CONTINUES

The easiest way to prepare the sticky buns is breaking down the process over 2 days, making the brioche the day before and assembling and baking the next day. For more delicate buns I recommend using the sticky caramel in two stages: put half in the pan and reserve the other half to pour on top when the buns come out of the oven. Doing so will prevent the exterior of the buns from becoming overly sticky.

1. For the brioche dough, sprinkle the yeast over the lukewarm water in a small bowl. Stir with a spoon to dissolve and let activate for 5 minutes.

2. In a stand mixer fitted with the dough hook attachment, combine the flour with the granulated sugar, salt, eggs, and dissolved yeast. Mix on low speed for 2 minutes or until a rough dough forms. Add half of the butter and mix on medium speed for 2 minutes. And the remaining butter and mix until well combined, about 2 minutes, stopping to scrape the sides of the bowl with a rubber spatula if necessary. Increase the speed to high and mix for 2 minutes to develop the gluten structure further.

3. Transfer the dough to a generously floured surface and knead into a ball. Lightly coat a medium bowl with nonstick spray and place the dough in it. Cover with plastic wrap and let it rise for 1½ to 2 hours, until doubled in size. Refrigerate for 2 hours or, even better, overnight.

4. The next day, remove the dough from the refrigerator and let it sit at room temperature for 1 hour. In the meantime, prepare the sticky caramel and cinnamon filling.

5. Place an oven rack in the middle position and preheat the oven to 350°F. Lightly coat the pan with nonstick spray.

6. To make the sticky caramel, melt the butter in a small saucepan over low heat. Split the vanilla bean lengthwise with a paring knife, scrape out the pulp with the back of the knife, and add both pulp and pod to the saucepan. Add the brown sugar and cream and bring the mixture to a boil while stirring with a wooden spoon. Simmer for 1 minute, turn off the heat, and carefully remove the vanilla bean with kitchen tongs or a spoon. Immediately pour half of the caramel into the prepared pan. Let the caramel cool completely. Reserve the other half for later.

7. For the cinnamon filling, scatter the pecans on a baking sheet and toast in the oven for 8 to 10 minutes, until a nut cut in half is golden inside. Let the pecans cool. Chop the toasted pecans into pieces no larger than a peanut.

8. In the stand mixer fitted with the paddle attachment, cream the butter and brown sugar until they form a paste. Add the cinnamon, nutmeg, and salt and mix until well combined. Add half of the pecans and mix on low speed until they're well distributed in the filling. Save the remaining pecans for later.

9. When it's ready, roll the chilled brioche into a 13-by-10-inch rectangle on a lightly floured surface. Spread the filling evenly over the brioche all the way to the edges with an offset spatula. Using both hands, roll the dough away from you to form a log (as you would a jelly roll). Rock the cylinder back and forth to tighten and elongate the log a bit. The log should now be

about 14 inches long and 2 inches thick. Using a chef's knife, trim ¼ inch off the ends and cut the log into 1½-inch-wide slices. Arrange the slices, cinnamon swirl facing up, atop the cooled sticky caramel in the pan, spaced 1 inch apart. Cover loosely with plastic wrap or a clean kitchen towel and proof at warm room temperature until the buns are puffy and soft to the touch, or until they no longer bounce back when you gently press with a moistened index finger, about 1 hour.

10. Place the pan of proofed buns on a rimmed baking sheet covered with aluminum foil to catch any drips—the foil will make cleaning up a lot easier. Bake for 20 minutes at 350°F. Then rotate the baking sheet and bake for another 20 minutes, until the buns are golden on top and the sticky caramel is bubbly. Let the sticky buns rest for 10 minutes. Using oven mitts, carefully invert the pan over a plate. Heat up the reserved sticky caramel in a small saucepan over low heat, stir in the reserved pecans, and immediately pour over the baked sticky buns. Let cool completely or serve while slightly warm. Leftovers will keep in an airtight container at room temperature for another day.

Variation

Cinnamon Buns

To make cinnamon buns, skip the sticky caramel. Fill the brioche with the cinnamon filling (with or without pecans) and shape the same way; just make sure to line the cake pan with parchment paper for easy release. Then follow the same instructions for proofing and baking.

Pain d'Amande

Equipment: 9-inch springform pan

For the dough

2 teaspoons instant yeast

½ cup (120 ml) lukewarm (98° to 105°F) water

1 cup (130 g) spelt flour

1 cup (135 g) bread flour, plus extra for dusting

2 tablespoons sugar

2 teaspoons kosher salt

1 teaspoon ground cardamom

1 large egg

1 tablespoon unsalted butter, at room temperature

For the butter block

1 cup (2 sticks/225 g) cold unsalted butter

For the almond cream

½ cup (80 g) whole raw almonds

¼ cup (50 g) sugar

6 tablespoons (¾ stick/85 g) unsalted butter, at room temperature

¼ cup (50 g) marzipan or almond paste

1 large egg

1 teaspoon almond extract

For finishing

1 large egg, beaten

2 tablespoons sugar

Confectioners' sugar for dusting

Although considered a bit kitschy, danishes are still very popular among pastry lovers. After all, who could refuse a flaky cheese danish, decorated with strips of white icing? Danishes belong to the family of laminated pastry, or viennoiserie in French, and despite their name, they were actually created by the Austrians, not the Danes.

Lamination involves layers of dough and butter that are progressively rolled and folded into a multileaf structure. Croissant dough and puff pastry are the other members of this family. Of all three, soft and malleable danish dough is the easiest to make. If you're new to lamination, this is a good place to start. Lamination projects are lengthy and best executed over 2 days. Schedule most of the lamination work for day one (4 hours including resting times), leaving assembly and baking for day two (1½ hours including rising time).

Traditional cardamom-flavored danish dough is best in sweet pastries, like this filled almond cake I call *pain d'amande*. Rather than shaping individual danishes, I make a large piece that can be baked in a cake pan and sliced like a cake. We make pain d'amande only on weekends at Friends & Family, and it sells out within a few hours. Many regulars order a whole one for special occasions. While undoubtedly delicious with morning coffee, it also makes a great dessert—just warm a slice in the oven and serve with whipped cream and fruit compote. It keeps for 2 days, so you could serve a few slices for breakfast on Saturday morning and enjoy leftovers for dessert on Sunday evening.

RECIPE CONTINUES

1. Sprinkle the yeast over the lukewarm water in a small bowl. Stir with a spoon to dissolve and let activate for 5 minutes.

2. In a stand mixer fitted with the dough hook attachment, combine the flours with the sugar, salt, cardamom, egg, butter, and the dissolved yeast. Mix on low speed just to incorporate. Increase the speed to medium and continue to mix until well combined, 2 to 3 minutes, stopping to scrape the sides of the bowl with a rubber spatula if necessary. Increase the speed to high and mix for 1 minute to develop the gluten further.

3. Transfer the dough to a lightly floured surface and knead into a ball. Lightly coat a medium bowl with nonstick spray and place the dough in it. Cover with plastic wrap and refrigerate for 1 hour.

4. For the butter block, lay the sticks of butter side by side in between two sheets of parchment. Let the butter sit at room temperature for 20 minutes to temper until malleable but not overly soft. Then flatten with a rolling pin to form a 7-inch square about ½ inch thick. In lamination, this butter packet is known as a butter block. If needed, you may use an offset spatula to help shape the butter block into the specified size. Refrigerate the butter block until the dough is finished resting.

5. At this point the butter block and the dough should be about the same temperature. To laminate, it is important that the butter not be too cold or it will crack and be hard to spread evenly over the dough. Soft, warm butter is equally problematic, because it will tend to leak out of the dough. To test the butter's readiness, press with your finger. If it resists but leaves an imprint, it is the right temperature.

6. Transfer the refrigerated dough to a lightly floured surface. Using a rolling pin, roll the dough into a 13-by-9-inch rectangle from the center out. The longer side of the rectangle should be closer to you. Visually divide the rectangle into thirds and place the butter block over the right two-thirds of the dough, leaving the left third uncovered. Fold the dough into thirds like a business letter that is to be placed inside an envelope, starting with the third without butter. Press the edges with the side of your hand to seal the butter in. We call this step "locking in the butter."

7. Next, do the first fold. Carefully roll the dough into another 12-by-8-inch rectangle and again fold like a business letter, wrap tightly with plastic, and refrigerate for 30 minutes. If butter squeezes out from the dough, patch it up by dusting the area with flour; this way it won't stick to the rolling pin.

8. Second fold: After the dough has chilled, roll into another 12-by-8-inch rectangle and fold like a business letter again. Refrigerate for another 30 minutes.

RECIPE CONTINUES

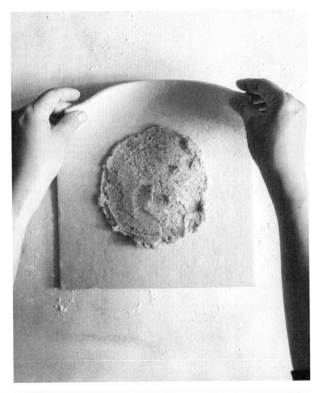

1. Lay the square of dough flat on a lightly floured surface. Put the almond filling in the middle and use an offset spatula to spread into a circle about 8 inches in diameter.

2. Fold the four corners of the square toward the center so the points meet in the middle. Corners should overlap slightly.

3. Pinch the edges of the dough to seal them together. You should have a square package with an X-shaped seam on top.

4. Gently place the dough package in the prepared cake pan seam side up.

9. Third and fourth folds: Repeat this process two more times, refrigerating for 30 minutes in between for a total of four folds. Let the dough rest in the refrigerator for 1 hour after the last fold.

10. On a lightly floured surface, roll out your chilled dough into a 12-inch square. Wrap with plastic and freeze to finish the pain d'amande the next day.

11. The next day, pull the dough from the freezer, leave it wrapped in plastic, and thaw for about 30 minutes on the kitchen counter.

12. In the meantime, make the almond cream. In a food processor, grind the almonds and the sugar to a fine meal. In a stand mixer fitted with the paddle attachment, cream the butter and the marzipan or almond paste. Add the ground almond meal, egg, and almond extract and mix to incorporate. Keep at room temperature until ready to use.

13. Lightly coat the springform pan with non-stick spray.

14. Lay the square of dough flat on a lightly floured surface and, using a knife or pastry wheel cutter, trim off about ¼ inch from the edges. Put the almond filling in the middle and use an offset spatula to spread the filling to form a circle about 8 inches in diameter. The circle of filling shouldn't touch the edges of the dough. Fold the four corners of the square toward the center so the points meet in the middle; they should overlap slightly. Pinch the edges of the dough to seal them together. You should have a square package with an X-shaped seam on top. Gently place the dough package in the prepared cake pan seam side up, cover with plastic wrap, and proof at room temperature for 1½ to 2 hours, until puffy and soft to the touch, or until the cake no longer bounces back when you press gently with a moistened index finger.

15. Place an oven rack in the middle position and preheat the oven to 350°F.

16. Brush the proofed pain d'amande with the beaten egg and sprinkle with the granulated sugar. Bake for 40 to 45 minutes, until the top is a rich mahogany brown. Let cool completely. To unmold, run an offset spatula or paring knife along the side of the pan and loosen the springform lock. Transfer to a cake plate. Put confectioners' sugar in a sifter and dust the surface generously. Slice into 8 wedges with a serrated knife. The pain d'amande keeps in an airtight container at room temperature for 2 days.

Sonora Wheat Croissants

MAKES 16 CROISSANTS
(8 CLASSIC CROISSANTS AND 8 PAINS AU CHOCOLAT)

For the dough

1½ teaspoons instant yeast

½ cup (120 ml) lukewarm (98° to 105°F) water

2 cups (260 g) Sonora wheat flour

2 cups (270 g) bread flour, plus extra for dusting

3 tablespoons sugar

1 tablespoon kosher salt

1 cup (240 ml) whole milk

1 tablespoon barley malt syrup

1 tablespoon unsalted butter, at room temperature

1 cup (180 g) bittersweet chocolate chips

For the butter block

2 cups (4 sticks/455 g) cold unsalted butter

For the egg wash

1 large egg, beaten

1 tablespoon heavy cream

If you're about to make croissants for the first time, brace yourself. Be ready to embark on a road of discovery that will bring some successes and, almost certainly, some failures. But persevere you must! Take comfort in knowing that every single baker who hopped on this adventure was once where you are today.

When I first developed this recipe, I was determined to include Sonora wheat flour in the dough. My goal was to make a croissant highlighting this important grain, so representative of the local Southern California grain-scape. Sonora is a soft, white, creamy flour with moderate gluten content. It's one of the oldest wheat varieties in North America and was a staple until industrialization pushed it out in favor of more modern wheats. Thanks to the Sonora, this soft and supple croissant dough is manageable for laminating at home. To strengthen the dough, this recipe contains equal parts Sonora and bread flour. High-gluten bread flour enables the dough to withstand the fermentation and lamination process, yielding pastries that stand tall and proud after baking.

Before you begin, keep in mind that lamination projects are lengthy and best executed over 2 days. My preference is to schedule most of the lamination work for day one, leaving the shaping and baking for day two. Aside from a trusted rolling pin and a pastry wheel cutter (see page 35), you won't need fancy equipment. It's also advisable to clear some space in the refrigerator. Laminating requires rolling the butter inside the dough and then folding the dough onto itself. After resting the dough in the refrigerator,

RECIPE CONTINUES

you're called to roll it and fold it again a few more times. This sequence is what allows the pastry to develop its characteristic flaky structure.

One batch of croissant dough will yield eight classically shaped croissants and eight pains au chocolat (or more if you cut them a bit smaller). The novice croissant baker can easily master these two traditional shapes. If you happen to fall for croissants as hard as I have, don't stop here. Make the dough over and over again and experiment with new shapes, fillings, and toppings. If making sixteen pastries at once sounds excessive, don't fret; the dough will keep in the freezer for 2 weeks. You could also save eight baked classic croissants to make the Halvah Croissants that follow.

1. For the dough, sprinkle the yeast over the lukewarm water in a small bowl. Stir with a spoon to dissolve and let activate for 5 minutes.

2. In a stand mixer fitted with the dough hook attachment, combine the flours with the sugar, salt, milk, barley malt syrup, butter, and dissolved yeast. Mix on low speed just to incorporate. Increase the speed to medium and continue to mix until well combined, 2 to 3 minutes, stopping to scrape the sides of the bowl with a rubber spatula if necessary. Increase the speed to high and mix for 1 minute to develop the gluten further.

3. Transfer the dough to a lightly floured surface and knead into a ball. Lightly coat a medium bowl with nonstick spray and place the dough in it. Cover with plastic wrap and refrigerate for 1 hour.

Opposite (left to right): Pains au chocolat, Halvah Croissants (page 316), classic croissants

4. Meanwhile, for the butter block, lay the butter sticks side by side in between two sheets of parchment. Let the butter sit at room temperature for 20 minutes to temper until malleable but not overly soft. Then flatten with a rolling pin to form an 8-inch square about ½ inch thick. In lamination, this butter packet is known as a butter block. If needed, you may use an offset spatula to help shape the butter block into the specified size. Refrigerate the butter block until the dough is finished resting.

5. At this point, the butter block and the dough should be about the same temperature. To laminate, it's important that the butter not be too cold or it will crack and be hard to spread evenly over the dough. Soft, warm butter is equally problematic, because it will tend to leak out of the dough. To test the butter's readiness, press with your finger; if it resists but leaves an imprint, it is the right temperature.

6. Transfer the refrigerated dough to a lightly floured surface. Using a rolling pin, roll the dough into a 12-inch square and put the butter block in the middle. Gently fold the excess dough on the sides over the butter, then fold the excess dough on the bottom and top toward the center until they meet in the middle. Seal in the butter by pinching the two flaps of excess dough together. Now you have a nice package of dough with a butter block inside it. We call this step "locking in the butter."

7. Next, do the first fold. Carefully roll the dough into an 18-by-10-inch rectangle, dusting additional flour over the work surface if needed. Fold into three even thirds like a business letter that is to be placed inside an envelope, wrap tightly with plastic, and refrigerate

RECIPE CONTINUES

for 30 minutes. You just put in the first turn. If butter squirts out in some patches of dough, dust the surface with flour so it doesn't stick to the rolling pin.

8. Second fold: After the dough has chilled, roll it into another 18-by-10-inch rectangle, dusting additional flour over the work surface if needed, and fold into thirds like a business letter one more time. Refrigerate for another 30 minutes.

9. Third and fourth folds: Repeat this process two more times, refrigerating for 30 minutes in between folds for a total of four folds. Let the dough rest in the refrigerator for 1 hour after the last fold.

10. Remove the dough from the refrigerator and roll into an 18-by-10-inch rectangle. Using a pastry wheel cutter, cut the rectangle in half to end up with two smaller rectangles, 9 by 10 inches each. Wrap each rectangle tightly with plastic and freeze overnight.

11. The next day, pull the dough rectangles from the freezer, leave them wrapped in plastic, and thaw for about 30 minutes on the kitchen counter.

12. Line two baking sheets with parchment paper.

13. To make the pains au chocolat: Use a rolling pin to roll one of the dough rectangles into a 12½-inch square. Use a pastry wheel to trim ¼ inch of dough from the edges of the dough rectangles. Cut one of the rectangles into four strips 3 inches wide by 12 inches long and then cut each strip into two 3-by-6-inch rectangles. (You should end up with eight rectangles.) To shape the pains au chocolat, orient the rectangles so that the shorter sides are parallel with your shoulders. Then line chocolate chips in two strips across each rectangle, one on the edge and another in the middle of the rectangle. Roll as you would a jelly roll. Place the shaped pains au chocolat seam side down on a prepared baking sheet, spaced at least 2 inches apart. Cover loosely with a kitchen towel and let them rise at room temperature for 2 hours, until puffy and soft to the touch or until they no longer bounce back when you press gently with a moistened index finger.

14. To shape the classic croissants, use a rolling pin to roll the remaining dough rectangle into a 14-by-10-inch rectangle. Next, cut into eight isosceles triangles (both long sides are equal in length) that are 3 inches at the base and 9 inches long. To do so, first orient the rectangle so that one of the long sides is parallel with your shoulders and directly in front of you on the work surface. Score very small notches every 1½ inches along the edge of the long side closest to you. Repeat to cut notches every 1½ inches along the edge of the other side. Now use a pastry wheel cutter to cut from the bottom left corner on a diagonal upward to the first notch on the top edge, which should be 1½ inches in from the left side. Then cut down the second notch on the bottom edge (3 inches in from the left side). Continue cutting in this zigzag pattern, using the 1½-inch notches to create eight isosceles triangles. You will also end up with two half-triangle pieces on the left and right sides. These can be rolled into funny-shaped croissants—they taste just as delicious. To shape the triangles into croissants, roll the bottom of the triangle toward the tip and press the tip to the bottom of the croissant to secure

the coil. Place the shaped classic croissants on a prepared baking sheet, spaced at least 2 inches apart. Cover loosely with a kitchen towel and let them rise at room temperature for 2 hours, until puffy and soft to the touch or until they no longer bounce back when you press gently with a moistened index finger.

15. Place an oven rack in the middle position and preheat the oven to 375°F.

16. Beat the egg and cream together. Brush the proofed croissants thoroughly with the egg and cream mixture. For optimal results, bake one sheet of croissants at a time. Bake the classic croissants first for 15 minutes. Then rotate the baking sheet and bake for 10 minutes more, until the croissants are a deep golden brown. Rotating the sheet halfway through the baking process will ensure that the croissants bake evenly. Repeat with the sheet of pains au chocolat. Let cool for at least 30 minutes before biting into them. Croissants should always be enjoyed the day that they're baked. But leftovers can be saved to make sandwiches, bread pudding or, if making classic croissants, the Halvah Croissants that follow.

Fold the dough into three even thirds like a business letter.

Halvah Croissants

½ cup (50 g) sesame seeds

5 tablespoons (70 g) unsalted butter, at room temperature

2 ounces (50 g) halvah, cut into ½-inch pieces

¼ cup (50 g) sugar

1 large egg

1 teaspoon vanilla extract

8 baked classic croissants (page 311)

Confectioners' sugar for dusting

This twice-baked croissant is a weekend favorite at Friends & Family. It's also a great way to use leftover croissants. Similar to traditional almond croissants, ours are split in the middle, then filled and topped with a butter-based paste enriched with halvah and sesame seeds. Halvah is a Middle Eastern confection made with tahini, somewhat of a cross between Italian torrone, milk fudge, and taffy. It can be found in Middle Eastern markets or specialty stores. Our preferred brand is Hebel & Co, made here in Los Angeles by our friend Katie Gurvin and her husband, Scott Hebel.

1. Place an oven rack in the middle position and preheat the oven to 350°F.

2. Scatter the sesame seeds on a baking sheet and toast for 10 to 15 minutes or until slightly golden. Let cool completely.

3. In a stand mixer fitted with the paddle attachment, cream the butter, halvah, and granulated sugar at medium speed until a uniform, lightened paste forms, 2 to 3 minutes. Add the egg and vanilla and mix to combine. Add the toasted sesame seeds and mix on low speed until the seeds are evenly distributed.

4. Line a baking sheet with parchment paper.

5. Split the croissants in the middle. Using an offset spatula, cover the bottom half of each croissant with a generous spoonful of halvah filling. Put the top croissant piece back on and frost generously with more filling. Place the filled and frosted croissants on the prepared baking sheet, spaced 2 inches apart. Bake for 10 minutes. Then rotate the sheet and bake for another 8 to 10 minutes. Rotating the baking sheet halfway through the baking process will ensure that the croissants brown evenly. Remove from the oven and let cool completely. Put the confectioners' sugar in a fine-mesh sieve and dust the tops generously. Enjoy the day that they're baked.

Opposite (from top): Vegan Pesto and Cherry Tomato Pizza (page 322), Artichoke Pizza with Fontina and Niçoise Olives (page 324), Smoked Salmon Pizza with Fennel and Red Onion (page 325)

Whole–Grain Pizza
Three Ways

Whole–Grain Pizza Dough

1 teaspoon instant yeast

¾ cup (180 ml) lukewarm (98° to 105°F) water

¾ cup (105 g) bread flour, plus extra for dusting

¾ cup (90 g) hard red wheat flour

2 teaspoons fine sea salt

About 1 tablespoon extra virgin olive oil

Pizza lovers, rejoice! Here's a pizza crust as flavorful as the toppings you put on it. The dough is very easy to prepare and makes enough for one 12-inch pizza. It can be baked directly on a pizza stone or on a baking sheet. If you plan ahead, you can make it the night before—the dough will develop a more complex flavor if allowed to ferment slowly in the fridge. But in a pinch, you can use it as soon as it's risen.

This recipe calls for equal amounts of hard red wheat flour and bread flour. The hard red will give it character, and the bread flour will make it extensible and malleable. Hard red wheat flour is easy to find at a good grocery store, independent mill, or specialty grain store. You may notice that some producers specify the red wheat varietal (such as Turkey Red, Red Fife, Yecora Rojo, or Joaquín Oro), while others simply call it "hard red wheat."

The dough will certainly pair well with traditional pizza toppings such as the Vegan Pesto and Cherry Tomato on page 322, but if you're craving something more out of the box try the Artichoke Pizza with Fontina and Niçoise Olives on page 324 or the Smoked Salmon Pizza with Fennel and Red Onion on page 325.

1. Sprinkle the yeast over the lukewarm water in a small bowl. Stir with a spoon to dissolve and let activate for 5 minutes.

2. Mix the flours and salt in a medium bowl and make a well in the center with your hands. Pour the dissolved yeast into the well and mix by hand until a rough dough forms. Turn the dough onto a lightly floured surface and knead for a few minutes, dusting with additional flour if necessary until it comes together in a uniform ball.

3. Transfer the dough to an oiled bowl, cover with a kitchen towel or plastic wrap, and let it rise until doubled in size, 1½ to 2 hours. You can refrigerate the dough now for later use. To do so, rub the dough with olive oil and put in a freezer bag. The dough will keep in the fridge for up to 2 days.

4. Place an oven rack in the lowest position, put a baking stone on it, and preheat the oven to 450°F. If you're making the pizza on a baking sheet, omit the baking stone.

5. Working on a floured surface, use your fingertips to pat the dough into a disk. Then drape it over your fists and carefully start stretching and expanding the dough to form a circle 12 inches in diameter. Alternatively, you can use a rolling pin to stretch the dough directly on the work surface. If using a baking sheet, roll the dough until a 16-by-12-inch rectangle and transfer it to a rimmed baking sheet generously brushed with olive oil. Your dough is now ready for topping and baking.

Vegan Pesto and Cherry Tomato Pizza

MAKES 1 PIZZA, SERVING 2 TO 4, OR 1 PAN PIZZA (ABOUT 15 BY 12 INCHES)

½ cup (70 g) whole raw almonds

1 cup (40 g) packed fresh basil

1 garlic clove

½ cup (120 ml) extra virgin olive oil, plus extra for drizzling

1 tablespoon fresh lemon juice

Pinch of kosher salt, plus extra as necessary

Pinch of red pepper flakes

1 cup (150 g) cherry tomatoes, cut in half

All-purpose flour for dusting (if using a pizza stone)

1 Whole-Grain Pizza Dough (page 320)

½ cup drained canned cannellini beans

Pesto is my secret weapon to make an array of tasty vegan dishes. While traditional pesto is made with Parmesan, it can be effectively "veganized" by replacing it with a hefty handful of nuts to make it creamy and rich in healthy fats. With vegan pesto as the sauce, the topping possibilities are endless, from shaved zucchini to sliced mushrooms or even parboiled fingerling potatoes. But at the height of the summer, when basil and the sweetest tomatoes are abundant, I prefer topping it simply with cherry tomatoes tossed in a bit more pesto. Cannellini beans make it a more substantial vegan dish, and toasted almonds sprinkled on top of the finished pizza as a garnish add the right amount of texture.

1. Place an oven rack in the middle position and preheat the oven to 350°F. Scatter half of the almonds on a baking sheet and toast in the oven for 8 to 10 minutes, until toasted and fragrant, and a nut cut in half is golden inside. Let them cool, then chop coarsely. Toss the chopped almonds with just enough olive oil to coat them in a small bowl. Season with salt and reserve as a garnish to finish the pizza when it comes out of the oven.

2. Switch the oven rack to the lowest position. Increase the oven temperature to 450°F. If baking with a pizza stone, put it on the oven rack.

3. Using a food processor, puree the basil and garlic with the ½ cup olive oil and the remaining almonds. You may need to stop every so often to scrape the sides of the bowl and help the basil puree evenly. Season with the lemon juice, pinch of salt, and red pepper flakes and pulse to combine. Gently toss the cherry tomatoes in a bowl with 2 tablespoons of the pesto. Taste and season with additional salt if necessary.

4. Generously flour the surface of a pizza peel. Transfer the stretched pizza dough (see page 321) to the prepared peel. Drizzle olive oil over the surface of the crust. Slide the pizza crust directly onto the stone and parbake for 10 minutes. Use the peel to remove the crust from the stone. Use an offset spatula to spread the remaining pesto over the parbaked crust. Sprinkle with the cherry tomatoes and cannellini beans. Slide the pizza back onto the stone and bake for another 5 to 10 minutes, until the edges of the crust have browned. Remove the pizza from the oven, garnish with the reserved toasted almonds, and drizzle with additional olive oil if desired. Serve immediately. If using a baking sheet, parbake the pizza with a drizzle of olive oil just the same. Then remove from the oven and finish the pizza as described above.

Variation

Ricotta, Pesto, and Cherry Tomato Pizza

Not a vegan? Try this version with creamy ricotta. Replace the cannellini beans with ¼ pound (155 g) whole-milk ricotta. Top the pizza with dollops of ricotta placed at random directly over the pesto and the cherry tomatoes. Finish with a light sprinkle of grated Parmesan in addition to the crunchy almonds.

Artichoke Pizza with Fontina and Niçoise Olives

One 14-ounce can artichoke hearts, drained

2 tablespoons extra virgin olive oil, plus extra for drizzling

1 tablespoon fresh lemon juice

2 garlic cloves, minced

½ teaspoon dried oregano

½ teaspoon red pepper flakes

Pinch of kosher salt

All-purpose flour for dusting (if using a pizza stone)

1 Whole-Grain Pizza Dough (page 320)

1 cup (115 g) grated Fontina

¼ cup pitted Niçoise olives, chopped

1 cup arugula

I have a personal rule for making pizza at home: Keep it simple. For me, homemade pizza should be a lazy weekend project, and once the dough is taken care of, I can't convince myself to do too much more. This artichoke pizza is a clear example of how a few ingredients can make a delicious meal without a great deal of time invested in making red sauce. In this recipe, briny Niçoise olives complement chunky marinated artichoke hearts while melty Fontina adds richness and substance. Finish with a handful of arugula right before serving to brighten it just enough. Make this pizza next time you want to impress dinner guests. They'll have no idea something so tasty could be so easy to make.

1. Combine the artichokes with the olive oil, lemon juice, garlic, oregano, and red pepper flakes in a bowl and season with salt. Marinate for 20 minutes.

2. Generously flour the surface of a pizza peel. Transfer the stretched pizza dough (see page 321) to the prepared peel. Drizzle olive oil over the surface of the crust. Slide the pizza crust directly onto the stone and parbake for 10 minutes. Use the peel to remove the crust from the stone. Cover the parbaked pizza with the grated Fontina. Place the marinated artichoke hearts and olives on top of the cheese, making sure they're distributed evenly throughout the surface. Slide the pizza crust back onto the stone and bake for 5 to 10 minutes, until the cheese is completely melted and the edges of the crust have browned. Remove the pizza from the oven and garnish with the arugula. Serve immediately. If using a baking sheet, parbake the pizza with a drizzle of olive oil just the same. Then, remove from the oven and finish the pizza as described above.

Smoked Salmon Pizza with Fennel and Red Onion

2 tablespoons extra virgin olive oil

½ cup (50 g) thinly sliced red onion

½ cup (50 g) thinly sliced fennel bulb, fennel fronds reserved for garnish

Kosher salt

½ cup (120 g) sour cream

1 large egg yolk

One 4-ounce (130 g) hot-smoked salmon fillet

All-purpose flour for dusting (if using a pizza stone)

1 Whole-Grain Pizza Dough (page 320)

¼ cup (30 g) grated Parmesan

1 cup (115 g) grated smoked mozzarella

Finely grated lemon zest

I first tried this flavor medley in Helsinki, where North Atlantic salmon is a source of pride. Instead of the common lox-style cold-smoked salmon sold in supermarkets, ask your fishmonger for a more substantial fillet of hot-smoked salmon. The fennel and red onion really complement the salty bites of succulent smoked fish, while smoked mozzarella pushes the smoky flavor and adds richness. Enjoy a couple of slices with a glass of white wine or serve skinny slivers as appetizers next time you throw a cocktail party.

1. Combine the olive oil, red onion, and fennel in a bowl and season with a pinch of salt.

2. Stir the sour cream, egg yolk, and 1 teaspoon salt together in a small bowl.

3. Rid the salmon fillet of skin (if any) and, using your hands, break the fish into flakes.

4. Generously flour the surface of a pizza peel. Transfer the stretched pizza dough (see page 321 to the prepared peel. Cover the surface with the red onion and fennel and sprinkle with the Parmesan. Slide the pizza crust directly onto the stone and parbake for 10 minutes. Use the peel to remove the crust from the stone. Use an offset spatula to spread the sour cream mixture over the parbaked crust. Sprinkle with the smoked mozzarella and flaked salmon. Slide the pizza back onto the stone and bake for another 5 to 10 minutes, until the cheese is completely melted and the edges of the crust have browned. Remove the pizza from the oven, garnish with the reserved fennel fronds, and grate a bit of lemon zest directly over it. Serve immediately. If using a baking sheet, parbake the pizza with the red onion and fennel just the same. Then remove from the oven and finish the pizza as described above.

Freekeh with Shiitake Mushrooms, Leeks, and Sugar Snap Peas

1 cup (150 g) freekeh

2 cups (480 ml) water

Kosher salt

2 cups (170 g) sugar snap peas

1 small leek, white and green parts

½ cup (120 ml) extra virgin olive oil

3 cups (140 g) shiitake mushrooms, stems removed and caps thinly sliced

2 cups (60 g) baby spinach

2 tablespoons fresh lemon juice, plus extra if necessary

Freekeh, like bulgur, is not a grain but rather a coarse meal made of broken wheat. Unlike bulgur, which is basically dried cracked wheat, freekeh is green wheat—typically durum—that's been smoked and cracked. Legend has it that a few hundred years ago a farmer lit his neighbor's wheat on fire over a dispute. The fields were still green, and the wheat didn't combust. When the fire died down, the affected neighbor collected the green wheat, removed the seeds, and cooked them. Imagine his surprise when he realized he had both salvaged his wheat and created an appetizing new dish. In many instances, freekeh is made by roasting green wheat rather than smoking it. But it's possible to find the smoked version in Middle Eastern markets. And every now and again I run into small wheat farmers who smoke green wheat and sell kernels whole, like the farro verde offered seasonally by Anson Mills.

We have featured this cold dish of freekeh with sautéed leeks, shiitake mushrooms, and sugar snap peas in our deli case at Friends & Family since we opened. Sometimes we use farro or Kamut, but I prefer freekeh. The texture of broken grain works nicely with the crunch of sugar snaps and the leathery feel of mushrooms. The subtle smokiness of freekeh combined with deep, earthy shiitakes makes an unexpected yet exciting bite loved by customers looking for a healthy, wholesome lunch.

1. Heat a medium saucepan over medium heat. Add the freekeh and toast in the dry pan, tossing until fragrant, 2 to 3 minutes. Add the water and 1 teaspoon of salt and bring to a boil. Reduce the heat, cover, and simmer for 15 to 20 minutes, until the freekeh is tender and the water has been fully absorbed. Spread the freekeh on a baking sheet to prevent it from clumping as it cools.

2. Meanwhile, remove the tough string that runs along the side of each sugar snap pea—the string is fibrous and hard to chew. Bring 2 quarts of water to a boil in a medium saucepan. Add 1 teaspoon of salt and blanch the sugar snap peas in the boiling water until they're bright green and tender, about 2 minutes. Immediately drain. Let cool completely. Cut each sugar snap pea into thirds at an angle.

3. Cut the leek in half lengthwise and slice the white and green parts into half-moons about ⅛ inch thick. Put in a bowl and cover with cold water to remove any dirt. Drain. If the leeks are still gritty, repeat the process one more time.

4. Heat a large sauté pan over medium-high heat and add half of the olive oil. Add the cleaned leeks and a pinch of salt and sauté until tender, about 5 minutes, stirring occasionally with a wooden spoon. Add the sliced mushrooms and sauté for another 4 to 5 minutes, until the mushrooms are fully cooked, adding more olive oil if necessary. Remove from the heat, transfer to a separate plate, and let cool completely.

5. Roughly chop the spinach and put in a large salad bowl. Add the freekeh, sugar snap peas, and sautéed leeks and mushrooms. Make a quick vinaigrette in a small bowl: Add the remaining olive oil to the lemon juice in a steady, slow stream while whisking vigorously. Add salt to taste. Add the vinaigrette to the salad and toss to combine. Check the seasoning and add more salt or lemon juice if necessary. Refrigerate until ready to serve or enjoy at room temperature. The salad keeps in the refrigerator for 2 days; after that the spinach and sugar snap peas will lose their brightness.

Kamut with Cherry Tomatoes, Cucumbers, and Fresh Herbs

SERVES 4

1 cup (180 g) Kamut berries

Kosher salt

¼ cup (60 ml) fresh lemon juice

2 tablespoons pomegranate molasses

⅓ cup (80 ml) extra virgin olive oil

1 cup (200 g) cherry tomatoes, cut in half

2 Persian cucumbers, cut in half lengthwise and then sliced into half-moons about ¼ inch thick

½ cup diced red onion

½ cup dill, minced

½ cup mint leaves, minced

½ teaspoon Aleppo pepper or freshly ground black pepper

This grain salad is loosely based on the Turkish salad nohut salatasi, which is traditionally made with copious amounts of chickpeas, loads of herbs, and an inspired vinaigrette with pomegranate molasses. Affordable and easy to find in Middle Eastern markets, pomegranate molasses adds sweetness and just enough sourness to the dish. In my version, cooked Kamut berries take the place of the chickpeas. In addition to fragrant herbs, the salad showcases crisp cucumbers and sweet cherry tomatoes, but you can really appreciate the toothy texture and earthy flavor of Kamut. The dish is meant to be thrown together with ease, but if you have extra time, I recommend marinating the cooked Kamut in the vinaigrette for a few hours, or even overnight, before combining it with the rest of the ingredients. It's comparable to tabbouleh and makes a great picnic or potluck contribution, especially if vegan friends are attending. If cooking for yourself, serve alongside grilled fish on a summer night for a delicious seasonal dinner.

Opposite (from top): Freekeh with Shiitake Mushrooms, Leeks, and Sugar Snap Peas (page 327); Kamut with Cherry Tomatoes, Cucumbers, and Fresh Herbs

RECIPE CONTINUES

1. Fill a large pot with 3 quarts of water and bring to a boil over high heat. Add 1 teaspoon of kosher salt and rain the Kamut berries over the boiling water. Reduce the heat, cover, and simmer for 45 to 50 minutes, until tender. Drain in a colander, then spread the grains on a baking sheet to prevent them from clumping as they cool.

2. Put the lemon juice and pomegranate molasses in a bowl. Add the olive oil in a steady, slow stream while whisking vigorously. Add the Kamut berries to the bowl and toss. If time permits, cover and marinate for a few hours or overnight in the refrigerator.

3. Combine the cherry tomatoes, cucumbers, red onion, minced herbs, and pepper with the marinated Kamut in a large salad bowl. Check the seasoning and add more salt if necessary. Serve immediately. Store leftovers in the refrigerator. The salad will keep for another day, but after that the tomatoes and cucumbers will lose their freshness.

Farro alla Pilota

SERVES 4

Kosher salt

2 cups (350 g) farro

½ cup (120 ml) extra virgin olive oil

4 ounces (115 g) salami, cut into small dice

1 small shallot, thinly sliced

4 garlic cloves, thinly sliced

1 cup (150 g) frozen peas (optional)

Pinch of red pepper flakes, plus extra if necessary

2 tablespoons minced flat-leaf parsley

¼ cup (20 g) grated pecorino or Parmesan for garnish (optional)

Finely grated zest of 1 lemon

If you're always on the lookout for quick, easy recipes to make for dinner after a long day at work, farro should be your trusted ally. In our house, farro ends up on the dinner table more than any other grain, and Farro alla Pilota is one of my favorite dishes to prepare with it. Traditionally made with rice, this dish is named after the piloti—the rice mill workers in charge of pearling or polishing rice. Compared to other berries, farro cooks quickly, in about 15 to 20 minutes. Think of it as pasta and boil until al dente in salted water. For this dish, buy unsliced salami you can dice and sauté in oil to render some of its fat and distill its piquant flavor. Part of what makes this satisfying dish work is biting into salty salami chunks. For a little extra richness, serve with a sprinkle of freshly grated Parmesan or pecorino.

1. Fill a medium pot with 4 quarts of water and bring to a boil over high heat. Add 1 teaspoon of kosher salt and rain the farro over the boiling water. Reduce the heat, cover, and simmer for 15 to 20 minutes, until tender but still toothsome in the center—similar to pasta cooked al dente. Drain in a colander, then spread the grains on a baking sheet to prevent them from clumping as they cool.

2. Heat a large skillet over medium-high heat. Add half of the olive oil and sauté the salami for 2 to 3 minutes, until slightly crispy. Add the shallot and garlic and sauté until softened, about 2 minutes. Add the remaining olive oil, the farro, and the frozen peas (if using)—it isn't necessary to thaw them previously, as the heat of the skillet will thaw them out quickly—and sauté for a few minutes, stirring frequently with a wooden spoon to make sure the kernels are well coated. Season with salt to taste and red pepper flakes as you stir. Turn off the heat, add the parsley, and stir to combine. Check the seasoning and add more salt or red pepper to taste. Transfer to a serving platter, sprinkle with cheese, and grate the lemon directly over the dish. Serve immediately. Store leftovers in the refrigerator. To reheat, sauté quickly in a skillet until warmed all the way through.

Acknowledgments

Mother Grains was written over a three-year period. I submitted the final manuscript in early March of 2019. A day later the city of Los Angeles announced a strict lockdown to contain the spread of the coronavirus. After losing most of our wholesale business, Friends & Family closed its doors temporarily, reopening eight weeks later with fewer bakers and very few customers. As we focused on rebuilding our bakery, copy editors and designers working remotely continued to put final touches on this cookbook. When the prolonged quarantine inspired a home-baking renaissance and grocery stores couldn't keep up with the demand for refined all-purpose flour, friends and acquaintances would reach out asking for recipes they could make with the few *weird* flours left on the shelves. Soon after they were making muffins with spelt, banana bread with buckwheat, or focaccia with rye flour. Funny how the pandemic that brought us to the brink of despair also taught us new ways to connect, learn, work, and even bake. It made me glad I had written this book—a project that would have never seen the light day without the love and support of my ever growing tribe. A todos, ¡muchas gracias!

Thanks to my husband, Daniel Mattern, for taking such good care of our home and our shop while I invested most of my time in *Mother Grains*. This book is yours as much as it is mine. In fact, so many of these recipes are indeed yours! I did most of my writing on my days off at our tiny Silverlake bungalow, in the good company of our cat, Gilbert. Thank you both for a dreamy space in which to live and work.

I'm grateful to my tenacious literary agent, Nicole Tourtelot, for always believing in me and finding the right home for *Mother Grains*.

I couldn't have asked for a better editor. Thanks to Melanie Tortoroli for mentoring me into becoming a legit cookbook writer. Your advice was always empowering and to the point. I'm grateful for your inclusive and respectful approach. I'm equally indebted to everyone at W. W. Norton & Company for trusting me to write this book.

Thanks to über-talented photographer Kristin Teig and stylist Nidia Cueva for creating gorgeous images full of sunshine. Thanks to David Thorne and Julia Meltzer for letting us shoot at the welcoming Elysian LA, and to Laura Ricci for assisting with food styling.

Thanks to the many writers who guided me through the writing process. Mary Singh and Corinne Kelly helped me polish the book in its initial stages. I was lucky to meet anthropologist Rossi Anastopoulo right at the beginning of this project. She contributed to the introduction of every chapter, gathering relevant information about each grain with untarnished curiosity and a great sense of humor.

Arielle Smolin copyedited and tested every recipe in this book with devotion. Thank you for your insights, impeccable language, and positive energy. I hope to return the favor when you are ready to write your own cookbook.

I enjoyed working with Maria Zizka who, with an inquisitive eye and unrivaled recipe testing skills, improved the final manuscript. This book is so much better because of you.

To my miller, friend, and ally in many battles, Nan Kohler, thank you for your endless ingenuity. *Mother Grains* would never exist without you and the many valuable lessons you have taught me throughout our five-year collaboration. Friends & Family is fortunate to call you its miller, and I look forward to many years of discovering new grains with you.

In 2000, pastry chef Kim Boyce took a chance on me and hired me as a pastry cook at Campanile. Kim's book, *Good to the Grain: Baking with Whole-Grain Flours*, was a catalyst for my own grain exploration. Thank you for twenty years of inspiration. I'm lucky to call you my friend and mentor.

In 2019, a grain pilgrimage took me all over Scandinavia, where I met like-minded bakers and millers. Martin Fjeld from Ille Brød, in Oslo, and Lars Petersen from Meyers Bageri, in Copenhagen, took the time to speak to me and show me their bakeries. Ronny Mikkelsen was my Danish guide and translator, and is responsible for my costly obsession with Royal Copenhagen porcelain. Fellow baker and writer Erica Landin-Löfving took me on an insider's tour of Stockholm's best bakeries, and later developed the Cardamom Bun recipe for this book. The unstoppable Eliisa Kuusela, another baker and writer in her own right, introduced me to the rye world of Finland, including a visit to Malmgård Estate, where I met their fearless founder, Kristina Creutz. Eliisa also shared her recipe for the Finnish Ring Bread. Thank you to each of you, for your hospitality and generosity.

Thanks to Rebecca Miller, of The Bread Bakers Guild of America, and Claudia Carter, of the California Wheat Commission, for their continued support and enthusiasm in anticipation of this cookbook.

Thank you to farmer Mai Nguyen and bakers Kate Pepper, Matthew James Duffy, Kristine Jingozian, Crystal White, Lucio Mejia, and Ellen King, who have enriched our bakers' grain experience by taking part in panel discussions, demos, and classes at Friends & Family.

Thanks to the women of the Silk Road Collective (Ferial, Feride, Leyna, Aliye, Claudia, Krissy, Leah, Karla, and Michelle) for involving me in events and conversations about diversified food systems, women entrepreneurship, food justice, community building, and social enterprise.

Thanks to the Los Angeles Bread Bakers—founder Erik Knutzen, and members Katie Turk, Dana Morgan, and Peter Hood—for hosting some of the first classes and events featuring ancient grains in our area.

Thanks to my business partners, Ash and Niroupa Shah, for believing in Friends & Family. We would have never made it this far without your friendship and support.

Thanks to my friends in the Los Angeles baking community—Clémence Gossett, Na Young Ma, Sarah Lange, Elizabeth Belkind, Dahlia Narvaez, Shannon Swindle, Meadow Ramsey, Jules Exum, Zoe Nathan, Sherry Yard, Christine Moore, Nicole Rucker, Genevieve Gergis, and Zack Hall, among many others—for answering my phone calls and text messages, whether I was asking annoying questions, requesting starter, or venting at ungodly hours. You all make me proud to be a baker in this city.

Thanks to the Friends & Family team who worked with me during the production of this book—Alison, Emily C., Emily W., Eva, Jenevieve, Joyce, Julietta, Maja, Olivia, Parker, Sarah, and Tony—and to all the bakers who have worked at Friends & Family over the years. I'm equally grateful to our sous chef, Shing (Coco) Kwok, our line cooks, baristas, and front-of-the-house staff. Your talent and hard work have come to define who we are. Friends & Family couldn't ask for a better crew!

Finally, thanks to the Thai Town and East Hollywood communities for your curiosity and support of the grain work that we do. Your open hearts are the fuel that keeps us baking with these mother grains.

Sourcing

This section lists artisans, farmers, millers, and producers from across the country. The majority offer their products online and ship nationwide. I highlight my preferred products from each provider, but keep in mind that availability varies throughout the seasons. Check the provider's website for up-to-date information.

Anson Mills

ansonmills.com
Based in South Carolina.
Ships nationwide.
Recommended products: aromatic buckwheat flour, toasted oat flour, blue cornmeal, Carolina Gold rice flour. When in season, seek their Farro Verde.

Arrowhead Mills

arrowheadmills.com
Comprehensive product line available in grocery stores and online shops.
Recommended products: organic buckwheat flour, brown rice flour, oat flour, rye flour.

Authentic Foods

authenticfoods.com
Products available in specialty stores and online.
Recommended product: brown rice flour.

Bob's Red Mill

bobsredmill.com
Based in Oregon.
Comprehensive product line available in grocery stores and online shops.
Recommended products: organic buckwheat flour, brown rice flour, oat flour, rye flour, and sorghum flour, as well as corn products such as polenta, yellow cornmeal, and corn flour.

Breadtopia

breadtopia.com
Great online store providing bread-baking ingredients and equipment.
Recommended products: bannetons, bench scrapers, lames.

Camas Country Mill

camascountrymill.com
Based in Oregon.
Popular West Coast mill.
Recommended products: organic barley, oat, and rye flakes; hard and red wheat flours.

Capay Mills

capaymills.com
Based in Northern California.
Provider of heritage grain flours milled to order. Available at selected Northern California farmers' markets and online.
Recommended products: Variety specific white and red wheat flours such as Chiddam Blanc de Mars and Marpacha.

Carolina Ground

carolinaground.com
Based in North Carolina.
Regionally grown and milled grains, available online.
Recommended products: spelt flour, Abruzzi rye flour.

Central Milling

centralmilling.com
Based in California and Utah.
Products available in specialty stores and online.
Recommended products: organic bread flours, California ground wheat flour, rye flour, buckwheat flour.

Conservation Grains

conservationgrains.com
Based in Montana.
Offers freshly milled flour, flour blends, and whole berries online.
Recommended products: Organic Gazelle rye flour, organic spelt flour.

Grist & Toll

gristandtoll.com
Based in California.
My top choice for artisan flour.
Offers quality, freshly milled flour online and at the Grist & Toll mill and retail shop, in Pasadena.
Recommended products: yellow and blue cornmeals, spelt flour, Sonora wheat flour, rye flour, hard white and hard red flours. When available, stock up on buckwheat and einkorn flours. Seek heirloom flours such as Wit Wolkering and Chiddam Blanc de Mars grown by small farmers in California when in season.

GrowNYC Grains

grownyc.org/grains
Based in New York City.
Marketplace for grains grown and milled in the Northeast.
Recommended products: any of the retail or preordered bulk bags available at the Grainstand in the Union Square farmers' market.

Hayden Flour Mills

haydenflourmills.com
Based in Arizona.
Family-owned and -operated mill offering flours online and in select retail locations.
Recommended products: stone-ground cornmeal, durum semolina, Sonora wheat flour.

Hebel & Co

hebelco.com
Based in California.
Artisanal halva available online and in Los Angeles retail shops, including Friends & Family.
Recommended product: vanilla halva.

If You Care

ifyoucare.com

Environmentally friendly kitchen and household products available in the online store and at retail locations worldwide.
Recommended product: sustainable parchment paper (roll or sheets).

Jacobsen Salt Co.

jacobsensalt.com

Based in Oregon.
Salt harvested from waters just off the Oregon coast. Available online and in retail shops nationwide.
Recommended products: kosher salt, pure flake finishing salt.

Jovial Foods

jovialfoods.com

Based in Connecticut.
A purveyor specializing in gluten free and einkorn wheat products.
Recommended product: organic whole-grain einkorn flour.

King Arthur Flour

kingarthurbaking.com

Based in Vermont.
Reputable supplier of flour, ingredients, baking mixes, baking equipment, and cookbooks. Available online and in retail stores nationwide.
Recommended product: unbleached all-purpose flour.

Lars Own

mypanier.com

scandinavianfoodstore.com

This is the brand of Swedish pearl sugar I use for topping Cardamom Buns. Available online via distributors such as myPanier or Scandinavian Food Store.

The Loveless Café

lovelesscafe.com

Based in Tennessee.
This beloved Nashville eatery is well-known for its Southern fare.
Recommended product: Sorghum syrup that is lighter in color with a more subtle flavor.

Maine Grains

mainegrains.com

Based in Maine.
A distributor of organic and heritage grains sourced from the Northeast, available online and in retail locations throughout the Northeast.
Recommended products: Øland wheat flour, whole spelt flour, buckwheat flour, farro, rye flour, corn flour.

Mandelin

mandelininc.com

Based in California
Producer of almond pastes and marzipan. Products available online and in selected retail locations.
Recommended product: natural almond paste.

Montana Flour & Grains

montanaflour.com

Based in Montana.
Sells high-quality flour and whole-grown kernels, as well as the trademarked ancient grain Kamut wheat. Available online.
Recommended products: Kamut berries, spelt flour, rye flour, hard white wheat flour.

Muddy Pond Sorghum Mill

muddypondsorghum.com

Based in Tennessee.
Providers of excellent quality, deep, dark sorghum syrup. Available online.
Recommended product: Sorghum syrup.

Rack Master

rackmaster.co.uk

Based in the UK.
Manufacturer of custom bench knives, baking molds, and pans, offering competitive shipping rates to the US.
Recommended products: stainless steel and coated loaf pans, bench knives, round cake pans.

Small Valley Milling

smallvalleymilling.com

Based in Pennsylvania.
Offers locally grown and milled organic flours and whole grain kernels in the online shop.
Recommended products: einkorn flour, emmer flour, spelt flour.

Sunrise Flour Mill

sunriseflourmill.com

Based in Minnesota.
Producer of stone ground heritage grains. Products available in their online shop and retail locations around Minnesota.
Recommended products: heritage rye flour, heritage fine cornmeal.

Weatherbury Farm

weatherburyfarm.com

Based in Pennsylvania.
Grower and miller of organic grain. Their flour is available for mail order or in-person pickup at the farm.
Recommended products: hard red and white bread flours, Danko rye flour, rolled oats, spelt berries.

Wild Hive Farm

wildhivefarm.com

Based in New York.
Mills small batches of organic grain purchased from local farmers. Available for purchase through their online shop.
Recommended products: whole-grain rye, emmer, and spelt flours; stone ground corn flour.

Equivalence Chart

INGREDIENT	VOLUME	WEIGHT IN OUNCES	WEIGHT IN GRAMS
BARLEY			
BARLEY FLAKES	1 cup	3.6	102
BARLEY FLOUR	1 cup	3.9	110
BARLEY KERNELS	1 cup	7	196
PURPLE BARLEY FLOUR	1 cup	4	112
BUCKWHEAT			
BUCKWHEAT FLOUR	1 cup	5.3	148
BUCKWHEAT GROATS	1 cup	6.5	182
CORN			
CORN FLOUR	1 cup	5.2	145
CORNMEAL, BLOODY BUTCHER	1 cup	5.5	154
CORNMEAL, BLUE	1 cup	5.7	160
CORNMEAL, WHITE	1 cup	5.8	162
CORNMEAL, YELLOW	1 cup	5.7	160
CORNSTARCH	1 tbs	0.3	8
HOMINY	1 cup	6	168
POLENTA	1 cup	5.8	162
OATS			
OAT FLOUR	1 cup	4.9	137
ROLLED OATS	1 cup	3.8	106
STEEL-CUT OATS	1 cup	6.5	182
RICE			
BROWN RICE	1 cup	7.2	202
BROWN RICE FLOUR	1 cup	5	140
PUFFED BROWN RICE	1 cup	0.65	18

INGREDIENT	VOLUME	WEIGHT IN OUNCES	WEIGHT IN GRAMS
RYE			
RYE BERRIES	1 cup	6.6	185
RYE FLAKES	1 cup	3.75	105
RYE FLOUR	1 cup	4.5	126
SORGHUM			
SORGHUM FLOUR	1 cup	5.7	160
SORGHUM GRAIN	1 cup	6.8	190
WHEAT			
ALL-PURPOSE FLOUR	1 cup	5	140
BREAD FLOUR	1 cup	4.75	133
EINKORN FLOUR	1 cup	3.8	106
FARRO	1 cup	6.6	185
FREEKEH	1 cup	5.3	148
HARD WHITE FLOUR	1 cup	4.5	126
KAMUT BERRIES	1 cup	6.7	188
OLAND WHEAT FLOUR	1 cup	4.5	126
SEMOLINA FLOUR	1 cup	5.9	165
SONORA FLOUR	1 cup	4.6	130
SPELT FLOUR	1 cup	4.7	132
WHOLE WHEAT FLOUR	1 cup	5.5	154
SALT			
FINE SEA SALT	1 tbs	0.5	14
KOSHER SALT	1 tbs	0.3	8
MALDON SALT	1 tbs	0.3	8
FATS			
COCONUT OIL	1 tbs	0.4	11
COCONUT OIL	1 cup	7.5	210
GHEE	1 tbs	0.5	15
GHEE	1 cup	8.5	240

INGREDIENT	VOLUME	WEIGHT IN OUNCES	WEIGHT IN GRAMS
MELTED BUTTER	1 tbs	0.4	11
	1 cup	7.3	204
OLIVE OIL	1 tbs	0.3	8
	1 cup	7.6	213
VEGETABLE OIL	1 tbs	0.3	8
	1 cup	7.6	213
SUGAR			
BROWN SUGAR, DARK	1 cup	8	224
CONFECTIONERS' SUGAR	1 cup	5.2	146
GRANULATED SUGAR	1 cup	7	196
TURBINADO SUGAR	1 cup	7	196
OTHER SWEETENERS			
BARLEY MALT SYRUP	1 tbs	0.6	17
	1 cup	11.5	322
CORN SYRUP	1 tbs	0.6	17
	1 cup	11.4	319
GOLDEN SYRUP	1 tbs	0.6	17
	1 cup	11.8	330
HONEY	1 tbs	0.6	17
	1 cup	11.6	325
MAPLE SYRUP	1 tbs	0.6	17
	1 cup	11	308
MOLASSES	1 tbs	0.7	20
	1 cup	11.7	328
SORGHUM SYRUP	1 tbs	0.6	17
	1 cup	11.3	316
NUTS			
ALMONDS, SLICED	1 cup	3.6	101
ALMONDS, WHOLE	1 cup	5.5	154
CASHEWS, WHOLE	1 cup	5	140
HAZELNUTS	1 cup	4.8	134
MACADAMIA NUTS	1 cup	4.8	134

INGREDIENT	VOLUME	WEIGHT IN OUNCES	WEIGHT IN GRAMS
PECANS	1 cup	3.5	98
PISTACHIOS	1 cup	5	140
WALNUTS	1 cup	3.2	90
SEEDS			
ANISE SEEDS	1 tbs	0.25	7
CARAWAY SEEDS	1 tbs	0.25	7
CHIA SEEDS	1 tbs	0.3	8
FLAX SEEDS	1 tbs	5.8	162
NIGELLA SEEDS	1 tbs	0.3	8
PEPITAS	1 cup	5.4	151
POPPY SEEDS	1 tbs	0.3	8
SESAME SEEDS	1 tbs	0.3	8
SUNFLOWER SEEDS	1 cup	5	140
DRIED FRUITS			
BLACK CURRANTS	1 cup	5.4	151
CHERRIES, DRIED	1 cup	6	168
COCONUT, SHREDDED	1 cup	2.5	70
CRYSTALLIZED GINGER, SLICES	1 cup	5.3	150
GOLDEN RAISINS	1 cup	2.56	168
MEDJOOL DATES	1 date	0.2	6
OTHER			
BLACK BEANS	1 cup	7	198
ENGLISH TOFFEE BITS	1 cup	5.25	147
CHOCOLATE CHIPS	1 cup	6.35	178
COCOA POWDER	1 tbs	0.25	7
	1 cup	4.1	112
PEANUT BUTTER, SMOOTH	1 tbs	0.5	14
	1 cup	8.75	245
PSYLLIUM HUSKS	1 tbs	0.3	8
SOURDOUGH STARTER	1 cup	7	198

Vegan Recipe Index

Gluten–Free Recipe Index

General Index

Note: Page references in *italics* indicate photographs.